ZERO TOLERANCE

EDITED BY ANDREA McARDLE
AND TANYA ERZEN

ZERO TOLERANCE

Quality of Life and the New Police Brutality
in New York City

New York University Press • *New York and London*

NEW YORK UNIVERSITY PRESS
New York and London

Library of Congress Cataloging-in-Publication Data
Zero tolerance : quality of life and the new police brutality in
New York City / edited by Andrea McArdle and Tanya Erzen.
p. cm.
Includes index.
ISBN 0-8147-5631-X (cloth : alk. paper) —
ISBN 0-8147-5632-8 (pbk. : alk. paper)
1. Police brutality—New York (State)—New York. 2. New York (N.Y.).
Police Dept. 3. Police administration—New York (State)—New York.
I. McArdle, Andrea, 1953– II. Erzen, Tanya. III. Title.
HV8148.N52 Z47 2000
363.2'09747'1—dc21   00-011660

New York University Press books are printed on acid-free paper,
and their binding materials are chosen for strength and durability.

Manufactured in the United States of America

10 9 8 7 6 5 4 3 2 1

Contents

     Paul Hoffman

9   Police Brutality in the New Chinatown   221
     **Committee Against Anti-Asian Violence:
     Organizing Asian Communities**

10   An Interview with Derrick Bell: Reflections on Race,
     Crime, and Legal Activism   243
     Andrea McArdle

11   Organizing at the Intersections: A Roundtable Discussion
     of Police Brutality through the Lens of Race, Class,
     and Sexual Identities   251
     Dayo Folayan Gore, Tamara Jones, and Joo-Hyun Kang

     Bearing Witness   271
     Bradley McCallum and Jacqueline Tarry

     Areas A, B, and C: An Afterword   282
     Andrew Ross

     Contributors   289

     Index   293

Foreword

Paul G. Chevigny

The police are a political lightning rod, especially for the sort of politics, so highly developed in the United States, through which a group carves out a place for itself in the system by recognizing its difference from others, while at the same time organizing to attack discrimination against it. It is easy to see why. In New York City, as in practically every other municipality larger than a village, the police are local. We have more than ten thousand police departments in this country, and even though employment in many of them is governed by civil service, they are sensitive to the society and the political structure in every place, big or small, where they work. Moreover, their work is structured so that they come in contact with the poorest and most marginalized people, even when other political actors do not. The common crimes that are at the heart of our penal codes—the assaults, thefts, and burglaries—as well as the category of "deviance" offenses, from disorderly conduct to narcotics, are given to the police. The white-collar crimes are rarely given to the police, and even when they are, most police rarely encounter them.

For a great many people—the poor and the dispossessed, the minorities, immigrants, and the thousands of others who are victims of crime, violators of city ordinances, as well as perpetrators of crime—the police are the cutting edge of government. They are the government agents who give orders in the street, divide people into those who are acceptable or suspicious based on their behavior and sometimes their appearance, and, as every child knows, have the power to make their orders stick, by force if necessary. It is inescapable that class relations, discrimination, and basic issues about rights, such as the right to free expression and the right to be free of arbitrary arrest and search, are embodied in police-community relations. It is little wonder that people who for one reason or another are treated by society as pariahs—either permanently as part of a suspect minority, or temporarily, for example because they are drunk or are urinating in a back alley (in a city where there are almost no public bathrooms)—are sometimes infuriated by the incursions of the police.

Combined with the rage is a large element of parochialism. Every city dweller sees his or her own police department as the paradigm. Every set of charges of police violence is insufferably bad, except when it is ignored by the citizenry. There are no better or worse departments, or more or less effective bureaucracies, because the police are almost totally local.[1] The local media hardly ever report scandals among out-of-town police, unless the events make it onto a network videotape. For example, suppose a terrible police scandal involving corruption and violations of civil rights were raging in, say, Los Angeles; preoccupied as we are with the dramatic incidents of police violence in New York City, we would probably be scarcely aware of it. *Mirabile dictu*, such a scandal does exist in Los Angeles as this is written, involving a cold-blooded shooting, a frame-up, and the reluctant review of thousands of convictions. That scandal may become familiar to people on the East Coast by the time this book sees print, but at this moment it is obscure here.

Knowledge about police abuses remains local also due to the fact that it is difficult to get nationwide information that compares cases or departments with one another. Until recently, the federal government made almost no effort to coordinate knowledge from different cities, and it made very little effort to enforce federal standards of civil rights against local law enforcement agencies. Since its powers were increased in 1994, the federal government has begun to try to draw minimal federal standards for police accountability, and to bring them to a few cities, but the project is still in its infancy.

The belief that each local scandal is the absolute worst is fed by the fact that systems of accountability, in New York City as in most other cities, are quite inadequate. We are free to draw our own conclusions about the prevalence of police abuses because we cannot have faith in decisions on cases of abuses by individual officers, and we cannot get reliable statistics about groups of cases. So people, even the police themselves, believe whatever they think is true about the police: that the number of civilian complaints is low because the police are either doing a good, clean job, or, on the other hand, because they are intimidating people to keep them from filing complaints; that the number of civilian complaints is high because police violence is on the rise, or, on the other hand, because there are more police and they are more proactive; that the percentage of substantiated complaints is low because the review agency is applying too high a standard of proof, or, on the other hand, because the complaints are the exaggerated rants of peevish malcontents. Police departments, including the NYPD, have resisted effective systems of accountability that would be transparent to the public in their procedures, evidence, and results. To a naive observer, this may seem puzzling; it would seem to be in the interest of the police to have the best possible relations with the residents of the city, and better accountability would seem to contribute to better relations. But perhaps the police are right, by their lights, to be leery of accountability because it is, as they fear, a proxy for control. Those who want accountability want change.

Some of those who most want change are the contributors to this volume of essays. The collection is sprawling and diverse, like the image of the city that is its model. Andrea McArdle and many of the writers here believe that some "disorder" is both useful and creative, meaning disorder, of course, in the sense of the diversity that supplies some of the energy to the city. A theme in this collection is that those proponents of the "broken windows" approach to law enforcement who think that disorder is criminogenic always run the risk of confusing diversity with disorder and of discouraging, even punishing, the racial, economic, and cultural abundance that makes New York what it is. There is a host of approaches to police reform here, almost all from the bottom up—from the point of view of the denizens of the city, whether they are police or not. There are some exceptions. Paul Hoffman's piece about international human rights, and even Andrea McArdle's chapter about police prosecutions concern top-down measures against police abuses. But even these are meant ultimately to supply ammunition to activists, to tell them where they can look for help. Most of the other essays are about the police at street level, about attitudes of the police themselves, about the work of the police or the media's representations of that work, or finally, about protests against the way the work is being done. A great strength of the collection is that proposals, however new or tentative, are being heard from groups who rarely get a hearing.

Police work has changed in the last generation through community policing efforts and the current fashion for quality-of-life or zero-tolerance policing. Through it all, however, the dynamics of ordinary police abuse—"street justice"—have not greatly changed. Most incidents of street justice—violent acts by police against people in the streets—are the result of incidents that police perceive as threats to their authority; in general, the police do not intend for the confrontation to end in violence but find that they cannot control the situation. Like so many acts of violence, these are cases of two people, usually men, each of whom has been challenged by the other, neither of whom feels like backing down; the nonpolice individual virtually always comes out the loser, even if he decides, too late, to back down. In light of these patterns, the essays about gender are welcome in this volume. The chapter by Amy Green is particularly suggestive that some conflicts might be different if more of the police officers were women instead of men, or if more officers tried strategies that the women Green interviewed used successfully.

Rather than focusing on the familiar old problems of street justice, the authors take a broad, radical view of the meaning of "police brutality"; for them it is on a continuum with other forms of police harassment, including those that are under the umbrella of "zero tolerance." Some commentators would take a narrower view. Jerome Skolnick and James Fyfe draw a distinction between "brutality" as a deliberately vindictive act to violate someone's rights, and "excessive force," which may be an error of judgment.[2] Others have distinguished between street justice, which is typically the excessive assertion of authority with a nightstick against those who defy it, and actual shootings, which are rarely deliberate violations of the rights of the person shot, but are terrible errors of judgment at worst. But those are lawyers' distinctions, made for the purpose of disciplinary proceedings or lawsuits. These essays, particularly those in the first part of the book, are from the consumer's perspective, and from this point of view those distinctions are almost arbitrary. If you are in the emergency room having your head stitched, it does not make much difference to you if the source of the blow was vindictive or an error of judgment.

Moreover, all the indignities that the police can visit on the denizens of the city are fuel for conflict with government, whether or not they result in physical injury; a sense of insult or discrimination can be an injury, and may well be experienced as "brutal." Those injuries may come from persistent patterns of stops and frisks against minority youths. They may, unfortunately, come also from actions that are perfectly legal and enforceable from the point of view of the police, from city ordinances or regulations that have been drafted to have a special impact on the poor, such as limitations on peddlers or automobile-windshield squeegee men, or that are enforced in a discriminatory manner, such as restrictions on trespassing. Here the police are again the lightning rod; they are getting blamed for enforcing policies that are not theirs but are those of the politicians who run the city. The important point for the authors of the essays is that the police take actions that hurt people, in the spirit and the pocketbook, if in no other way, and we must accept that the police will be the targets of rage whether an act is their own policy or not. The police are already facing that fact; as Jennifer Wynn's essay shows, some police are hesitant about supporting zero-tolerance policing.

The editors' and authors' perspectives are especially important during our present stage of neoliberal policies, including reduction of assistance to poor and disabled people and increasing economic inequality. The unskilled are increasingly ignored in the economy, and rentals in the city, when they are available, are more and more out of reach for the poor. Some say that the incarceration of nearly two million people, predominantly minorities, in the United States is an effort at social control of those who are viewed as refuse by society.[3] It is clear that other features of the criminal justice system, especially the efforts in the streets, have parallel purposes. Quality-of-life policing, including stops and frisks as well as the vigilant enforcement of minor infractions, is a form of surveillance, not only to obtain information, but to create a prevailing sense of police presence as a deterrent to crime as well as to "disorder." In this volume, we see this clearly in the essays by Tanya Erzen, by the Committee Against Anti-Asian Violence: Organizing Asian Communities, and by Jennifer Wynn. So it is natural—in fact, practically required—that those affected should see all the police tactics, whether physically violent or not, as dedicated to the same purpose: the control of the poor and marginal in the interests of the "orderly."

This volume may be seen as a tribute to, or at least a hope for, the failure of current police tactics and the repressive policies they advance. The authors remind us that the tactics are not working well to intimidate those at whom they are directed; instead, they are causing protest and grassroots calls for police accountability and reform. It is natural that those who are victimized by repressive tactics should be alarmed and want them to end; their protests, however, are not likely to change police-community relations much without support from the larger society. That should remind us that government policies of heightened personal security—the fear of crime, the blame placed on the alleged leniency of the courts, the demand for more police presence, the media support for tougher law enforcement, the longer prison sentences, the drive to build prisons, the death penalty—are directed just as much, if not more, at those who are unlikely to be the victims of police harassment as to the poor and marginalized.

Indeed, the policies have been much more successful with the "establishment" than with their actual targets. Heather Barr's essay about the treatment of mentally ill people as criminals is indicative of this effect in a particularly subtle way. She tells the familiar story about how the mentally ill were released from hospitals in the past few decades, with the assumption that they would receive other, more rehabilitative care. What they got instead, as Barr tells us, were charges of crime and incarceration; a large percentage of those incarcerated as criminals today are mentally ill. This change in policy has done nothing for the social control of the mentally ill. Besides sending them into situations that are bound to make them sicker, it has raised the crime rate and frightened the supposedly sane and respectable with the depredations of criminals. Thus the change has also prompted calls for more security through the criminal justice system, while facilities for the mentally ill remain too few. Voters do not support expenditures for the mentally ill; they want to spend money to protect themselves. So if the politicians can call mental illness a crime and frighten us with it, we will vote for them and pay for the programs they endorse on behalf of our security, which we consider money well spent.

The politicians and the media have persuaded us, and indeed we have persuaded ourselves, that crime is dangerous and out of hand, that we ought to stop handcuffing law enforcement, that rights are standing in the way of security, that more repression will make us safer. The politicians have competed with one another in frightening us with the seeming depredations of the poor, the dispossessed, and even the mad, and have promised us safety. And in fact we have been rewarding the politicians who are the most flamboyant in pushing the promise of repression. We are responsible for the policies which many of the authors here protest, and we can help put a stop to such measures. The targets of police abuse in the city cannot do it by themselves.

NOTES

1. See Henry Weinstein, "Rampart Police Probe May Now Affect 3000 LA Cases," *Los Angeles Times*, December 15, 1999, just one of many stories in this newspaper.

2. Jerome Skolnick and James Fyfe, *Above the Law: Police and the Excessive Use of Force* (New York: Free Press, 1993).

3. See, generally, Joseph Davey, *The New Social Contract: America's Journey from Welfare State to Police State* (Westport, Conn.: Praeger, 1995).

Acknowledgments

This anthology began as a collaborative project for the American Studies Program at New York University's Graduate School of Arts and Science. The group project—a distinguishing feature of the program's model of interdisciplinary scholarship—put the project authors (Tanya Erzen, Leota Lone Dog, Andrea McArdle, and Eric Tang, who first proposed the project) in an extended conversation about the brutal effects of New York City's high-intensity campaign against urban disorder and crime. Although not all of the original collaborators remained involved in the project as editors, those of us who did benefited from the ideas of the original group, as well as the generosity of many others. The list of those who helped this project take shape is long, and although there is a risk that in naming particular individuals we will seem to overlook others, we would like to acknowledge some special contributions. First, the intellectual and moral support of our American Studies faculty— the director of American Studies, Andrew Ross, as well as Lisa Duggan, Phillip Brian Harper, Nikhil Pal Singh, and George Yudice—and our graduate colleagues has been key. We also wish to thank our editor at New York University Press, Eric Zinner, who, along with the able assistance of Cecilia Feilla, guided this project to completion. Thanks also to the late Peter Cicchino, Andrew Darien, Steven Donziger, Douglas Lasdon, Hyun Lee, Philomena Mariani, Bradley McCallum, Eric Tang, Stephane Tonnelat, and Elaine Unkeless for information and help along the way. We are grateful to Dean John Sexton of NYU School of Law for extending crucial research and administrative support. In addition, we wish to acknowledge the NYU School of Law Lawyering Program founder, Anthony Amsterdam, and the director, Peggy Cooper Davis; School of Law faculty members Derrick Bell, Paul Chevigny, Jerome Skolnick, Anthony Thompson, as well as the Lawyering Program faculty; Brian Arthur, Abigail Caplowitz, Richard McKewen, and Susan Schroeder, who provided valuable research assistance with funds from the School of Law, including the Filomen D'Agostino and Max E.

Greenberg Research Fund; and Sandra Scott, Carrie Ortiz, Stephen Rechner, and Talib Saahir, for administrative and clerical assistance and their infinite patience. Our special thanks go to Andrew Ross, who has advised and encouraged us in this project from the beginning.

Enough! Vicinity of Federal Courthouse, lower Manhattan, April 15, 1999. (Photo by Andrea McArdle.)

Introduction

Andrea McArdle

Diallo
      Louima
Huang
      Rosario
Baez
      Bumpers
ENOUGH!

ON APRIL 15, 1999, posters bearing this message in Brooklyn's Cadman Plaza and lower Manhattan communicated more than any speech, march, or courtroom debate could. The names inscribed on the posters documented the grief of mothers, fathers, spouses, and children whose loved ones had been killed or gravely wounded by police officers. As part of a new community activism galvanized by the police shooting of Amadou Diallo in front of his Bronx residence on February 4, 1999, the posters formed an iconography of protest. The names were metonyms for police violence and the harassment, humiliation, and indignities that many men and women experience routinely in New York City. The posters declared that New York City residents had lost all tolerance for "zero tolerance," the catchphrase for New York's harsh crackdown against disorder and crime. Frustration and rage crystallized in the posters, as families and entire communities were moved to action.[1] Three names in particular had become the code words for zero tolerance, New York's new police brutality:

Amadou Diallo. A street vendor from Guinea, West Africa, Diallo was struck by nineteen of forty-one bullets fired by officers of the NYPD Street Crime Unit. The multiple rounds punctured Diallo's spleen, kidney, liver, aorta, intestines, and spinal cord. The officers claimed that they opened fire after Diallo had apparently reached for a weapon (it was actually his wallet). The officers— Sean Carroll, Edward McMellon, Richard Murphy, and Kenneth Boss—were indicted on charges of intentional and reckless murder, and, after being granted a change of trial venue to Albany County, were acquitted of all charges on February 25, 2000.[2]

Abner Louima. This thirty-year-old Haitian immigrant was arrested and detained in the 70th Precinct on August 9, 1997, following a fracas outside a Brooklyn nightclub. Some time later, he was taken away by ambulance and underwent emergency surgery to treat injuries to his intestine and bladder. Louima recounted from his hospital bed the lurid details of an incident at the station house in which he was battered and sodomized with a wooden stick. At the May 1999 trial in federal court, Officer Justin Volpe pleaded guilty to violating Abner Louima's civil rights in connection with the assault, and was later sentenced to thirty years' imprisonment; Charles Schwarz was convicted by a jury of holding Louima down during the station-house attack. On March 6, 2000, he was convicted with officers Thomas Wiese and Thomas Bruder of fabricating a report to exonerate Schwarz. The remaining three defendants in the earlier trial—against whom Louima's testimony was uncorroborated—were acquitted. Schwarz was sentenced on June 27, 2000, to fifteen years and eight months in prison for his participation in the assault on Louima and the subsequent conspiracy to cover up his involvement in the attack. Thomas Wiese and Thomas Bruder were each sentenced to five-year prison terms for their role in the cover-up conspiracy. In a separate prosecution, former officer Francisco Rosario was convicted by a federal jury on June 21, 2000, of two charges of conspiring with his police partner to make a false statement to federal authorities concerning events he witnessed in the Louima case. Rosario's partner previously had pleaded guilty to similar charges.[3]

Anthony Baez. The twenty-nine-year-old unarmed Latino man died on December 22, 1994, from asphyxiation after he was arrested

by New York City police officer Francis Livoti for disorderly conduct. Livoti ordered Baez and his three brothers to stop playing
an early-morning football game in front of their parents' home
after the football had struck Livoti's parked patrol car. When
Baez refused to put his hands behind his back for rear-cuffing,
Livoti placed his arm around Baez's neck in a chokehold, although the NYPD had banned that procedure, and kept Baez
face down on the ground. Within an hour of the arrest Baez was
dead from neck and chest compression, with asthma as a contributing condition. Acquitted of criminally negligent homicide,
Livoti was indicted on federal civil rights charges, convicted on
June 26, 1998, after a jury trial, and later sentenced to a term of
90 months.[4]

Within a month of the Diallo verdict, a fourth name was added to
this roster. Patrick Dorismond, an unarmed twenty-six-year-old Haitian American security guard, was fatally shot in an altercation with an
undercover officer who had approached him to buy drugs. Mayor
Rudolph Giuliani's disclosure of Dorismond's minor criminal record
shortly after the shooting provoked widespread criticism and additional community-based protest.[5]

As empowering as the posters and the protests have been to a broad
spectrum of people, these rallies invoked the most visible, and tragi-
cally familiar, form of police brutality in the U.S., in which the targets
have been black and Latino young men. Yet, police brutality in New
York City is a multidimensional phenomenon referring not only to the
hyperviolent responses in the Diallo, Louima, Baez, and Dorismond
cases, but to an entire set of public-order police practices directed
against homeless people, vendors in Chinatown, and sexual minorities.
The complexity of the problem requires a commensurate response, involving a range of strategies and activism, scholarly and otherwise.

This collection, bringing together the work of scholars, lawyers,
journalists, and activists, is a form of collaborative activism. It is framed
as a response—and a challenge—to an official narrative that connects
New York City's declining crime rates to intensified law enforcement. It
sketches out a definition of police brutality more encompassing than
the use of excessive physical force, and analyzes its deeper connections
to larger economic, political, and social structures. It identifies—and
then teases apart—the connections we believe to exist between the

exercise of raw power memorialized in the posters, and the day-to-day violence that accompanies the city's campaign to police the "quality of life." Offering perspectives from law and society, urban theory, cultural studies, and the visual arts, among others, the essays assembled here complement, and provide a counterpoint to, the work of criminologists and police scholars on this subject. At the same time, they demonstrate the possibilities for bridging interdisciplinary scholarship and activism, of grounding scholars' work—theory, ethnography, historiography—in the needs and concerns of everyday life.

With its focus on conditions in late-twentieth-century New York City, one aim of this anthology is to situate violent policing within a larger economic and political context. The city's more pronounced neoliberalism under the Giuliani administration—a market-oriented, prodevelopment, antiwelfare stance[6]—has fostered a climate that encourages, even rewards, aggressive law enforcement. Police brutality proliferates in an urban space that increasingly has lost its public character—where public resources are reassigned from the care and improvement of citizens (used here in the broadest sense of the word) to tax abatement for private redevelopment. The convergence of redevelopment and anticrime policies underpinning the city's position as a global center of entertainment, retailing, and financial services has entailed the strategic deployment of the police to secure urban spaces and effectively reconstitute them as private. The wide-ranging stories of police abuse that are part of the fabric of daily life in New York City—the shower of bullets that killed Amadou Diallo, the sweeps of homeless people from public places, the routinized harassment of gays and lesbians—cannot be fully understood without attending to the political and economic imperatives that drive them.

The anthology interrogates New York's idiosyncratic version of James Wilson and George Kelling's influential "broken windows" theory, which posits a connection between community disorder—visual and behavioral—and crime.[7] Since 1994, during the two Giuliani administrations, the city's successful initiatives to maintain public order and create a new urban esthetic have coalesced in the relentlessly promoted "Quality of Life" campaign. With its punitive, "tough love" enforcement ethic aimed at an array of low-level offenses, New York's variant of quality of life is often linked, and sometimes equated, with "Zero Tolerance," a strict, results-oriented approach to enforcement. The explosion of interest in public-order initiatives reflects a broader trend that has taken hold in the 1990s, when the rate of more serious crime began its decade-long decline throughout the United States. By targeting less serious offenses, the public-order approach is a significant reorientation of a crime-control policy that for three decades had focused attention and resources on attacking serious crime and "diverting" relatively minor infractions from the criminal justice system.[8] New York City's version of public-order policing fits within this trend; it is a preemptive strategy to prevent the occasion of serious crime and a streamlined version of a more traditional crime-fighting program, manifest in the controversial stop-and-frisk practices of the city's Street Crime Unit.

In the years since New York City has so famously embraced it, the Quality of Life program and Zero Tolerance, its less euphemistic alter ego, have become prototypes of aggressive public-order initiatives. Even as a few cities have pointedly distanced themselves from this model, Zero Tolerance is ripe for export to many other localities within and outside the United States that are rethinking their own order-maintenance policies:[9] in Baltimore, where quality-of-life ideology has entered the public discourse, where a "zero tolerance" approach became the focus of the city's recent mayoral campaign, and the new administration has called upon former NYPD personnel to help craft a tough-on-crime policy;[10] in San Francisco, where, in the city's efforts to respond to homelessness, police issued 20,000 citations for trespassing, camping, and park curfew violations in 1999 alone; in Sacramento, where police cooperate with business groups to evacuate homeless people from shopping and tourist districts; and in Britain, where Prime Minister Tony Blair's embrace of zero-tolerance policing has been characterized by some critics as "macho policing."[11] Beyond its use by urban police agencies, the stringent requirements of a zero-tolerance approach have deployed in a range of institutional settings. The policy is credited with improving conditions at Rikers Island, New York City's largest detention facility,[12] and is used in schools across the country to underpin strict disciplinary policies for both minor and more serious infractions.[13]

In a sociopolitical climate that has taken an increasingly authoritarian turn, intensified law enforcement of this sort is offered as an unmitigated good. Yet, if the presumed linkage between disorder and crime has a surface plausibility, its claims have not been substantiated. In a recent essay, Bernard Harcourt applies law-and-society perspectives to examine the city's assertion that public order is maintained, and serious crime reduced, by enforcing low-level criminal codes. Finding no empirical evidence based on existing studies that such a causal link exists,[14] Harcourt illuminates the way that the city's policies create a set of expectations in which disorder-to-crime has a common-sense appeal. The city's resort to surveillance and intelligence gathering through video cameras, interrogation, frisking, and fingerprinting consolidates the category of the "disorderly."[15] Once in existence, this construct is used to justify policies that treat the disorderly person as one who "needs to be policed, surveyed, watched, relocated, controlled"—*disciplined* but not rehabilitated, to revise Michel Foucault.[16] The knowledge produced by these criminalizing strategies of visibility thus becomes the occasion for a further exercise of power. (Turnstile jumpers and public drinkers may have pending arrest warrants that come to light during the processing of a Quality of Life offense).[17] This "network of visual authority," borrowing Stephane Tonnelat's evocative phrase, is enforced by the ubiquitous NYPD as well as the surveillance cameras of the global corporations that have come to define the "new" Times Square.[18]

The use of surveillance and an aggressive management of public space are crucial to New York City's combined crime-control and order-maintenance initiatives. The stop-and-frisk campaign of the Street Crime Unit, at various times the focus of five government investigations and a federal lawsuit,[19] is one of the more notorious ways in which the NYPD occupies space. Running roughshod over the Fourth Amendment's ban against unreasonable searches, Street Crime plainclothes officers reported stopping 45,000 persons to search for weapons in 1997 and 1998, and out of that number they arrested 9,500.[20] A report issued in November 1999 by New York State attorney general Eliot Spitzer compiled voluminous data confirming that blacks in New York City were stopped six times more frequently, and Latinos four times more frequently, than whites. And in June 2000, a report of the U.S. Commission on Civil Rights pointed to NYPD data that "strongly suggests" that the NYPD uses racial profiling in stops, frisks, and searches. The report also recommended establishing an independent mechanism to investigate serious cases of police abuse.[21]

The rationale for these public-order and stop-and-frisk practices—to prevent incipient criminality—recalls a similar justification offered for enforcing the now-discredited vagrancy and loitering laws.[22] Almost thirty years ago, the United States Supreme Court invalidated laws that cast a wide net to arrest and prosecute persons based on an unsubstantiated suspicion of criminal conduct. As Justice William O. Douglas, author of the Court's opinion in *Papachristou v. City of Jacksonville*,[23] understood, these laws targeted "poor people, nonconformists, dissenters, idlers" on the "extravagant" theory that unspecified crimes would be "nipped in the bud."[24] The potential for arbitrary or discriminatory application was obvious. The Court treated the targeted activities—walking, strolling, lingering—as part of the "unwritten amenities" deserving judicial protection from the law's vague proscriptions.[25]

In the same way, the city's public-order campaign seems a regression to these vagrancy laws, aimed at creating a safe and sanitized environment from which the detritus of homeless people, squeegee men, street vendors, and young men and women of color can be swept away. This initiative infringes on amenities of life that should be considered subject to constitutional protection, as an aspect of the "liberty" protected by the Fourteenth Amendment's due process clause, if not the Fourth Amendment's ban against unreasonable seizures.[26] The city's crackdown on homeless people in the wake of several incidents of apparently random violence demonstrates the way that the city uses law enforcement mechanisms to control access to public space. Targeting homeless persons who sleep on the streets, New York City police commissioner Howard Safir announced that if these homeless individuals did not accept proffered services, "we will either summons them or arrest them."[27] Undeterred by an abysmal record before the courts on constitutional issues such as the right to free expression,[28] Mayor Rudolph Giuliani offered his constitutional analysis of this policy initiative: the right to sleep in the street "doesn't exist anywhere. The founding fathers never put that in the Constitution."[29]

The mayor's "textualist" interpretation notwithstanding, the campaign to evict homeless people from city spaces arguably infringes a host of constitutional protections, including the right to travel (or not),[30] and the right to be protected against criminal prosecution for one's status (e.g., homelessness)[31] or for involuntary conduct connected to that status (sleeping in the street made necessary by the city's failure to provide adequate shelter).[32] In New York City, the conclusion seems inescapable that the enforcement of criminal codes defining low-level offenses has become the preferred way of banishing ill-fitting people from the city's public spaces.

As Richard Sennett suggests, this sort of "purification" response to the fear of urban disorder encourages insularity and a shrinking base of experience for city dwellers.[33] When diverse city residents interact in chance encounters, the heightened risk for "complexity of confrontation and conflict" is precisely the antidote to a stultifying, if safe, lack of lively connection with others.[34] Far from an endorsement of crime, Sennett's abiding faith in the liberatory potential of disorder and diversity offers an alternative vision of the city, and a set of ideas about the quality of urban life, fundamentally at odds with the current regime of order-maintenance policing.

If Sennett's conception of a good city life entails the flourishing of its public spaces, New York City's trajectory has been in the direction of increasing privatization. The transformation of Times Square into a three-ring, theme-park tourist attraction, and the gentrification of neglected residential enclaves such as the Lower East Side illustrate this trend. The politics and economics of privatization generate their own set of questions, such as how the global economics of postindustrial capitalism produces segregated city spaces and who, to borrow Henri Lefebvre's classic formulation, has the "right to the city."[35]

Lefebvre's work addressed the ways in which uses of space signify logics of prohibition and control. The "law" imposed by a city's spatial arrangements is bound up with a sense of order, and disorder. In *The Production of Space*, Lefebvre elaborated the idea of an "abstract" space associated with capitalism that conceals within itself the reinforcing power of the state.[36] The Quality of Life campaign, by contrast, makes no effort to disguise the revanchist spirit[37] with which business concerns and the city government have aligned themselves to control access to the city's redeveloped spaces. Efforts to limit street vendors' zone of operations in Chinatown,[38] and the campaign to zone more sexually explicit entertainment along the margins of the city,[39] are just two instances of police cooperation with more established business interests.

In New York City, the public-private sector nexus borders on the incestuous. The city's thirty-nine Business Improvement Districts (BIDs), established in the 1980s to spearhead a form of private-public initiative, augment the city's order-maintaining apparatus by providing private security and street-cleaning services.[40] Policies begun in the 1980s with the Quality of Life campaign have encouraged a backlash against the poor and downwardly mobile by reassigning public spaces to private use. (The conversion of Christadora House, a settlement house bordering Tompkins Square Park in the Lower East Side, to a luxury cooperative,[41] and the city's recent auction to a private developer[42] of Charas/El Bohio, a Latino cultural space in the same neighborhood, come to mind.) In the same vein, urban geographer Neil Smith has shown that the city's enshrining of global capital and the entertainment industry in midtown involves uses of space that are explicitly class- as well as race-based.[43] In Times Square, the NYPD cracks down on street vendors, religious and political dissidents,[44] and the homeless at the same time that the city has granted multiple tax exemptions to development sites and major corporate tenants to induce these companies to remain in the city.[45]

This anthology interrogates whether political space exists to challenge current city policies and policing practices that deny public access to urban space. As Neil Smith reminds us, "The problem today is not that there is no politics, but that there is precious little political movement."[46] Urbanists Jane Jacobs and Manuel Castells, in their distinct ways, have contributed useful models of local activism in relation to city policies. Although their work was done in the 1960s and 1970s, their common focus on grassroots participation, what anthropologist James Holston might call "insurgent citizenship,"[47] offers a vision of an engaged citizenry that is worth considering in the contemporary context.

Jacobs has long argued for a diversity and density of use in the service of a "lively urbanity."[48] The kind of intensive street use she advocated in *The Death and Life of Great American Cities* anticipated the active street culture of San Francisco's gay community that Castells documented. If urban neighborhoods could function as "mundane organs of self-government,"[49] she suggested, it would be possible for politically engaged citizens to resist the city's top-down postwar urban renewal policies that produced forbidding islands of use, the physically segregated high-rise structures that were so destructive of a sense of community—and safety.[50] In what seems today like a blueprint for genuine "community" policing, Jacobs sketched out how neighborhoods could take responsibility for their own collective well-being; watchful eyes on well-traveled streets are a more effective deterrent to crime than stepped-up enforcement by the police.[51] Castells's studies of the failure of either San Francisco's politically and culturally mobilized Latinos or gays to develop coalitions or longer-term strategic alliances can be an object lesson for those people in New York who have most keenly felt the effects of zero-tolerance policing.[52]

The possibility of the kind of engagement suggested by Jacobs and Castells holds out some hope for New York City's besieged communities. There have been pockets of resistance throughout the Giuliani years, though until recently community activism has lacked a consistent focus or the backing of a broad-based coalition of groups to sustain it. The forty-one shots fired at Amadou Diallo have helped to generate what may be a near-consensus that the city's culture of policing, and the political culture that produces it, do not respect human rights. An immediate challenge facing the diverse communities in New York whose experience of zero-tolerance policing has been an increase in police violence is to develop a coalitional strategy for a human rights agenda that, at the same time, recognizes and respects differences.

There are many points of connection among these essays. Each in its own way amplifies the concerns that have animated this project: New York City's use of aggressive order-maintenance and crime control strategies to abet economic redevelopment and privatization; their devastating impact—materially and symbolically—on the city's more marginalized residents; the need for a coordinated antibrutality strategy among targeted communities. A special benefit of an anthology is that it affords the opportunity to put multiple ideas in conversation, to bring both links, and suggestive differences, into sharper focus. The relationships among these ideas have suggested the organizational framework that we have adopted.

The first section, "Policing the Quality of Life," focuses attention on the social costs of the Quality of Life initiatives. In addition to the essays by Tanya Erzen and Heather Barr noted in Paul Chevigny's Foreword, Sasha Torres uses the lens of cultural studies to examine how television generates and sustains consensus around the Giuliani administration's approach to policing. The next section, "The Police," featuring essays by Amy S. Green, Jennifer Wynn, and Andrea McArdle, examines dimensions of professional police identity and socialization and their relationship to the city's political and legal culture.

The essays in the concluding section, "Activism," illuminate the range of strategies needed—from U.S. and international legal remedies and grassroots organizing to innovative pedagogies—to launch a multifaceted antibrutality campaign. In addition to contributions by the Committee Against Anti-Asian Violence and Paul Hoffman previously noted in the Foreword, this section includes a roundtable discussion by Joo-Hyun Kang, Dayo Gore, and Tamara Jones of the Audre Lorde Project that analyzes police interactions with urban communities in terms of the intersections among the social categories of gender, sexuality, race, and class. Also featured is an interview with lawyer-scholar-author–civil-rights activist Derrick Bell, who reflects on the complexities of attempting to work within a system to change it. Journalist Andrew Hsiao offers a short history of the rise of the grassroots anti–police brutality movement in New York City, tracing the "odyssey" into activism through which family members have turned their grief into leadership of community organizing efforts. The photo essay created by artists Bradley McCallum and Jacqueline Tarry, inspired by their public artwork *Witness: Perspectives on Police Violence*, suggests the ways in which visual culture and the spoken word—testimony—can serve as a powerful form of public advocacy. Andrew Ross's Afterword highlights the collection's overarching attention to the ways in which policing, crime, and the economy are connected, shoring up the city's "privatizing revolution."

The tense relations between the NYPD and the city's less empowered communities are a product of many forces. The militaristic, crime-fighting ethos of police culture valorizes aggressive responses and a siege mentality that sees danger in difference. Lacking a functioning system of accountability, the NYPD is in deep denial about the ways in which it has criminalized, and brutalized, difference. Yet it would be misguided to think of the NYPD as a monolith, or to assume that the problem of police violence is one that the NYPD has created, or can resolve, on its own. This anthology hopes to show that police brutality and the policing function more generally are part of the deep structure of a globalized, neoliberal society. Contemporary New York City typifies the move toward redevelopment, internationalization, deregulation, and privatization[53] that marks this new politico-economic order—and that has put so much pressure on the city's dwindling public spaces. The zeal with which some NYPD officers have embraced Quality of Life policing and more confrontational anticrime strategies is a symptom of a much broader, and deeper, social pathology manifested in an

indifference to poverty, the exploitation of labor, and the devaluing—
and demonizing—of racial, ethnic, and sexual minorities.

Yet the city also can be a crucible from which its embattled residents
can emerge strengthened, a site for a reinvigorated politics. James Holston and Arjun Appadurai remind us of this crucial fact: "With their
concentrations of the nonlocal, the strange, the mixed, and the public,
cities engage most palpably the tumult of citizenship."[54] Only an exercise of citizenship, a "substantive" form of citizenship that includes a
full measure of human rights,[55] holds out the possibility of countering
these forces that encourage and enable police brutality. Framing activism—grassroots movements, legal advocacy, public pedagogy, and
even electoral politics—in terms of citizenship rights situates the struggle and the contestants at the center of a reinvigorated democratic project. A citizenship frame supplies a language that accords with ideas of
human dignity, agency, and community engagement. This collection offers various ways of thinking about citizenship struggles and about the
right to the city that must be their point.

POSTSCRIPT

Since this book went to press in mid-summer of 2000, Zero Tolerance
has remained a centerpiece of city policy. When Police Commissioner
Howard Safir retired from service, Mayor Giuliani selected city Corrections Commissioner Bernard Kerik to replace him—ensuring that there
would be no retreat from Zero Tolerance for the balance of his mayoral
term. [See Jennifer Wynn's essay in this collection for a discussion of
Kerik's Zero Tolerance-style management at Rikers Island.] During this
same period, the Patrolmen's Benevolent Association, battling with city
negotiators over salary issues, sponsored a series of controversial ads
portraying the dangers to police of Zero Tolerance policing—while the
NYPD initiated a multimillion-dollar recruitment campaign featuring
caring and courageous officers at work in the city's communities, in its
effort to reverse the falloff of applicants for police work. And as a Manhattan grand jury voted not to indict the detective who had fatally shot
Haitian American Patrick Dorismond, finding that the shooting of the
unarmed security guard was not intentional, the irretrievable consequences of Zero Tolerance policing was brought home again to the city
residents who remain its most likely targets.

NOTES

1. See, e.g., Jodi Wilgoren, "Turning Protest Signs into Substance," *New York Times*, 17 April 1999: B3; Jodi Wilgoren, "Push to Turn Rally into a Broader Movement," *New York Times*, 14 April 1999: B6.

2. See, e.g., Dan Barry, "2 Sides Recommend Diallo Jury Hear Reduced Charges," *New York Times*, 17 February 2000: A1, B6; Amy Waldman, "Judge in Diallo Case Allows Jury to Consider Lesser Charges for Officers," *New York Times*, 18 February 2000: B6; Jane Fritsch, "Four Officers in Diallo Shooting Are Acquitted of All Charges," *New York Times*, 26 February 2000: A1.

3. See, e.g., Alan Feuer, "Ex-Officer Details Surge of Rage as He Began Attack on Louima," *New York Times*, 18 February 2000: A1, B6; Joseph P. Fried and Blaine Harden, "The Louima Case: The Overview; Officer Is Guilty in Torture of Louima," *New York Times*, 9 June 1999: A1, B8; Alan Feuer, "Three Are Guilty of Cover-up Plot in Louima Attack," *New York Times*, 7 March 2000: A1. Alan Feuer, "3 Ex-Officers Are Sentenced for Roles in Louima Torture," *New York Times*, 28 June 2000: B3; Alan Feuer, "Officer Convicted of Lying in Last of the Louima Cases," *New York Times*, 22 June 2000: B3.

4. Matthew Goldstein, "Officer Acquitted of Homicide; Judge Found Proof at Trial Inadequate," *New York Law Journal*, 8 October 1996: 1; "'Minor Dispute' Becomes a Senseless Homicide," *New York Times*, 22 February 1997: 25.

5. See, e.g., William K. Rashbaum, "Undercover Police in Manhattan Kill an Unarmed Man in a Scuffle," *New York Times*, 17 March 2000: A1; Randall G. Archibold, "Giuliani's Reaction to Police Shooting Is Felt in Suburbs," *New York Times*, 31 March 2000: B1; Bob Herbert, "In America: The Mud-Slingers," *New York Times*, 20 March 2000: A23; Adam Nagourney with Marjorie Connelly, "Giuliani's Ratings Drop over Actions in Dorismond Case," *New York Times*, 7 April 2000: A1.

6. See, e.g., discussion of neoliberalism in David Garland, "Governmentality and the Problem of Crime: Foucault, Criminology, Sociology," *Theoretical Criminology* 1 (1997): 173, 182–184.

7. For an extended discussion of Kelling and Wilson's thesis, see Tanya Erzen's essay in this collection.

8. See David Garland, "Overall Perspective on Crime Is Not the Problem: Criminology, Crime Control, and 'The American Difference,'" 69 *U. Colo. L. Rev.* 1137, 1148–1149 (1998). See also Debra Livingston, "Police Discretion and the Quality of Life in Public Places: Courts, Communities, and the New Policing," 97 *Colum. L. Rev.* 551, 576, 578–580 (1997).

9. See Neil Smith, "Giuliani Time: The Revanchist 1990s," *Social Text* 57, vol. 16 (Winter 1998): 1,9. See also Fox Butterfield, "Cities Reduce Crime and Conflict without New York–Style Hardball," *New York Times*, 4 March 2000: A1.

10. See, e.g., Peter Hermann, "Residents Frustrated over Crime; New Po-

lice Leaders Hear Angry Comments at a Council Forum; 'The City Is Dying'; Public Meetings Are Prelude to Daniel Confirmation Hearings," *Baltimore Sun,* 19 January 2000: 1B; Peter Hermann, "Police Hire N.Y. Officer as Deputy; Norris, Credited with Crime Reduction, to Work under Daniel," *Baltimore Sun,* 10 January 2000: 1A.

11. Evelyn Nieves, "Homeless Defy Cities' Drives to Move Them," *New York Times,* 7 December 1999: A1, A18; Jason Bennetto, "Law and Order: Blair Turns to Zero Tolerance for Crime; Penal Reformers Have Warned against Introducing 'Macho Policing' That Could Lead to Inner-City Riots," *Independent* (London), 30 September 1998: 8.

12. Christopher Drew, "An Iron Hand at Rikers Island Drastically Reduces Violence," *New York Times,* 8 November 1999: A1, B6.

13. Dirk Johnson, "Schools' New Watchword: Zero Tolerance," *New York Times,* 1 December 1999: A1, A21.

14. See, generally, Bernard E. Harcourt, "Reflecting on the Subject: A Critique of the Social Influence Conception of Deterrence, the Broken Windows Theory, and Order-Maintenance Policing New York Style," 97 *Mich. L. Rev.* 291, 308–342 (1998). Cf. Debra Livingston, "Police Discretion," at 581–583 (noting some suggestive, though not conclusive empirical research, linking disorder with crime, and public-order policing with crime reduction).

15. Harcourt, "Reflecting on the Subject," 341–342, 363–365.

16. Id. at 363–365.

17. See, e.g., id. at 341.

18. The quoted language is from a paper, "The Extras of Times Square," that Stephane Tonnelat presented at a conference, "Shaping Conflicts," held at the Graduate Center of the City University of New York on April 14, 1999. An architect and urban planner, Tonnelat is completing a joint Ph.D. degree program in urban planning at the Institut d'Urbanisme de Paris, University Paris XII, and in environmental psychology at the Graduate School of the City University of New York.

19. Kevin Flynn, "U.S. to Hear Complaints about Police," *New York Times,* 26 May 1999: B9.

20. Kit R. Roane, "Spitzer Threatens Subpoena on Frisk Data," *New York Times,* 16 May 1999: Metro 39.

21. See Kevin Flynn, "Racial Bias Shown in Police Searches, State Report Asserts," *New York Times,* 1 December 1999: A1, B5; Kevin Flynn, "Rights Panel Scolds Police on Race Issues," *New York Times,* 27 April 2000: B1; Steven A. Holmes, "Commission Says Independent Prosecutors Should Investigate Claims of Police Abuses," *New York Times,* 17 June 2000: B3. See United States Commission on Civil Rights, *Police Practices and Civil Rights in New York City* 187–190, 190–235 (June 2000).

22. Debra Livingston, "Police Discretion," at 592–593, 599–601.

23. 405 U.S. 156 (1972).

24. Id. at 171.

25. Id. at 164.

26. Three justices of the United States Supreme Court—Justices Stevens, Souter, and Ginsburg—recently endorsed this view in *City of Chicago v. Morales*, 119 S. Ct. 1849, 1857–1858 (1999).

27. Elisabeth Bumiller, "In Wake of Attack, Giuliani Cracks Down on Homeless," *New York Times*, 20 November 1999: A1, B3.

28. See Susan Sachs, "Giuliani's Goal of Civil City Runs into First Amendment," *New York Times*, 6 July 1998: B1, B6.

29. Id.

30. See, e.g., *Shapiro v. Thompson*, 394 U.S. 618 (1969). See, generally, Harry Simon, "Towns without Pity: A Constitutional and Historical Analysis of Official Efforts to Drive Homeless Persons from American Cities," 66 Tul. L. Rev. 631, 649–660 (1992).

31. See, e.g., *Robinson v. California*, 370 U.S. 660 (1962). See Simon, "Towns without Pity," 660–664; Juliette Smith, "Arresting the Homeless for Sleeping in Public: A Paradigm for Expanding the Robinson Doctrine," 29 Colum. J. L. & Soc. Probs. 293, 309–318 (1996).

32. See Smith, "Arresting the Homeless," 319, 330–335.

33. Richard Sennett, *The Uses of Disorder: Personal Identity and City Life*, 9–12, 42, 70–73, 80–82 (1970).

34. Id. at 123–124, 141–149.

35. Henri Lefebvre, *Writings on Cities*, 158, trans. and ed. by Eleonore Kofman and Elizabeth Lebas (Blackwell, 1996).

36. Henri Lefebvre, *The Production of Space*, 278–291 (Donald Nicholson-Smith, trans. Blackwell, 1991). Similarly, David Harvey's studies have demonstrated that private capital maintains itself through urban institutions and practices. Not only do cities offer a constantly renewable source of labor, opportunities for employment and education for labor, and a locus of ideas and technological innovation, but a city's built environment, infrastructure, and institutions of local government supply governance, managing, and coordination functions. David Harvey, *The Urban Experience* 23–24, 43–54 (Johns Hopkins University Press, 1989).

37. The term is discussed in Neil Smith, *The New Urban Frontier: Gentrification and the Revanchist City*, 45 (Routledge, 1996).

38. For an extended discussion of the campaign against Chinatown's vendors, see the essay by the Committee Against Anti-Asian Violence: Organizing Asian Communities in this collection.

39. See Zoning Resolution of the City of New York, 15 December 1960, as amended N950384 ZRY, 25 October 1995, and codified as sections 12-10, 32-01, 42-01, 52-77, 52-734, 72-40 of the Amended Zoning Resolution. See also Mike

Allen, "New York Begins to Raid and Close Adult Businesses," *New York Times*, 2 August 1998: 1, 35; "Legal Boundaries for the City's Sex Trade," *New York Times*, 2 August 1998: 35.

40. See, e.g., Charles V. Bagli, "Business Group Fails to Mollify Giuliani," *New York Times*, 24 September 1998: B5; Thomas J. Lueck, "The Mayor's Reach," *New York Times*, 5 April 1998: 33.

41. See, e.g., Smith, *The New Urban Frontier*, 22.

42. "Still Mourning; Latino Group Loses 2 Treasured Murals," *New York Times*, 21 November 1999: City Section, 8; Andrew Jacobs, "A New Spell for Alphabet City," *New York Times*, 9 August 1998, City Section: 1, 10–11.

43. Smith, "Giuliani Time," 7.

44. See, e.g., Jayson Blair, "2 Officers Charged in Theft of Street Vendors' Wares," *New York Times*, 30 June 1999: B3; Kit R. Roane, "Police Stole Peddlers' Wares, an Officer Tells Investigators," *New York Times*, 16 January 1999: B2; Benjamin Weiser, "Deal Allows Partial Return of Preachers to Times Sq.," *New York Times*, 18 December 1998: B4; Susan Sachs, "City Is Sued over Handling of Times Sq. Rallies," *New York Times*, 25 August 1998: B2.

45. See, e.g., Charles V. Bagli and Randy Kennedy, "Disney Wished upon Times Sq. and Revived a Dream," *New York Times*, 5 April 1998: 1; Charles V. Bagli, "Companies Get Second Helping of Tax Breaks," *New York Times*, 17 October 1997: A1 ff.

46. Smith, "Giuliani Time," 17.

47. James Holston, "Spaces of Insurgent Citizenship," in *Cities and Citizenship*, 166–168, James Holston, ed. (Duke University Press, 1999).

48. Jane Jacobs, *The Death and Life of Great American Cities* 275 (Vintage, 1992) (1961).

49. Id. at 114.

50. Id. at 42–46.

51. Id. at 31–32, 35–37.

52. See, generally, Manuel Castells, *The City and the Grassroots*, 106–170 (University of California Press, 1983).

53. Saskia Sassen, "Whose City Is It? Globalization and the Formation of New Claims," in *Cities and Citizenship*, 182–186, 183, n. 4, James Holston, ed. (Duke University Press, 1999).

54. James Holston and Arjun Appadurai, "Cities and Citizenship," in *Cities and Citizenship*, 2 (James Holston, ed., Duke University Press, 1999).

55. Id. at 4, 11–12, 14.

PART I

POLICING THE QUALITY OF LIFE

I

Turnstile Jumpers and Broken Windows

Policing Disorder in New York City

Tanya Erzen

IT IS RUSH hour in a crowded subway station in New York, and amid the jostling and general mayhem, a man bounds over a subway turnstile instead of swiping a card or paying a token. On the other side, a transit cop spots the fare evader mid-leap, and is waiting as he clears the turnstile. The officer slaps him with a fine and hauls him down to jail. When the suspect's name is run through the system, the officer discovers that the turnstile jumper is wanted for robbery and assault. By nabbing him in the subway and cracking down on minor offenses in general, this officer has solved one more crime and locked away one more criminal. While this scenario is my creation, the Quality of Life campaign in New York credits itself with just this sort of crime busting. Its logic rests on the idea that New York is a city where graffiti taggers, turnstile jumpers, and kids in a public park are either already criminals or simply criminals in the making. Underlying New York's Quality of Life campaign is the belief that leniency toward even minor offenses like fare beating in the subways reduces the city's quality of life and creates a culture that encourages more serious crime.

It is the apparently seamless link between a decrease in violent crime, an increase in police officers on the street, and an intensified Quality of Life campaign that has justified an ongoing program of force and harassment portrayed as an integral, legitimate step toward reducing crime in New York. For everyone deemed capable of creating disorder, from panhandlers to neighborhood teenagers to the homeless, the

Quality of Life initiative represents a concerted assault upon the right to exist in the city and to move in public spaces. The campaign's premise is two-pronged. First, the same people who jump a turnstile or wash a windshield may very well be felons and robbers, rapists and burglars. Second, a broken window, a trash-strewn street, or a homeless person asleep on a bench symbolize disorder. This disorder initiates a snowball effect whereby drug dealers, vandals, and other urban predators begin to engulf a neighborhood.

These ideas are not inventions of the Giuliani administration, but the actual product of the "broken windows theory," coined in 1982 by George Kelling and James Wilson in a widely cited article in the *Atlantic Monthly*. Kelling and Wilson believe that an area that appears disorderly implicitly sanctions more serious crimes. Thus, a causal link exists between physical disorder and actual crime.[1] Based on the premise that orderliness is equivalent to control, the theory assumes that visual disorder imbues people with a sense of fear and the menace of crime. With the Giuliani administration, the term "visual disorder" has become malleable enough to encompass people sleeping on benches, roaming public parks, washing windshields, and panhandling.

From the concept of broken windows emerged other studies that have come to serve as the operating manuals of the Quality of Life campaign. In 1990, Wesley Skogan conducted a survey of 13,000 residents in forty residential neighborhoods in Atlanta, Chicago, Houston, Philadelphia, Newark, and San Francisco, buttressed by field researchers' observations in ten of the forty neighborhoods. In his book, *Disorder and Decline: Crime and the Spiral of Decay in American Neighborhoods*, he established that disorder fosters social withdrawal, sparks concern about neighborhood safety, and plays an important role in urban decline.[2] His surveys found a broad consensus in these neighborhoods in identifying loiterers, vandalism, drug sales, gang activity, and public drinking as problems. Several forms of physical disorder were closely related to these disorderly behaviors: commercial sex shops; vandalism consisting of graffiti and damage to public spaces such as schools, bus shelters, street signs, vending machines, and dilapidated buildings. These findings have become fundamental texts in the oeuvre of quality-of-life literature. Yet, there are key questions that these theories do not address. Who is the community being protected? Who or what is disorderly? Does cracking down on quality of life offenses reduce crime? And, most importantly, does the Quality of Life initiative result in more daily police violence and harassment?

Proponents of the broken windows theory claim to speak on behalf of common, decent people in neighborhoods whose quality of life is being adversely affected by various forms of disorder. In the case of the campaigns to rid the New York subways of homeless people and graffiti, George Kelling and Catherine Coles, in *Fixing Broken Windows*, claim that it was not bankers or stockbrokers who demanded a safer subway environment, "it was working persons of all races who relied upon public transportation and craved decent and civil means of travel."[3] Separating those who cause disorder from the community members who want a safe, orderly place to live, both books distinguish between the rights of "disorderly" individuals and broader community claims. Kelling and Coles assert that "bands of teenagers congregating on the streets" present a disorder problem without addressing how those teenagers might be part of that same community or neighborhood. They avoid dealing with why a gathering of people on the street heralds the breakdown of the social order. What are the social and cultural implications when residents of a neighborhood do not have the right to congregate in a public place?

While the centerpiece of the Quality of Life initiative is the concept of disorder, what exactly constitutes disorder remains somewhat ambiguous. Kelling and Coles define disorder as "behavior that violates widely accepted standards and norms of behavior, and about which a broad consensus exists, in spite of racial, ethnic and class differences"[4] and "in its broadest social sense, disorder is incivility, boorish and threatening behavior that disturbs life, especially urban life."[5] Skogan tells us that social disorder is a matter of behavior such as catcalling, sexual harassment, drinking, and prostitution, while physical disorder includes ill-kept buildings, trash-filled lots, and alleys with rats.[6] According to the broken-windows theory, disorder is demarcated from more serious crimes like rape, murder, and assault to include "aggressive panhandling, street prostitution, drunkenness, and public drinking, menacing behavior, harassment, obstruction of streets and public spaces, vandalism and graffiti, public urination and defecation, unlicensed vending and peddling, unsolicited window washing of cars and other such acts."[7]

The Quality of Life initiative serves a psychological function as well as a punitive one; enforcement against these "crimes" restores a feeling of safety even if actual crime levels remain the same. One resident sums up this logic: "People have an implicit, causal theory about why things are littered—that somehow it's out of control, the city is not paying attention. So, by removing graffiti you may not have changed other things, but you make people feel as if you have."[8] An example is the way the administration heralds the ability of police officers to decipher graffiti-covered walls and thus solve local crimes, but in actuality no such link has been established.[9] In the Quality of Life campaign, it is assumed that people will perceive clean (devoid of homeless, panhandlers, graffiti) as safe areas. George Kelling writes, "For most people, New York's crime problem comes down to the well-founded belief that society has ceded control to those who are on the margin of or outside the law, and therefore that anything might happen in such places."[10] In the language of the broken windows theory, life in cities is synonymous with urban warfare. Fred Siegel, a professor at Cooper Union, writes: "New Yorkers understand that entering public places leaves them open to what have become the indignities of everyday interaction. In the East Village and on Upper Broadway, 'thieves" markets set up by predatory peddlers block the sidewalks. On nearly every street, homeless men panhandle aggressively, often 'rough tailing' passersby. Even those who drive must pay a toll to not-so-subtle shakedown artists, the 'squeegee men.'"[11] By focusing on fear of crime, the Quality of Life campaign skirts the accusation that it is engaging in a form of social control. Not only does the campaign strive to impose order on the built environment; it seeks to create a notion of the public good that is above politics, while sanctioning violence and harassment against certain people and populations.

The campaign juxtaposes the idea of a city that had proliferated out of control and the claim that cosmetic changes like erasing graffiti and removing newsstands and bus shelters are what have made a difference in reducing the number of dangerous felonies.[12] The ubiquitous posters of a white cop and young black man talking amiably underneath the caption "NYC needs CPR (Courtesy, Professionalism and Respect)" exemplify this strategy. The Giuliani administration has used cultural representations effectively, from the mantra of "cleaner, safer, brighter" to justify zoning laws and homeless evictions, to subways signs that are supposed to create a shared sense of the negative effects of panhandling. A Municipal Transit Authority (MTA) public service message from 1996 read:

> I'm SOOOO glad I got this seat. GOOD, now I can relax. (deep breath). Haven't even seen a panhandler for a while. WHOOPS, spoke too soon. TeRRIFic. MY LUCK he HAD to pick this car. Hey. HEY, buddy. Over here—over my head. See that? It says it's *illegal*. *Come onnnnn!* Can't I just SIT HERE without getting hassled?!!!! *Change* ? . . . yeah, THIS is what I'd like to change.

This poster was intended for the assumed community that shared a mutual exasperation with panhandlers on the subway. As a representation of a monolithic urban mindset, the ads and the campaign's justification as crime control shift the focus from problems of homelessness and economic disparity to a notion of public order and disorder. By invoking an abstract concept of order, the ad disguises the repercussions of the campaign on real people's lives.

While the eradication of some disorder sounds like a palatable idea to some, the lingering question is whether it results in a decline in crime. To justify the Quality of Life initiative, the Giuliani administration has assembled an impressive array of statistical information about the decrease in crime. However, no statistics have proven that arresting people for drinking beer in public reduces murders. Kelling and Skogan differentiate between the national crime problem and the continuum of local disorder problems on a neighborhood level. Some police officers contend that focusing on minor offenses will lead to a decrease in major problems, and that officers will now have specific guidelines when faced with thorny issues like panhandling as part of a unified strategy for addressing street disorder.[13] Whether crime has actually decreased is subject to debate considering that misdemeanor arrests have increased by 50 percent.[14] Previously, most people accused of minor offenses were given desk appearance tickets, which included a court date, and were then released. Under Giuliani's administration, the practice has shifted to detaining people accused of even minor misdemeanor offenses for the purpose of verifying their identities and whether any outstanding warrants exist. After being written up and detained, thousands have their charges dismissed by prosecutors who deem the arrests "flawed."

Another explanation for the overall decrease in crime and the

increase in misdemeanor arrests is the way that the Giuliani administration and the NYPD have implemented programs like Compstat.
Compstat is a computer system that systematically maps and compares high crime areas in the city. Precinct commanders meet weekly
with the commissioner and people from probation, parole, and the
district attorney's office. Each commander is required to give a formal
presentation highlighting crime results and statistics in his or her
precinct. Their charts track crime reports and arrests by the week,
day, and hour as well as concentrations of drug trafficking, shooting,
burglary, and robberies.[15] In one meeting, Louis R. Anemone, then
chief of department, asked a narcotics supervisor to explain why
there were few Saturday arrests. "It's a tough area, but aren't we
doing anything on Saturday? Your arrests are low on Saturday. Aren't
they selling dope on Saturday? I want you to balance this. I certainly
don't want you setting a pattern where they know you won't arrest
them on Saturday."[16] Officers and commanders who want to keep
their jobs have a tangible incentive to make as many arrests and issue
as many Quality of Life summonses as possible.

Aside from its implementation by the police, the initiative's effort
to link questions of disorder and crime has garnered significant support
among certain New York City residents. A quality-of-life survey conducted by the Commonwealth Fund in New York in 1992 found that
people feel the city government has the primary responsibility for aspects of life that give them the most concern: the number and quality of
available jobs, safer and cleaner streets and parks, and better schools.[17]
In an unsystematic survey conducted by the *New York Times* City Section in 1994, New Yorkers were asked what they saw as the quality of
life issues in their neighborhoods. The impressionistic responses ran the
gamut from traffic congestion, drugs, car radios, unlicensed vendors,
vacant lots, panhandling, social service programs, homeless enclaves,
prostitution, graffiti, in-line skaters, to motorcycle noise.[18] The Commonwealth survey also found that three out of five New Yorkers stated
that five "qualities"—dirt (43%), graffiti (40%), homeless people (34%),
noise (31%), and panhandlers (29%)—have created a sense of disorder
on the streets and reduced the quality of life for themselves and their
families.[19]

While it is understandable that some of us wouldn't want alley rats
and litter on our sidewalks, what happens when this extends to people
sleeping on benches and meeting on stoops?

HOW THE ROTTING APPLE WAS REDEEMED

Like most tales of redemption, the Quality of Life campaign invokes, if only to displace, a decline-and-fall narrative. And where better to begin than the grimy New York subways? The Quality of Life initiative has its origins in the 1987 and 1988 subway campaign spearheaded by William Bratton, then head of the New York City Transit Authority (NYCTA), in collaboration with the Metro North Police Department and Long Island Railroad Police Departments. According to George Kelling and Catherine Coles, two highly visible phenomena were creating a quality-of-life crisis in the subways—graffiti and disorderly behavior—which they claim the media translated into "the homeless problem."[20] Kelling and Coles write that the homeless were turning the subways and Grand Central Terminal into "gigantic surrogate shelters."[21] Rather than deal with homelessness, Bratton and the police study group that was set up to address the subway issues contended that the subway problem was a problem of disorderly behavior. Captain Richard Gollinge cautioned officers that disorderly behaviors, rather than homeless persons, should be targeted. Kelling and Coles write that the "outrageous and illegal behavior" in the subways was perpetrated by a "large number of petty and serious criminals."[22] What they meant by "disorderly and outrageous behavior" was panhandling and begging, and in 1989 Operation Enforcement went into effect to cleanse the subways. As the NYPD Transit Force began to crack down on panhandling and the eradication of graffiti, "police discovered that a high percentage of those arrested for fare beating either were carrying illegal weapons or had warrants outstanding for their arrest on felony charges."[23] When Bratton became commissioner of the New York City Police Department in 1993, the idea that petty offenses led to more serious crime in the subway became the blueprint for the Quality of Life campaign to "restore order" on the streets of New York.

With Bratton, the Quality of Life initiative relocated outside the subway, defined by the notorious squeegee campaigns that arrested men and women who washed the cars of motorists driving into the city and then demanded payment for their services. Kelling and Coles describe the threat the squeegee men represented: "The behavior of squeegeers toward occupants of cars varied. Many squeegeers worked hard, running back and forth between cars, even climbing on the bumpers of trucks to wash windows. . . . Nevertheless, others behaved in a manner clearly calculated to menace: if drivers said no to them, these squeegeers would drape themselves over the hoods of cars to prevent them from moving . . ."; "Squeegeers were not merely a troubled population. They were capable of considerable mayhem. Citizens had good reason to be fearful."[24] Again, the logic of the Quality of Life initiative supposedly found support in the fact that, of the squeegee men arrested, half had previous arrests for serious felonies such as robbery, assault, burglary, larceny, or carrying a gun, and half had arrests for drug-related offenses. Although Kelling and Coles do not cite statistics for these allegations, the implication was clear: subway graffiti artists, panhandlers, and window washers were sowing disorder *and* were apt to commit more serious crimes.

The Quality of Life program itself was begun as a pilot project in the West Village in Manhattan under the auspices and coordination of the Sixth Precinct in March 1994. It went citywide in July 1995. The West Village was chosen as the pilot site because it is a tourist destination, with an inordinate number of bars and a large weekend influx of people. According to Officer Mike Singer, the 6th Precinct issues more Quality of Life summonses than the whole Borough of Manhattan combined. In 1997, the precinct issued 7,400 summonses that fell into three main categories: public urination, drinking in public, and noise.[25] When offenders are given a summons they are required to produce some form of identification, and if an ID is unavailable they must go to the station house and have someone verify that they are from the neighborhood. People who cannot present proof of residency are promptly arrested and often sent to central booking as part of the new and improved "get tough on quality of life offenses" prong of the campaign. Since the campaign went into effect, 70 percent of the summonses are answered in court. In the most significant departure from previous protocol, those who do not come to court have a warrant issued for their arrest.[26] A plainclothes anticrime unit, a boroughwide task force for street peddling, a homeless task force to "encourage" homeless men and women to move from parks to shelters, and an antigraffiti unit of twenty-five officers are included in many precincts as part of the citywide campaign.[27] Unlike misdemeanor and felony complaints, summonses for many of the most commonly cited Quality of Life offenses can only be issued on the basis of observed conduct, not on a report of a violation. As a result, surveillance has been intensified in neighborhoods like the West Village in order to boost the number of arrests and citations.

The actual Quality of Life enforcement options consist of a list of twenty-five offenses that include panhandling, window washing, leaving property such as mattresses, shacks, or structures on public streets, the removal of residential trash, urinating in public, disorderly behavior on park department property, disorderly behavior in transit facilities, public consumption of alcoholic beverages, operation of a sound-reproduction device without a permit, street vending without a permit, public lewdness, open fires, unreasonable noise, and loud motorcycles (Appendix 1). In part, the Quality of Life initiative entails implementing laws of questionable legality that have honed the program even further. The "nuisance abatement" statute allows the NYPD to bring actions in state supreme courts seeking the judicial closing of locations where criminal activities occur. The "police padlock law" authorizes the police department to issue orders to close specific locations where two arrests have taken place and a third arrest occurs. Operation Chariot keeps people from driving to New York City to buy drugs, and Operation Soundtrap targets boom boxes.[28] Police officers have wide discretionary powers to determine what constitutes appropriate behavior in public spaces and what behavior will be tolerated to make an area "safe" for the "community."

If, as Mayor Giuliani claims, his administration has reduced the amount of violent crime in New York City, then has the Quality of Life initiative also led to an increase in brutality against the homeless and other populations? Although they are not named explicitly, homeless men and women have been the most obvious targets of the Quality of Life campaign, and are the most likely to be considered the visual and social emblems of disorder. Section 16-122 of the New York City Administrative Code makes it

> unlawful for any person to leave any box, barrel, bale of merchandise or other movable property upon any public street or in any public place. It is also unlawful under this section for the person to erect in public spaces any shed, building or obstruction. An Environmental Control Board Notice of Violation may be issued for this violation to a properly identified violator if the offense occurs in the officer's presence. If the offender cannot be properly identified, he or she may be arrested (as this section of law has both civil and criminal sanctions).[29]

Urinating and defecating in a public place is a misdemeanor under the Quality of Life enforcement codes.

Removal of the homeless has always been a key part of the enforcement options, and as noted, their presence was a crucial factor in the subway campaigns of the 1980s. In recounting these campaigns, Kelling stresses the distinction between homelessness and criminality.

"While homelessness was a factor that aggravated the situation in the subway, few genuinely homeless individuals sought refuge there. The most significant problem was outrageous and illegal behavior by a relatively large population of subway users, some of whom appeared to be homeless but many of whom were not, a high proportion of whom were severe alcohol and drug abusers and/or seriously mentally ill, and many of whom were using the subway as shelter."[30]

The subway campaigns and the erection of public shelters code are both very clear about trying to distinguish homelessness from disorderly acts in order to avoid the accusation of targeting homeless individuals. Kelling also emphasizes that homelessness is not a result of structural issues like poverty or unemployment, but exists as a choice for many people: "A significant subgroup of those identifying themselves as homeless are actually using an identity of homelessness as a camouflage for carrying out criminal acts. Neither the mentally ill and substance abusers, nor those who live on the streets by hustling and unlawful activity, should be permitted to threaten the viability of social and commercial life in our cities by repeatedly crossing the boundaries of civil and lawful behavior."[31]

This rhetoric resonates eerily with invectives about the homeless in the wake of a heavily publicized attack on Nicole Barrett by a man who was assumed to be homeless and mentally ill and turned out to be neither. Being homeless is deemed to be wanton and deliberate disorderly behavior that is preferably pushed out of view. Giuliani didn't mince words when he summed up his administration's views on homelessness in connection with the Barrett case, "Streets do not exist in civilized societies for the purpose of people sleeping there, bedrooms are for sleeping."[32]

The Equality of Life Campaign, operating out of Hudson Guild, challenges the Quality of Life initiative and defends homeless men and women who have been issued summonses. According to Jennifer Levy, a lawyer for the organization, homeless people are routinely cited and fined for these offenses.[33] In addition, they are cited for misusing park benches or taking up more than one seat on the subway. Levy stated that there are weekly sweeps of parks in Chelsea and the West Village, and the possessions of the homeless residents of these parks are often destroyed. When the lawyers at the Hudson Guild persuade the men and women in these cases to go to court, the charges are routinely dismissed, indicating that the charges function more as a concerted form of harassment. The courts are so clogged by cases involving the Quality of Life campaign that new civil judges are being assigned to deal with these offenses.[34] Ironically, in the case of the homeless, removing them from streets and park benches does not reduce violent crime because homeless persons, in their often vulnerable positions living on the street, are more frequently the victims of violent crimes.[35] Despite this fact, the Giuliani administration contends that crime is being averted as a result of the sweeps.

In addition to the disparate effect of the Quality of Life initiative on homeless people, the Public Lewdness code has been used to target gay men in an arbitrary and homophobic manner. The Gay and Lesbian Anti-Violence Project (AVP) documents that men are often arrested simply for being somewhere where it is suspected that gay sex may occur. In a two-day period at a World Trade Center public restroom, Port Authority Police recorded sixty-seven arrests for public lewdness.[36] In 1997 alone, the AVP recorded an 80 percent increase in police harassment and abuse complaints. Most of these cases came from individuals who had been targeted by police in "cruising areas" or near the Times Square sex businesses that are now being replaced in a larger redevelopment scheme.[37] The code, as made part of the Quality of Life initiative, actually reads:

> A person is guilty of Public Lewdness, Penal Law 245.00, a misdemeanor, when he/she intentionally exposes the private or intimate parts of his or her body in a lewd manner or commits any other lewd act (a) in a public place or (b) private premises under circumstances in which he or she may readily be observed from either a public place or from other private premises and with the intent that he or she be so observed. Public lewdness does not require that the intimate parts of the body be exposed, but that a person conducts himself or herself in a manner that most reasonable people would characterize as lewd, which may include actions such as prolonged,

deliberate manipulation of the clothed genital area, drawing attention to the genital area by pointing, gesturing, etc.[38]

Embedded in this code is an assumption that everyone knows "lewd"
when they see it, just as perceptions of disorder are assumed. Yet, the language leaves the enforcement of the code wide open for abuse by police.

The code also creates a seamless connection between lewd or sexual behavior and crime. Whitney Brown, a lawyer at the Gay and Lesbian Anti-Violence Project, confirmed that two gay men were recently
arrested for public lewdness near their home, beaten, placed on Rikers
Island, and then evicted from their apartment.[39] The code neglects to
mention whether consensual sexual acts in one's home that are observed from a public place like the street are grounds for arrest. Despite
the fact that "public" masturbation typically occurs in secluded areas
and is usually not a violent crime, men such as these are treated as sexual predators who victimize and sully the "public good" and public
standards of behavior. Arrests for public-lewdness violations are almost
exclusively confined to gay men rather than heterosexuals, enforcing
the idea that only gay men engage in public sex. Brown also stated that
through her experience, young men of color who are arrested for public lewdness are often assumed to be hustlers, while middle-class white
gay men are less likely to be sent to central booking.[40] As an arbitrary
construct brimming with moralistic undertones, lewdness is not only
problematic as a legal category, but its targeted use needlessly creates a
sense of shame and stigmatization for those accused of it.

POLICING COMMUNITIES

The most damaging repercussion of the Quality of Life initiative is the
way in which it has led to increased harassment in certain neighborhoods and against certain people, including, but not limited to, the
homeless and those people suspected of public lewdness. Across the
board, charges of police brutality have been on the rise since the incep-
tion of the Quality of Life initiative. Complaints lodged with the Civilian Complaint Review Board (CCRB) were up 20 percent for the first
five months of 1998; the CCRB received 2,176 complaints against police
officers for the period of January through May 1998 in contrast to 1,818
complaints during the same period in 1997.[41] For the entire calendar

year 1998, there was a 4.1 percent increase in complaints filed with the CCRB over the previous year.[42] The Equality of Life Campaign, the Audre Lorde Project, and the Gay and Lesbian Anti-Violence Project have documented instances of police brutality that demonstrate that the campaign has generated tolerance for aggressive measures and sustained harassment.[43] These organizations are still compiling statistics, but the documented brutality occurrences are representative of the harassment and violence of the campaign in general. Aside from these statistics, the fact that the Quality of Life initiative disproportionately affects populations like the homeless who have less access to legal recourse means that many instances of violence and harassment go unreported. The campaign also enables officers to act upon racial and gender biases they may have when they enter the police department—under the guise of enforcement of "unified guidelines." Officers who are already burdened with a difficult job are then forced to make arbitrary and highly individual judgments, raising the possibility of an increased use of force and harassment.

In theory, the local aspect of the Quality of Life initiative should foster greater "courtesy, professionalism, and respect" between officers and community members. Bratton wrote in 1995 that "reclaiming the public spaces of New York is a long-term strategy that puts precinct commanders in a position to mount their own local efforts against quality of life offenses."[44] However, despite the campaign's avowals of sensitivity to neighborhoods, surveillance of disorderly behavior has taken the place of actual mutual collaboration between officers and residents of a neighborhood. Bernard Harcourt writes: "The primary engine of community policing in New York may be the enhanced power of surveillance offered by a policy of aggressive misdemeanor arrests."[45] Surveillance operates as the new form of community policing.

The original idea of community policing was to focus more attention on working partnerships between the police and community that could potentially play an important role in reducing crime and promoting security. According to Robert C. Trojanowicz and David Carter, community policing evolved from the era of policing when beat officers were involved in communities and performed a number of social services. As conceptions of the police role changed in the early twentieth century, police departments began to measure their performance by the growth and decline in the rate of serious crimes. With the arrival of the police patrol car before World War I, police officers were brought under centralized authority and the mandate of the police was solely about controlling crime.

The first community policing projects were begun in the late 1960s in response to the large-scale uprisings that occurred in many urban areas of the United States.[46] Community policing was envisioned as a means to defuse and control massive public disorder. After the riots of the sixties, police departments realized it was necessary to mitigate the alienation between officers and the communities, instituting police/community relations programs. Initially, these programs failed to bridge the hostility in many neighborhoods because the officers assigned to the programs were those who had been unsuccessful in other capacities. Finally, departments began to recruit more educated and enthusiastic officers who were put back on beats in the community. These officers functioned as full-fledged law officers, but with the added mandate of working directly with citizens to help them solve the plethora of problems that had eroded the community's overall quality of life. Foot patrol programs in Newark, New Jersey, and Flint, Michigan, demonstrated that citizens fear not only crime, but also disorder, because they rightly perceive that "urban predators" can tell when a neighborhood is on its way up, or down, and that criminals parasitically feed on neighborhoods in obvious trouble. As community policing officers successfully solved crimes, the idea of community policing gained legitimacy and grudging respect, and motor patrol officers were rotated into foot patrol.[47]

Trojanowicz and Carter emphasize that community policing is a philosophy and not a specific tactic. "It is a proactive, decentralized approach, designed to reduce crime, disorder, and by extension, fear of crime, by intensely involving the same officer in the same community on a long-term basis, so that residents will develop trust to cooperate with police by providing information and assistance to achieve those three crucial goals."[48] The philosophy of community policing opposes traditional policing methods that are incident-driven, hierarchical, and standardized and replaces them with a strategy that is decentralized and flexible.[49] Community policing employs a variety of tactics, ranging from park-and-walk to foot patrol, to immerse the officer in the community. The premise of the Quality of Life initiative was similar; officers were to deal with local, neighborhood problems rather than emphasize large-scale crime-control policy. The original "broken windows" theory also contended that police should be more neighborhood oriented, and that there should be more officers deployed on foot who attend to minor disorder problems in neighborhoods.

Trojanowicz and Carter stress that community policing is about controlling crime and disorder in a community. This supports the premise of the current Quality of Life campaign because the authors see the community policing officer (CPO) acting as a uniformed armed presence to deter crime. Equally important, he or she also takes action with citizen assistance to resolve problems before they erupt as crime. Like Kelling and Bratton, they argue that, because physical and social disorder cluster closely with crime, the CPO also acts as the liaison to public and private agencies in dealing with problems like neighborhood decay. In keeping with the current Quality of Life campaign, improved police/community relations is a welcomed by-product of community policing, not its primary goal. Instead, New York City's Quality of Life campaign draws on the idea of community-police cooperation, but its approach is standardized rather than tailored to specific communities. "The idealized notion of community policing, in which beat cops organize a community to solve its problems, has always struck me as unrealistic. . . . Something else is happening in New York City—the reorganization of police resources and police strategies, including civil enforcement tactics to help communities counter the problems that afflict them."[50]

The fact that the concept of "community" in community policing is imprecise and idealized engenders difficulties in actually implementing it. As applied in New York City, community policing has become a shield for the biased policies of a campaign that is geared toward the community interest of some as opposed to others. The Giuliani administration has capitalized on the success of community policing initiatives to justify the enforcement options of the Quality of Life campaign. It equates the evictions of homeless people, and the harassment of immigrants and gay people, with policing and protecting a community's "quality of life."

According to theorists of community policing, the level of the fear of crime is indicative of whether there have been successful police interventions into the quality of life of a community. If the tangible results of community policing often fall short of the ideal of its rhetoric,[51] the most pernicious manifestation of communities policing themselves is the phenomenon of citizens' groups that have emerged specifically to enforce the ideas of "quality of life." As a mode of activism, the "quality of life" politics of these groups emphasize the accountability of municipal government and business interests to the local community, often expressed as an opposition between the neighborhood and outsiders. The Giuliani administration has capitalized on the fact that these communities often hold the local government responsible for, and as the enforcer of, Quality of Life concerns.[52] The new activists are "community rebels" who resist the siting of social service facilities in their neighborhood like AIDS treatment centers or homeless shelters in defense of the safety of their families and the "quality of life" in their neighborhoods.[53] According to new community activists, the right to the city is only valid as long as it conforms to specific notions of quality of life. That does not include the right that would allow homeless people to sleep in parks or teenagers to congregate on a corner.[54]

The Quality of Life initiative revolves around conceptions of community and disorder that substantially limit the right of any person to sleep, walk, congregate, vend, or listen to music in public spaces. While the initiative has effectively banished anyone whose behavior disrupts the order and safety of a community, its claims to reducing more serious crime are flimsy at best. In fact, the number of homicides in the city increased by 6 percent in 1999 over the previous year and for the first quarter of 2000, the number of homicides increased by 13 percent over the same three-month period in 1999.[55] If crime control connotes clogged civil courts and increased misdemeanor arrests, then the campaign has been successful. Thus far, even the Giuliani administration has been unable to prove that turnstile jumpers and squeegee men are violent criminals in waiting. And as a result of Quality of Life policing and surveillance, more people are targets of harassment and violence by police officers who are driven to make as many arrests as possible because of the prevalence of programs like Compstat. It is important not to dismiss the real fears that many people in New York have about crime. However, it is an accepted part of life in a large city that one inevitably interacts with a myriad of people on the streets. Forcing teenagers to disband and fixing a broken window may make us feel better, but does it make New York safer or only more sanitized?

Activism against police brutality cannot ignore the consequences of the Quality of Life initiative in favor of more visible police violence. Appalling instances of police brutality like the shooting of Amadou Diallo instigated protests and marches, but the daily harassment of the homeless and others remains largely uncontested. The most dangerous consequence of the increasing severity and number of arrests under the Quality of Life initiative is the potential for more brutality on the part of arresting officers. The very vagueness of the enforcement options and the arbitrary way in which community and disorder get defined leave too much discretion to the police. Too often the result is heightened harassment and violence. By handing over the informal power to define deviance to police officers and some community members, we have relinquished our right to live in a democratic and diverse city. If there is an incivility in the new New York City, surely this is it.

APPENDIX

Editors' note: Following are selections from the NYPD Quality of Life Enforcement Options Reference Guide for police officers. Some portions of the editors' copy were unreadable or unavailable, and the omitted text is indicated by asterisks.

Quality of Life Enforcement Options
A Reference Guide
Revised July 18, 1996

Panhandlers in Public Places

Penal Law Section 230.43 (1), Loitering for the Purposes of Begging, has been declared unconstitutional and is therefore unenforceable. *Loper v. New York City Police Department*, 999 F. 2d 699 (2d Cir. 1993). However, those who beg and, in the process, also annoy, harass, or alarm passersby by engaging in such activity as pushing, shoving or otherwise having physical contact with passersby may be charged with violation of Penal Law Section 240.26 (1), Harassment, in the second degree, a violation. Panhandlers who engage in such activity as following passersby, (Penal Law Section 240.26(2)), making menacing gestures or other conduct that annoys, harasses or alarms passersby (Penal Law Section 240.26(3)) can also be charged with harassment.

Panhandlers who impede pedestrian traffic can be charged with Penal Law Section 240.20 (5), Disorderly Conduct, a violation.

All of the aforementioned offenses are violations and must occur in the police officer's presence for the officer to take enforcement action. Properly identified violators may be issued a universal summons returnable to Criminal

Court. In addition, for any harassment charge, we must have a willing complainant before any enforcement action can be taken.

Panhandlers in Streets and Roadways

Panhandlers who operate in the streets and roadways by approaching vehicles stopped in traffic lights or other reasons can be charged with violation of Penal Law Section 240.20 (5), Disorderly Conduct, a violation, if they impede the flow of traffic.

In addition, the following Sections of the New York City Traffic Regulations apply to panhandlers in streets and roadways.

1. Section * *(e) (1) of the Traffic Regulations prohibits standing in a roadway in order to talk with, sell or offer to sell to anyone in a vehicle.

2. Section 2 * * of the Traffic Regulations prohibits the * * *

3. Section 3 * *(d) of the Traffic Regulations prohibits any person, other than an occupant or prospective occupant of a passenger vehicle from opening, offering to hold open, hold open or close or offer to close any door of the vehicle. (This shall not apply to such acts when intended as a social amenity without * * *- doorman or other persons employed by owners of the abutting premises.

4. Section 4 * * *(5) of the Traffic Regulations states that no person shall hail or procure for another, not in his or her social company, a taxi or other passenger vehicle.

All of the above mentioned offenses are violations that must occur in the presence of the police officer before he/she may take enforcement action. A universal summons returnable to Criminal Court may be issued to a properly identified violator.

* * *

Panhandlers on Transit Authority Property

Panhandling on Transit Authority Property such as the subways and subway system, buses and bus terminals, etc. is prohibited under Transit Authority Rule 1050.6 (b), a violation. Use of this section of law to prevent begging within the subway system was upheld as constitutional in *Young v. New York City Transit Authority*, 903 F.2d 146 (2nd Cir. 1990). A police officer must personally observe a violation of this section of law before taking enforcement action. A universal summons returnable to Criminal Court may be issued to a properly identified violator.

Window Washers

Persons who approach vehicles in traffic, or about to stop in traffic, for the purpose of washing windshields may be charged with violating New York City Traffic Regulation 4.04 (*)(3), a violation. Should the person's activity impede traffic flow, the person may also be charged with a violation of Penal Law Section 240.20 (5), Disorderly Conduct, a violation. A police officer may issue a universal summons for these violations to a properly identified violator, returnable to Criminal Court, provided the offense occurs in his/her presence. In Patrol Boroughs Manhattan North and South, prior to issuing the universal summons for the violation, a police officer must determine whether this is the subject's third violation, in which case, an arrest will be made. (A DAT may be issued, if the defendant qualifies. See Operations Order #31, s 94).

Structures, Shacks, Mattresses and Other Property on Public Streets

Section 16-122 of the New York City Administrative Code, a violation, makes if unlawful for any person to leave any box, barrel, bale of merchandise or other movable property upon any public street or in any public place. It is also unlawful under this section for the person to erect on any public street or in any public place any shed, building or obstruction. An Environmental Control Board Notice of Violation may be issued for this violation to a properly identified violator if the offense occurs in the officer's presence. If the offender cannot be properly identified, he or she may be arrested (as this section of law has both civil and criminal sanctions).

Refuse in Public Areas

Section 16-128 of the New York City Administrative code grants the Commissioner of Sanitation broad power to remove refuse and to keep the streets and other public places clean. Therefore, the Commissioner can remove or dispose of any vehicle, cardboard box, barrel, bale of merchandise or other movable property left in a public place. If a police officer becomes aware of such property abandoned in a public space, the Department of Sanitation can be requested to remove it.

Removal of Litter

Section 16-113 (7) (b) of the New York City Administrative Code, a violation, states that no unauthorized persons shall remove garbage placed by householders or their tenants within the stoop or area line, or in front of houses or lots, for removal, unless requested by residents of such houses. A police officer, who personally witnesses this offense, may issue a universal summons, returnable to Criminal Court. However, this section does not apply to public litter baskets.

Urinating in Public and Related Offenses

Urinating or defecating in a public place is a violation of the New York City Heath Code Section 153.09, a misdemeanor. Spitting in public is a violation of a Health Code Section 131.03, a misdemeanor. An officer may issue a universal summons, returnable to Criminal Court, to a properly identified violator of either of these sections of law.

Disorderly Behavior on Parks Department Property

There are several pertinent sections of the Parks Department Regulations that prohibit disorderly behavior on Parks Department property and are potentially useful enforcement tools for police officers. These are all misdemeanors. Members can issue a universal summons to a properly identified violator returnable to Criminal Courts. They include:

Section 1-04 (l)(8) prohibits engaging in any form of sexual activity;

Section 1-04 (m) prohibits using a park bench so as to interfere with its use by others,

Section 1-04 (o) prohibits camping, or erecting or maintaining a tent, shelter, or camp without a permit,

Section 1-04 (q) prohibits using any water fountain, drinking fountain, pool, sprinkler, or any other water contained in the park, for the purpose of washing himself or herself, his or her clothing, or other personal belongings. This subdivision shall not apply to those areas within the parks that are specifically designated for personal hygiene purposes (i.e., bathrooms, shower room, etc.), provided, however, that no person shall wash their clothes or personal belongings in such areas, nor shall any person who has not been using a facility under the jurisdiction of the Department for * * * purposes be permitted to use a shower room within said facility for personal hygiene purposes.

Section 1-04 (c) (1) prohibits littering in any park. This section also prohibits a person from taking in, dumping within, carrying through any park, or depositing in any parks receptacle any refuse generated or collected on property outside the jurisdiction of the Parks Department.

Section 1-04 (l) (5) prohibits the obstruction of pedestrian or vehicular traffic within any park. This section also prohibits the interference with or encumbrance of, the obstruction of or the rendering dangerous of any part of a park or park road.

Section 1-05 (p) (2) prohibits the leaving of personal belongings unattended within or adjacent to any park.

Section1-05 (s) (1) Exclusive children playgrounds. "Adults allowed in playground areas only when accompanied by a child under the age of twelve (12)."

Section1-05 (s) (2) Exclusive senior citizen areas. Certain areas of a park may be set aside for citizens 65 years of age and older, for their quiet enjoyment and safety."

"All exclusive areas will be specifically designated as such and signs will be posted informing the public of this designation."

Disorderly Behavior in Transit Facilities

Transit Authority Rule 1050.7, a violation, prohibits certain disorderly conduct on Transit Authority property, including subways and the subway system and buses and bus terminals. The prohibited behavior is as follows: no person on or in any facility or conveyance shall:

1050.7 (a) litter, dump garbage, liquids or other matter, create a nuisance, hazard or unsanitary condition (including, but not limited to, spitting, urinating, except in facilities provided).

1050.7 (l) conduct himself or herself in any manner which may cause or tend to cause annoyance, alarm or inconvenience to a reasonable person, or create a breach of the peace;

1050.7 (j) occupy more than one seat on a platform or conveyance, lie on the floor, platform, stairway, landing, or conveyance, or block free movement on a station platform or conveyance;

1050.7 (k) commit any act which causes or may tend to cause injury or harm to oneself or to any other person including, but not limited to riding a bicycle, skateboard, roller skates, in line skates, or any self-propelled or motor-propelled vehicle. This provision does not apply to the * * * or motor- propelled wheelchairs or similar devices by a non-ambulatory individual.

A police officer who personally observes any of the aforementioned violations of law may issue a universal summons to a properly identified violator, returnable to Criminal Court. In lieu of the issuance of a summons, Transit Authority Rule 1050.11 empowers a police officer to eject from the facility any person observed violating any of the aforementioned rules provided, however, said persons had notice of such rule.

Public Consumption of Alcoholic Beverages

The public consumption or carrying of an open container of alcoholic beverages in a public place by persons is prohibited by Administrative Code Section 10-125 (2) (b), a violation. This section of law does not apply to such activity at a block party, feast or similar function where a permit has been obtained. A police officer must personally observe a violation of this section of law before taking enforcement action. A universal summons returnable to Criminal Court may be issued to a properly identified violator.

Consumption of Alcoholic Beverages in a Vehicle

The drinking of an alcoholic beverage by an operator or passenger of a vehicle, being driven upon a public highway, is prohibited by Section 1227 (1) of the Vehicle and Traffic Law, a traffic infraction. The person in possession of the alcoholic beverage is the violator. A universal summons may be issued for this violation if the offense occurs in the officer's presence. Such summons are returnable to the Traffic Violations Bureau.

Public Consumption of Alcoholic Beverages on Parks Department Property

Parks Department Regulations Section 1-05 (1) (3), a misdemeanor, prohibits except where specifically permitted by the Parks Commission, the consumption of any alcoholic beverage in any park, playground, beach, swimming pool or any other park facility or property. This section prohibits the possession of alcoholic beverages on any park's property or facility. Additionally, this section also prohibits any person from bringing, possessing, or consuming any controlled substance, as defined in Section 220.00 of the New York State Penal Law, on any parks department property or facility. Parks Department Regulation Section 1-05 (f) (2) prohibits the appearance, in any park or park facility, by any person under the influence of alcohol or other drug to the degree that he may endanger himself, other persons or property, or unreasonably annoy persons in his vicinity. A universal summons may be issued for a violation of either of these sections of law. Such summonses are returnable to Criminal Court.

Public Consumption of Alcoholic Beverages in Transportation Facilities

Transit Authority rule 1050.7 (g), a violation, prohibits the consumption of alcoholic beverages of possession of any open container of alcoholic beverages on Transit Authority Property, including subways and the subway system, and buses and bus terminals. Officers who personally observe a violation of this section of law may issue a universal summons, returnable to Criminal Court, to a properly identified violator.

Public Consumption of Alcoholic Beverages By Minors

Section 65 (1) of the Alcoholic Beverage Control Law, a misdemeanor, states that no person shall sell, deliver, or give away or permit or procure to be sold, delivered or given away, any alcoholic beverage to any person actually or apparently under the age of 21 years. Section 65 (2) prohibits the sale of alcoholic beverages to any visibly intoxicated person. A police officer may issue universal summonses for these misdemeanor offenses to properly identified violators.

Section 65 (b) of the Alcoholic Beverage Control Law, a violation, prohibits the purchase or attempted purchase of an alcoholic beverage by persons under 21 years of age through fraudulent means. A police officer may issue a universal summons for this misdemeanor offense to properly identified violator, over the age of 16, returnable to Criminal Court.

Section 65 (c) of the Alcoholic Beverage Control Law, a violation with a civil penalty only, prohibits the possession of an alcoholic beverage with intent to consume by persons under the age of 21 years. Only a universal summons, returnable to Criminal Court, may be issued as a violation of this section. An arrest may not be effected for a violation of this section, even if the officer cannot properly identify the violator.

In addition to the prohibitions mentioned above, Section 260.20 (2) of the Penal Law, Unlawfully Dealing With a Child, a misdemeanor, prohibits any adult from giving or selling an alcoholic beverage to a person less than 21 years of age. A properly identified violator can be issued a DAT for this offense. This law does not apply to the parent or guardian of a child.

Street Vendors

The sale of all types of merchandise and services in public places of the City of New York is regulated by the General Vendor Provisions in Title 20 of the

Administrative Code. Those general vendors who are operating without a Department of Consumer Affairs license are in violation of Section 20-453 of the Administrative Code, a misdemeanor. An Environmental Control Board Notice of Violation should be issued for selling or displaying for sale merchandise and services in public places. In addition to the issuance of an E.C.B. Notice of Violation, the goods of a an unlicensed general vendor should be seized and vouchered for forfeiture. Special rules apply to the vendors of written materials such as books, baseball cards, greeting cards, etc., and religious articles. Prior to taking enforcement action against vendors of these items, the officer concerned should contact the Legal Bureau at 212-374-5400, or the Manhattan South Peddler Task Force.

The sale of consumable food items in public places of the City of New York is regulated by the Food Vendor Provisions of Title 17 of the Administrative Code. Food vendors must possess a permit for their cart and a license for the operator of the cart. If either one of these items is missing, the food cart must be seized and vouchered for forfeiture. If the vendors license is missing, an Environmental Control Board Notice of Violation should be issued for a violation of Section 17-307 (b) of the Administrative Code, a misdemeanor. If the cart does not have a permit, an Environmental Control Board Notice of Violation should be issued for a violation of Section 17-307 (b) of the Administrative Code, a misdemeanor. Special rules apply to licensed food vendors. Prior to taking enforcement action against a licensed food vendor, the officer concerned should contact the Legal Bureau at 212-374-5400, or the Manhattan South Peddler Task Force.

Sound Reproduction Devices

A sound reproduction device is any sound device or apparatus, or any device or apparatus for the amplification of any sounds from any radio, phonograph, sound-machine or sound-producing device, or any device or apparatus for the reproduction or amplification of the human voice or other sounds. Operation of a sound reproductive device without a permit is a violation of Section 10-108 (2) (d) of the Administrative Code, a misdemeanor. An officer may issue a universal summons, returnable to Criminal Court, to a violator of this section and seize the sound reproduction device as evidence. Children more than eleven, but less than sixteen years of age, should be issued a juvenile report for violation of this section of law and the sound reproduction device will NOT be seized. For further information regarding sound enforcement consult Interim Order No. 73, Series 93, or consult the Legal Bureau at 212-374-5400.

Unreasonable Noise, Not Involving Sound Reproduction Devices

A police officer who receives complaints for unreasonable noise should make a Activity Log entry listing the names and addresses of the complainants. The officer has several choices regarding noise enforcement action (as per Interim Order 73, s. 94). He or she may issue a universal summons, returnable to Criminal Court for Disorderly Conduct, Penal Law Section 240.20 (2), a violation. In the alternative, the officer may issue an Environmental Control Board Notice of Violation for violation of Section 24-218 of the Administrative Code, a misdemeanor.

Cars with Excessively Loud Radio Devices

The operator of a motor vehicle playing a radio or other device at an excessive volume (i.e. a "boom box car") may be charged with Penal Law Section 240.20, Disorderly Conduct, a violation of Administrative Code Section 24-210, Unreasonable Noise, a misdemeanor. Because of the difficulty in determining what level of sound is excessive, whenever possible, an officer who has been trained in sound enforcement and has the use of a sound meter should be assigned to this enforcement. With a proper sound level reading, the vehicle may be seized pending disposition of the case pursuant to Vehicle and Traffic Law Section 375 (47) (a).

Public Lewdness

A person is guilty of Public Lewdness, Penal Law 245.00, a misdemeanor, when he/she intentionally exposes the private or intimate parts of his or her body in a lewd manner or commits any other lewd act (a) in a public place, or (b) private premises under circumstances in which he or she may readily be observed from either a public place or from other private premises, and with intent that he or she be so observed. Public lewdness does not require that the intimate parts of the actor be exposed, but that a person conducts himself or herself in a manner that most reasonable people would characterize as lewd, which may include actions such as prolonged deliberate manipulation of the clothed genital area, drawing attention to the genital area by pointing, gesturing, etc.

Open Fires

Section 24-149 of the air pollution provisions of the New York City Administrative Code prohibits the use, maintenance or kindling of any open fire so as to cause * * *, exempted from the law are residential barbecues, barbecues in approved locations on Parks Department property and outdoor fires used in conjunction with tar kettles and asphalt melting equipment.

*   *   *

Erection of Public Shelters

Section 16-122 of the New York City Administrative Code makes it unlawful for any person to leave any box, barrel, bale of merchandise or other movable property upon any public street or in any public place. It is also unlawful under this section for the person to erect in public spaces any shed, building or obstruction. An Environmental Control Board Notice of Violation may be issued for this violation to a properly identified violator if the offense occurs in the officer's presence. If the offender cannot be properly identified, he or she may be arrested (as this section of law has both civil and criminal sanctions).

Loud Motorcycles

The lack of, or the removal of, baffling plates in the mufflers of vehicle engines, particularly motorcycles, creates unreasonable noise and is a cause of community concern. Motorcycles in this condition are said to have "straight pipes", and can be excessively and unreasonably loud. Members of the service who personally observe a motorcycle operating with "straight pipes" may issue a properly identified operator a universal summons, returnable to the Traffic Violations Bureau, for a traffic infraction under Section 375 (31a) of the New York State Vehicle and Traffic Law. Operators whose motorcycles possess a partially removed or interchangeable baffling system may be issued a universal summons for a traffic infraction under Section 375 (31b). In the event a member of the service, because of lack of experience, is unable to determine if the reason for the excessive noise emanating from a motorcycle is because of "straight pipes," an Environmental Control Board Notice of Violation may still be issued for the violation of "unreasonable noise" under Section 24-213 of the Administrative Code. When issuing a Notice of Violation for this offense, the member should make an Activity Log entry of the type of location (i.e. residential, commercial, etc.); name and address of complainants, if available; and the distance from which the motorcycle could be heard. Members who have been trained in the use of sound meters can enforce Section 386 of the Vehicle and Traffic Law and Section 24-232 of the Administrative Code against motorcycles and other vehicles with unreasonably loud engines. Both of these offenses are violations that require the offender to exceed a certain, measured decibel level.

*   *   *

NOTES

1. George Kelling, "The Broken Windows Theory," *City Journal*, Spring 1982, 23–34.

2. Wesley Skogan, *Disorder and Decline: Crime and the Spiral of Decay in American Neighborhoods* (New York: The Free Press, 1990).

3. George L. Kelling and Catherine M. Coles, *Fixing Broken Windows: Restoring Order and Reducing Crime in Our Communities* (New York: Martin Kessler Books/The Free Press, 1996), 4.

4. Ibid., 5.

5. Ibid., 14.

6. Skogan, *Disorder and Decline*, 21.

7. Ibid., 15.

8. Janny Scott, "The Mellowing of the Quintessentially Crabby City," *New York Times*, 9 February 1997: sec. 1, 39.

9. Recent articles in the *Times* talk about how law enforcement squads have begun treating graffiti tags as evidence. Thirty graffiti arrests last year in the Gowanus Housing Project in Brooklyn led to the recruitment of two informers who led the police to several top drug dealers. See Clifford Krauss, "Decoding Graffiti to Solve Bigger Crimes," *New York Times*, 4 October 1996: Metro.

10. George Kelling, "Measuring What Matters: A New Way of Thinking about Crime and Public Order," *City Journal*, Spring 1992, 24–25.

11. Fred Siegel, "Reclaiming Our Public Spaces," *City Journal*, Spring 1992, 36.

12. One piece of the campaign is to "reduce clutter" on New York's busiest corners by imposing a uniform appearance on sidewalk structures by placing the design, construction, and maintenance of all bus shelters and newsstands under a single contract that would go to the highest bidder. See Jonathon Hicks, "Street Newsstands and Bus Stops are Giuliani's Latest Concern," *New York Times*, 14 April 1995: B1.

13. George James, "Police Project on Street Vice Goes Citywide," *New York Times*, 6 July 1994: B1.

14. See, e.g., Bernard E. Harcourt, "Reflecting on the Subject: A Critique of the Social Influence Conception of Deterrence, the Broken Windows Theory, and Order Maintenance Policing New York Style," *Michigan Law Review* 97, no. 2 (November 1998): 332; Ford Fessenden and David Rohde, "Dismissed before

Reaching Court, Flawed Arrests Rise in New York," *New York Times*, 23 August 1999: A1.

15. David Anderson, "Crime Stoppers," *New York Times Magazine*, 9 February 1997: 47.

16. Ibid.

17. This is based on a survey of 2,800 residents in all boroughs conducted between April and September 1992. The respondents rated as negative: safety on the streets (88 percent), air quality (86 percent), street maintenance (83 percent), police protection (67 percent), and parks (49 percent). The survey was conducted by Louis Harris and Associates for the Manhattan Institute, and the results were part of a special issue on quality of life in spring 1992.

18. See Todd Purdum, "What Makes Us Angry," *New York Times*, 7 August 1994: sec. 13, 1.

19. The Commonwealth Fund, "Improving the Quality of Life in New York City Program," Survey of New York City residents, survey questionnaire, 17 September 1993, 10.

20. Kelling and Coles, *Fixing Broken Windows*.

21. Ibid., 120.

22. Ibid., 124.

23. Ibid., 134.

24. Ibid., 142.

25. This was one of three conversations with Officer Singer on April 29. He stated that since 1990, the precinct has incrementally increased its force and that this has correlated to a decrease in crime. He added that the precinct does not have many repeat offenders, which according to him indicates that the Quality of Life program is working. The number of officers has gone up from 123 to 240, and the additional officers are hired as beat officers. He believes the sight of the officers on the street keeps people from committing crimes.

26. Conversation with Officer Singer.

27. Ibid.

28. William Bratton, "The New York City Police Department's Civil Enforcement of Quality-of-Life Crimes," *Journal of Law and Policy* 3 (1995): 448–450.

29. Quality of Life Enforcement Options, 3. See Appendix to this chapter.

30. Kelling and Coles, *Fixing Broken Windows*, 122.

31. Ibid., 67–68.

32. Nina Bernstein, "A Homeless Man Challenges New York City Crackdowns," *New York Times*, 22 November 1999: A1.

33. Jennifer Levy, a lawyer at the Equality of Life campaign, spoke to me on several occasions about the work her organization is doing to fight the Quality of Life initiative. The organization has three lawyers who represent the homeless in court, advise them about their rights when they are arrested, and

train them to act as activists for other homeless men and women. As a result of the disproportionate negative effects of the Quality of Life initiative on the homeless, the lawyers and the Center for Constitutional Rights are bringing a suit against the police. In addition, homeless activists have implemented workshops in shelters throughout the city to explain the campaign and the legal rights that the homeless have when they are targeted.

34. Clyde Haberman, "Crime Down, but Courts Are Clogged," *New York Times*, 3 January 1997: B1.

35. Brad Lichtenstein, "Yet Another Reason to Arrest the Homeless," *New York Times*, 24 October 1994: A16.

36. These statistics were made available to me by the Gay and Lesbian Anti-Violence Project, an organization that deals with bias crimes as well as defending men who are prosecuted under the public lewdness code. Whitney Brown, the lawyer with whom I spoke, stated that in a World Trade Center bathroom on a day in January, there were twenty-nine arrests; there were thirty-four on another day.

37. Gay and Lesbian Anti-Violence Project statistics.

38. Quality of Life Enforcement Options, 9. See Appendix of this chapter.

39. According to Brown, unlike the case of the homeless who are frequently hauled down to court, public lewdness summonses are never dropped in court. The Gay and Lesbian Anti-Violence Project is the only organization fighting public lewdness in the city, and it either files complaints against the city or makes reports to the Civilian Complaint and Review Board (CCRB). Suing the city if someone sustains injuries is an endless process that begins with filing a claim within ninety days of an injury, after which there is a hearing, talks, and usually settlement. When I interviewed Brown, almost all of her cases were still in the hearing stage. Simultaneously, the CCRB is making the criteria for substantiation of a case of abuse on the part of the police while arresting men for public lewdness more difficult. Almost 97 percent of public lewdness cases involve physical or verbal abuse, and Brown estimates that 95 percent of the men arrested are subjected to slurs, while 50 percent are beaten physically by the police. Brown spoke of one recent case that involved a gay black man who had purchased two bags of groceries for his mother who lived outside the city and went to Penn Station to board a train. While he was in the bathroom, two police officers entered and charged him with public lewdness, threatened to rape him, and beat him up. None of these statistics addresses the fact that it can be deeply humiliating to withstand the court process on a public lewdness charge after experiencing brutality by the police.

40. This information is incomplete in that it comes from the statistics of the Gay and Lesbian Anti-Violence Project and does not include men who don't seek legal counsel.

41. "Complaints against the Police Rise," *New York Times*, 11 June 1998: A25.

42. *Civilian Complaint Review Board Report for 1998*, 3.

43. Both organizations are currently compiling statistics on the number of brutality cases their organizations deal with. The Gay and Lesbian Anti-Violence Project did a Freedom of Information Law request for the numbers of men cited for public lewdness in January 1996, but were unable to get accurate numbers because the lewdness charges are mixed in with undifferentiated misdemeanors. The Equality of Life campaign has had difficulty in compiling accurate statistics because of the significant numbers of homeless people who they believe never report incidences of harassment or brutality.

44. Bratton, "The New York City Police Department's Civil Enforcement of Quality-of-Life Crimes," 448–450.

45. Harcourt, "Reflecting on the Subject," 342.

46. Robert R. Friedman, *Community Policing: Comparative Perspectives* (New York: St. Martin's Press, 1992), 25.

47. Robert C. Trojanowicz, *Community Policing: How to Get Started* (Cincinnati: Anderson Publishing, 1994) and Robert C. Trojanowicz and David Carter, "The Philosophy and Role of Community Policing," The National Neighborhood Foot Patrol Center, 1988.

48. Ibid., 12. See also Samuel Walker, *A Critical History of Police Reform: The Emergence of Professionalism* (Lexington, Mass.: Lexington Books, 1992) and Robert M. Fogelson, *Big City Police* (Cambridge, Mass.: Harvard University Press, 1977).

49. Although they are not part of all community policing models, standard elements include the continuous assignment of police units to specific neighborhoods or beats, the implementation of a knowledge base regarding the problems, cultural characteristics, and resources of a neighborhood, the use of formal and informal mechanisms to involve community people in identifying problems, and the delegation of responsibility to the community police unit to address crime and order maintenance problems in the neighborhood that fall under the term "quality of life."

50. Trojanowicz, *Community Policing*.

51. A central flaw in community policing models is that it is rarely coupled with actual power sharing with the community and tends to function as an umbrella term for disparate policies like public relations, crime prevention, crime control, and beat officers. Similarly, a further issue is that as officers become integrated into communities they may begin to wield too much power, and officer parochialism and corruption will increase. Currently, the Community Patrol Officer Project in New York has been virtually abandoned in lieu of the Quality of Life campaign, which has appropriated the rhetoric about controlling disorder and addressing quality of life issues.

52. See Steven Gregory's essay on community activism in the Corona area of Queens in "Race, Rubbish and Resistance," in *Race*, Steven Gregory and

Roger Sanjek, eds. (New Brunswick, N.J.: Rutgers University Press). There are countless examples of community activism in the name of quality of life, such as the Quality of Life Task Force, which formed in Queens to prevent the siting of a sex club.

53. Vivian Toy, "Sex Shops Greet Law with Wink and Lawsuit," *New York Times*, 16 October 1996: B1. Most of the New Community Activism has taken root in primarily working-class areas of the city. Karen Koslowitz, a councilwoman for the Rego Park area of Queens where a Quality of Life Coalition has formed to prevent the citing of sex businesses, sums up this new type of activism: "These places have a right to exist, but not in residential areas where they bring down property values and destroy the quality of life."

54. Heather MacDonald, "The New Community Activism: Social Justice Comes Full Circle," *City Journal*, Autumn 1993, 44–55.

55. William K. Rashbaum, "Rising Murder Rate Defies Latest Push against Crime," *New York Times*, 5 April 2000: B3.

2

Policing Madness

People with Mental Illness and the NYPD

Heather Barr

James

James[1] grew up in Brooklyn in a middle-class family where he was the oldest of three children. He was a junior in college studying engineering when he was hospitalized for the first time and diagnosed with paranoid schizophrenia. He has been in and out of hospitals dozens of times since then. His family took care of him for years, but eventually his parents died and his siblings left the city.

Today, James is homeless. He sleeps in a park, eats out of garbage cans, panhandles, and drinks malt liquor to help him cope with the voices he hears in his head. He does not see a psychiatrist; he has neither benefits nor insurance.

James hears things other people do not. He hears agents from the FBI planning to capture him, kidnap him, and hurt him. He often talks back to the voices he hears.

One day, James is standing on a busy corner arguing loudly with the voices in his head and waving his arms for emphasis. He is blocking pedestrian traffic and a police officer tells him to move along. James looks at the police officer and sees one of the FBI agents coming to get him. He flails his arms, hitting the officer and knocking him down.

James is arrested and charged with disorderly conduct, assaulting a police officer, and resisting arrest. Assaulting an officer is a felony. James spends several hours at the nearby precinct, several more hours at Central Booking, several more hours in a pen below the courthouse, several more hours in a pen behind the courtroom, and finally, about 30 hours after hitting the police officer, James meets his lawyer.

The lawyer knows immediately that there is something wrong with James. Thirty hours of moving from one cage to another have not helped James collect himself. He is disheveled and smelly and detoxing from alcohol; he is barefoot, talking loudly to himself, and there is a cut and a bruise on his face where another prisoner punched him for being too noisy.

At arraignment, the assistant district attorney assigned to the case is amenable to lowering the charges. She has reviewed the paperwork and agrees with the defense attorney that James probably did not mean to hit the police officer. She, like the defense attorney, can tell just by looking at James that he has psychiatric problems.

James is offered the opportunity to plead guilty to misdemeanor assault and receive a sentence of 10 days of community service. The defense attorney tells James it's a good deal and he should take it. James pulls himself together enough to get through the procedure of pleading guilty. His defense attorney tells him where and when to go for the community service and, as an afterthought, suggests that James see a doctor and get some medicine.

James agrees to everything and walks out of the courtroom barefoot into a cold rainy night. He still has no benefits or insurance or any idea where he might find a doctor, if he wanted one. He loses the piece of paper with the information about community service almost immediately. He goes back to the park where he usually sleeps. He does not show up for community service. Three weeks later, James is found sleeping in the entrance foyer of a building on a snowy night. He is arrested for trespassing, and the judge wants to send him to jail because he didn't do his community service last time.

Gidone (Gary) Busch

Gidone (Gary) Busch grew up on Long Island in a loving family. He completed college and enrolled in the prestigious Mount Sinai Medical School before symptoms of psychiatric illness began to trouble him. He left medical school and spent several years in Israel, where he became increasingly involved in the study and practice of Judaism. During his time in Israel, he was also hospitalized several times and treated for schizophrenia.

When he returned to New York, Busch settled in Borough Park, a section of Brooklyn that is home to a community that is predominantly made up of Hasidic Jews. There, Busch pursued his religious studies with several of the community's rabbis, wrote poetry, and earned a reputation in the community as a person who lived to help others.² He also became engaged to a young woman named Netanya.

On August 30, 1999, at 6:40 p.m., the NYPD received a 911 call regarding "an emotionally disturbed Jewish man who is armed with a knife and taking drugs at 1619 46th Street."³ This is the address of the basement apartment where Busch lived with his roommate, a previously homeless man whom he had recently taken in. At 6:45, two officers arrive at Busch's apartment and, observing that Busch appears to be experiencing a psychiatric crisis, follow NYPD procedure by calling for a supervisor and the Emergency Services Unit, a unit of officers specially trained in handling psychiatric emergencies.

Within two minutes, two sergeants and two additional officers have arrived. The Emergency Services Unit has not. The six officers try to contain Busch in his apartment by using pepper spray. Their efforts fail and they retreat from the apartment up the basement stairs. Busch follows them, waving a small hammer used in religious rituals. One of the sergeants is hit in the arm with the hammer, but Busch is moving away from the officers, still holding the hammer, when four of the six open fire.⁴ Busch was shot twelve times, eleven of them with hollow-point bullets, and was killed immediately. He was thirty-one years old.

Busch's tragic death led to an outburst of protest, both in the Borough Park community where he lived and in the larger community. Police Commissioner Howard Safir defended the officers, saying that the officers' lives were in danger and explaining that in shooting to kill rather than simply to disarm or disable Busch, they were following NYPD policy. Mayor Rudolph Giuliani called the shooting "unfortunate," then, with typical tact, snapped at reporters, "Would you like to have a hammer inserted in your brain?"⁵ A grand jury investigation ended with a decision not to indict any of the officers involved in the shooting. Busch's family retained the "O.J. Dream Team," Johnny Cochran, Peter Neufeld, and Barry Scheck, to explore the possibility of a civil lawsuit.

INTRODUCTION

James and Gidone Busch's stories are disturbingly common ones in this city where psychiatric services are crumbling, the criminal justice system is continuously expanding, and police have virtually no training or resources for handling people in psychiatric crises. In New York City, over one million people suffer from mental illness,[6] over 100,000 people live with severe and persistent psychiatric problems such as schizophrenia,[7] and an estimated 12,000 mentally ill homeless people live on the streets.

The New York City Police Department responds to *every* 911 call regarding a person in psychiatric crisis, regardless of whether a crime has been committed. Each year, the New York City Police Department responds to at least 50,000 calls designated as involving EDPs ("emotionally disturbed persons" in police jargon). As responsibility for dealing with the mental health needs of poor people has increasingly shifted from the mental health system to the criminal justice system, the New York City Police Department has been forced to become the first intake procedure for admission to the state's largest psychiatric facility—Rikers Island.

Recent trends in New York's mental health and criminal justice systems have led to increasing contact between acutely mentally ill people and the police. Continued downsizing of psychiatric hospitals, fragmentation and underfunding of community mental health services, and the impact of welfare reform on people with disabilities have made it increasingly difficult for New Yorkers with serious mental illnesses to access the psychiatric services they need to live in the community.

At the same time that the mental health system has been turning increasing numbers of seriously mentally ill away without the help they need, recent shifts in New York City's criminal justice policies have created a declining tolerance for public disorder. "Quality-of-life" crime enforcement, Mayor Rudolph Giuliani's brainchild (with a tip of the hat to James Q. Wilson and George Kelling's "broken windows" hypothesis), drastically changed police behavior in New York City. Police now arrest people for public disorder offenses such as drinking in public and public urination that in the past would have been cause for a reprimand, if that. The population most affected by this change: the homeless, particularly those who, because of mental illness, act out in conspicuous ways.

The impact of shifts in mental health and criminal justice policies on people with mental illness has been striking. Rather than crisis intervention services, New York City has the police. Increasingly, jails and prisons have replaced hospitals for mentally ill New Yorkers. On any given day, there are close to 8,000 mentally ill people in New York State's prisons and jails. Some of these people are serving long sentences in the state prison system; many others are spending short periods of time at Rikers Island on relatively minor misdemeanor charges. In 1997, 15,000 New York City jail inmates were treated for serious mental illnesses, and more than 33,000 required mental health services.[8] Fifteen to 20 percent of city jail inmates are mentally ill; 7 to 8 percent of state prisoners are.[9]

The "criminalization of mental illness" in New York City has had a profound impact on the New York City Police Department. The city offers virtually no mental health crisis services, so police are forced to deal with all emergency situations, regardless of whether criminal behavior is involved. The department has done almost nothing to prepare officers for these duties, providing almost no training on crisis intervention to regular officers. Difficulty accessing emergency mental health services leads officers to arrest people they would prefer to hospitalize.

This chapter will describe the changes in New York City's mental health and criminal justice systems that have created this situation and will discuss some of the unintended consequences of the fact that, in New York City, mental illness has become primarily a criminal justice issue.

THE DETERIORATION OF NEW YORK'S MENTAL HEALTH SYSTEM

Serious deficiencies plague the New York City and New York State mental health systems. These deficiencies, some long-standing, others the result of recent policies, are, along with the shifts in the city's criminal justice system described below, the backdrop for the new challenges New York City police face in dealing with people with serious mental illnesses.

Deinstitutionalization

New York, like every other state in the United States, has pursued "deinstitutionalization"—the closure of state psychiatric hospitals that used to provide long-term care (and housing) to people with serious mental illness. Begun in the 1950s, deinstitutionalization was a result of pharmacological advances that, for the first time, made it possible to control many of the symptoms of serious mental illness, as well as a growing recognition that conditions in state hospitals were poor at best and, very often, downright cruel.While many proponents of deinstitutionalization were focused on providing humane treatment to people with mental illness, the plan also held promise from a fiscal perspective. At its height, the New York State psychiatric hospital system housed 93,000 people; as poor as the services may have been, they were not cheap. Today, the cost of keeping a patient in a state hospital for a year is $135,000. Advocates of deinstitutionalization argued that closing these hospitals and reallocating the money to fund comprehensive community mental health services would give people with mental illness a better life by making them part of the community.

Government bean counters probably realized early on what it would take advocates decades to understand: there was enormous political will to save money by closing the hospitals, but virtually no political will to spend the savings on the community mental health services patients would need to survive outside the hospital. The Bazelon Center for Mental Health Law estimates that, nationwide, state spending on treatment for the seriously mentally ill is one-third less than it was in the 1950s.[10]

In New York, as in many other states, money saved through the closure of state psychiatric hospitals went into the state's general fund and was used to pay for other things—bridges and roads and, very likely, prisons. At the same time that New York's hospitals were closing, the state's prison system was rapidly expanding; in 1973, state prisons housed 12,500 prisoners;[11] today there are 72,000 state prisoners in New York.

The downsizing of New York's state hospital system has been drastic and was not an isolated event—it continues today. From the 93,000 beds that were available in 1972, our hospital system has shrunk to 6,000. In 1999, the state Office of Mental Health planned to eliminate another 500 beds, and the governor described a long-range plan to reduce the number of beds to 4,500. For decades, very little of the money saved through hospital closure was invested in community mental health services.

Former state hospital patients were discharged to unsafe housing, to families unable to deal with their problems, or simply to the streets. Outpatient mental health programs were scarce, crowded, and required patients to come to them, demanding a level of insight and motivation that is rare in people who had been institutionalized for years or decades. Supportive housing with on-site psychiatric services was virtually nonexistent in New York until the early 1990s. The result was that thousands of seriously mentally ill New Yorkers became homeless, living in shelters or on the streets, their illnesses going untreated.

The New York/New York Agreement and the Community Mental Health Reinvestment Act

In 1990, a glimmer of hope appeared. After long negotiations, then-Governor Mario Cuomo and then-Mayor David Dinkins signed what was known as the New York/New York Agreement. The New York/New York Agreement was a five-year plan for the city and the state to jointly fund the construction and operation of 3,600 new units of permanent housing for mentally ill homeless people in New York City. Five years later, the units had all been built and filled and the population of the city's shelter system had dropped by over 3,000 people.[12]

In 1993, the mental health community had another reason to hope that better days were coming. New York State passed the Community Mental Health Reinvestment Act, legislation designed to ensure that for the next five years money saved from future hospital closures would be invested in community mental health services. Advocates celebrated, although they realized that reinvestment funding would come only at the cost of additional hospital downsizing (that many feel we can no longer afford), and that this legislation did nothing to redress the decades of money lost to the mental health system as a result of the 75,000 beds already closed.[13]

Bad days were ahead, though. In 1994, George Pataki defeated Mario Cuomo to become New York's governor. As Governor Pataki took office, several key deadlines for the mental health community loomed on the horizon: 1995 marked the end of the first New York/New York Agreement, and the Community Mental Health Reinvestment Act was set to expire in 1998, if not renewed. New Yorkers with mental illness and their advocates quickly realized that they could expect little help from the new gubernatorial administration.

A vigorous and well-organized statewide campaign for a second New York/New York Agreement led not to the 10,000 beds needed to house New York City's estimated 12,000 seriously mentally ill homeless people, but rather to a five-year plan to build only 1,500 beds. Even this agreement was a major concession by Governor Pataki, who yielded only after being assailed by church leaders and, notably, even Mayor Giuliani, himself no friend to the homeless. Reinvestment fared no better. Rather than the five-year extension of the legislation that advocates asked for, the governor agreed only to a one-year extension "to assess where we are and how to proceed."[14]

Today, the state's mental health system is in terrible trouble, with no relief in sight. In spite of the Reinvestment Act, the state's mental health budget has been decreased by $40 million over the last five years.[15] State hospitals have downsized to the point that staff must discharge even the most chronic and institutionalized patients, including those with histories of serious violent behavior. Mental health services in the community, particularly beds in New York/New York supportive housing programs, are so scarce that these patients have little chance of obtaining a discharge plan that will provide them with services adequate to maintain their psychiatric stability in the community. In the absence of an appropriate plan, they are discharged anyway, to the shelters or the streets, where their psychiatric symptoms quickly return, frequently leading to encounters with the NYPD. Acute care hospitals are also downsizing, creating pressure to shorten patient stays; New York City's public hospital system has closed 19 percent of its inpatient psychiatric beds in the past four years.[16]

Community mental health programs—clinics, day treatment programs, case management programs, even psychosocial clubhouses—have long waiting lists. Supportive housing, unquestionably the most important community service for people with serious mental illnesses, is so scarce that a monthly vacancy report is just a list of zeros; hundreds of mentally ill homeless applicants may vie for a single precious vacancy. Welfare reform has created huge new obstacles to accessing services by depriving thousands of indigent disabled people of Medicaid benefits. Without access to community mental health services, there is no continuity of care for people leaving hospitals, jails, or prisons where they have been receiving psychiatric treatment. The system is in disarray; advocates for people with mental illness unanimously agree that thousands, perhaps tens of thousands, of people with mental illness in New York City are not getting the services they desperately need.

Kendra's Law

January 3, 1999, the day Andrew Goldstein pushed Kendra Webdale to her death from the 23rd Street subway platform, marked a violent collision between New York's mental health and criminal justice systems and the first time Governor Pataki demonstrated any real interest in mental health issues. Suddenly, the state's treatment of people with mental illnesses—an issue that had been virtually invisible because it concerns the underfunding of an unpopular group with very few constituents—became a key political issue in Albany.

An involuntary outpatient commitment demonstration project had been running for two and a half years at Bellevue Hospital. The purpose of the program was, through judicial intervention, to compel patients leaving the hospital to remain compliant with mental health treatment. The Bellevue program had been created through legislation that required that it be evaluated; a sunset provision ended the program in June 1999. By January 1999, the evaluation had been completed; it showed that while all clients had benefited from the enhanced services available through the program, those subject to court orders had fared no better on any measure than a control group receiving identical services without the coercive order.[17] Legislation to renew and expand the program was languishing in the legislature; its passage seemed uncertain, and the governor seemed uninterested.

With the death of Kendra Webdale, the issue had new urgency. Webdale, an attractive young woman who had moved to New York City from upstate New York, was a most sympathetic victim and her family was quick to become involved in state mental health politics. Goldstein, Webdale's killer, is a seriously mentally ill man with a long history of hospitalizations for schizophrenia and a pattern of violent behavior during periods of psychiatric deterioration. Webdale's family, the governor, and even some members of the mental health advocacy community seized upon outpatient commitment as a fitting memorial to Kendra Webdale and a strategy to avoid future tragedies.

As the newly renamed "Kendra's Law" moved toward making outpatient commitment a statewide program with broad eligibility criteria, its proponents studiously avoided acknowledging the obvious: Andrew Goldstein had not refused treatment, the state had repeatedly refused *him* mental health services that he knew he needed.[18] Reporters documented the fact that Goldstein, who had a history of violent behavior resulting from his mental illness, had repeatedly sought services such as case management, supportive housing, and even long-term hospitalization at Creedmoor, one of New York's drastically downsized state hospitals.[19] The mental health system's response was consistent refusal; either the beds were full, the waiting list was too long, or Goldstein just wasn't judged to need the services badly enough.[20]

Goldstein's story, a painful case study of the way New York has failed its mentally ill citizens, was ignored. Kendra Webdale's death, a tragedy that would have motivated a less cynical legislature to allocate substantial funding to repair the state's broken mental health system, led instead to Kendra's Law, an unfunded mandate that coerces treatment without making treatment available. At best, Kendra's Law may have little effect; at worst, it will divert the funds necessary to administer the program from treatment services, leading to fewer services overall and a reallocation of existing services that favors patients with activist families at the expense of the truly marginalized, particularly homeless people.

New York State's mental health system had its day in the sun in 1999. For once, everyone in the state was thinking about and talking about how we should treat people with mental illness. If there was ever a window of opportunity to repair our state's devastated mental health system, this was it—and we missed it.

THE EXPANSION OF NEW YORK'S CRIMINAL JUSTICE SYSTEM

The last six years have been a time of drastic change in New York City's criminal justice system. Mayor Rudolph Giuliani, elected in 1993 after a fiercely partisan campaign focused on criminal justice and public safety issues, moved quickly to institute sweeping changes in New York City's law enforcement system. Other shifts in the city's criminal justice system, such as the proliferation of Business Improvement Districts (BIDs)[21] and community courts, were underway before Mayor Giuliani was elected, but dovetailed neatly with the harsher system he sought to implement. BIDs and community courts are important developments because they are both examples of ways in which the criminal justice system has expanded beyond its traditional public function to encompass partners from the private sector. This section will highlight some of the key shifts in New York City criminal justice policies that have, in recent years, forced police into their new role as the mediators of psychiatric disturbance.[22]

Quality-of-Life Crime Enforcement

Throughout his campaign to become New York City's mayor, Rudolph Giuliani touted his intention to dramatically change NYPD practices, to strictly enforce laws prohibiting "quality of life" crimes, and to reduce crime in New York City. Once in office, Giuliani began implementing a "zero-tolerance" policing strategy based on criminologists James Q. Wilson and George Kelling's hypothesis that vigorously combating minor public disorder offenses (such as vandalism, public drinking, and disorderly conduct) would lead to a reduction in more serious criminal behavior as well.

Giuliani's early efforts focused on "squeegee" people (people who clean windshields at intersections), petty drug dealers, and prostitutes. Subsequent targets included sidewalk vendors, taxi drivers, truant children, and jaywalkers. People drinking in public, urinating in public, and jumping subway turnstiles were also zealously rounded up.

Mayor Giuliani claims great success in his war on crime. The mayor's office reports that between 1993 and 1997 felony complaints in New York City dropped by 44.3 percent, and murders and nonnegligent homicides dropped by 60.2 percent.[23]

From the beginning, critics of Giuliani's policing policies raised concerns about the impact these policies would have on people of color, the poor, the homeless, and people with mental illness. Many critics also viewed these new policies as flagrantly violating thousands of New Yorkers' civil rights, noting, for example, that the number of arrests tossed out by prosecutors as meritless had more than doubled, to five hundred per day.[24] Some New Yorkers expressed concern that as the mayor bragged about how sharply crime had dropped, the total number of arrests[25] and the number of people in jail in New York City continued to rise. Commentators pointed out that crime rates had fallen just as drastically in many other cities, including ones that adopted much kinder community policing models as opposed to zero tolerance.

"Quality-of-life" crime enforcement got a real boost, however, in the summer of 1996, with the arrest of John Royster, Jr. Royster was accused of the murder of an elderly woman as well as brutal attacks on three other women, a crime spree that had frightened New Yorkers and fed tabloid headlines for weeks. His arrest resulted from fingerprints found at the scene of the murder. These fingerprints were matched to a set that had been taken when Royster was previously arrested for jumping a turnstile—an offense that, prior to the Giuliani administration, very likely would not have led to a formal arrest and fingerprinting. The mayor and his supporters gained powerful ammunition against critics of quality-of-life policing, and it became clear that this strategy was here to stay as long as Giuliani was mayor.

While neither Giuliani nor police commissioners focused explicitly on arresting homeless people until late 1999, the homeless were clearly the primary target of many of the city's Quality of Life campaigns. Many of the offenses now being vigorously prosecuted are inevitable results of life on the streets. Activities that nonhomeless people perform legally all the time—drinking a beer, changing clothes, urinating—become crimes when they are done on the street. Other activities that are not legal but that people with homes do without detection, such as drug use, are far more likely to lead to arrest when done on city sidewalks. Petty economic crimes such as jumping subway turnstiles or selling used items on the sidewalk are also committed primarily by the very poor, often the homeless. To a homeless person who lives in the subway, jumping a turnstile may be the only way to get "home," whereas to a person who can easily afford to pay $1.50 the hassle of getting caught is certainly not worth the money.

Finally, while quality-of-life crime enforcement has led to the arrest of New Yorkers from all walks of life, there is no question but that discriminatory enforcement is an issue. No one would seriously suggest that young men in suits carrying beer bottles or peeing in a doorway on their way home from after-work drinks are *as likely* to be arrested as a homeless man doing the same thing. In a perverse way, this makes sense. Quality-of-life crime enforcement is intended, by definition, to root out the people who most contribute to the now-changing image of New York City as unsightly, irritating, and unfriendly to residents and tourists. The bond trader urinating in a doorway is unsightly at that moment, but the homeless person wears unsightliness like a badge, even when sitting quietly on the sidewalk.

Mentally ill homeless people are even more unsightly. Homeless people drinking, peeing, or sitting on the sidewalk are, if anything, less tolerated by police if they appear psychotic. Researchers have found that police are more likely to arrest the mentally ill. Sometimes behaviors that are clearly psychotic symptoms, for example gesturing and yelling in response to auditory hallucinations, are dealt with as quality-of-life offenses and lead to arrest (many psychiatric symptoms can be viewed as disorderly conduct). Visitors to New York City these days often exclaim about how tidy the city looks and how few homeless people they have seen; to see many of New York City's homeless people today, it is necessary to visit Rikers Island.

While quality-of-life crime enforcement could, from its beginning, be viewed as an undeclared war on the homeless, in November 1999 in New York City the declaration was made explicit. On November 16, 1999, Nicole Barrett, a twenty-seven-year-old woman who had recently moved to New York City from Texas, was waiting to cross the street at 42nd and Madison when a stranger walked up and hit her in the head with a six-pound paving brick. Barrett was hospitalized and remained in a coma for several days. In spite of the attack taking place in the middle of the day on one of the busiest corners in Midtown Manhattan, several weeks went by before an arrest was made. In the interim, the media raged. Witnesses reported that the attacker looked like a homeless person, and the tabloids assumed that anyone who could do such a thing must be mentally ill. Three days after the attack, the *New York Daily News* devoted the entire front cover of the paper to a headline screaming, "Get the Violent Crazies Off Our Streets."

Mayor Giuliani offered his solution the same day during his weekly radio show; he promised to arrest the homeless. "Streets do not exist in civilized societies for the purpose of people sleeping there," the mayor said. "Bedrooms are for sleeping."[26] The same day, Police Commissioner Howard Safir explained that police would be visiting homeless encampments more often and would offer homeless people shelter and services, but if this help were refused and homeless people "don't obey, we're going to arrest them."[27]

Advocates for the homeless reacted with disbelief, in part because a city policy announced a month earlier sought to bar homeless people from the bedrooms of last resort—the city's shelter system. In November the city described plans to require all shelter residents to comply with its welfare-to-work program and promised to evict those who did not comply from the entire shelter system. Together, the two policies meant that homeless people unable to comply with workfare would be thrown on the streets; once there they would be arrested for refusing to go to a shelter due to the mayor's determination that sleeping on the streets is illegal. Twenty-three homeless people were arrested during the weekend following the mayor's announcement.[28]

Mayor Giuliani's decision to arrest the homeless drew criticism from many quarters, including the Reverend Al Sharpton, Tipper Gore, Andrew Cuomo, the leader of the Central Conference of American Rabbis and other religious leaders,[29] and New York senatorial candidate Hillary Rodham Clinton. Between one and five thousand protesters attended a rally against the policy on December 5,[30] and ten people were arrested at another protest the following day.[31] In a strange footnote, after weeks of public hysteria about "violent crazies" and dozens of arrests of homeless people, an arrest was made in the Nicole Barrett case. The man arrested, a longtime petty criminal named Paris Drake, was neither homeless nor mentally ill.[32]

Business Improvement Districts

Another sign of the decreasing tolerance for disorder generally and mentally ill/homeless people specifically is the growing presence and power of Business Improvement Districts (BIDs) and their security forces. Many BIDs were up and running before Mayor Giuliani took office, but their activities and priorities complement the mayor's "zero tolerance" policing. BIDs have been very successful in New York at improving business but, in doing so, have often trampled upon the rights of the homeless and the mentally ill.

BIDs are a rapidly spreading and increasingly popular approach to urban renewal. The first BID, New York City's Grand Central Partnership, was founded in the late 1980s; since then at least one thousand BIDs have appeared all across the U.S., including at least thirty-four in New York City alone.[33] The creation of the first BID and the ongoing popularity of the concept grew out of the concerns of business owners who saw commercial districts in which their establishments were located becoming both less aesthetically pleasing and less safe, and business revenues declining as a result. The BID was a model by which business owners could create their own organizations to address these issues while receiving government recognition and assistance.

BIDs in New York are formed under state law (the BID Act) that permits a special tax to be imposed upon property owners within the BID's boundaries.[34] In 1994, when BIDs were a relatively new idea, New

York City BIDs had already collected over $30 million from their members.[35] The special taxes collected under the BID Act are used to fund the activities of the BID. Functions performed by BIDs vary from one to the next, but commonly include sanitation, graffiti removal, market support, and improvements such as fixing or installing street lights, landscaping, seasonal decorations, etc. A well-funded BID, such as many of the lower Manhattan BIDs, may perform a wider range of functions, including security patrols, park maintenance, outreach to homeless people, operation of shelters, and distribution of food to the homeless.

There is little question but that BIDs have been successful at their goal of assisting business communities. Significant changes wrought by BIDs in New York City include the dramatic rehabilitation of Bryant Park. The Grand Central Partnership was begun at a time when the Mobil Corporation and Philip Morris Incorporated were threatening to move their offices because of the squalid condition of the neighborhood. Today the terminal is illuminated by lights at night, street lights are maintained, and a forty-two-member security force patrols the area from 8 a.m. to 11 p.m. Police report that crime has fallen sharply since the BID began operations in 1989.[36] Other Manhattan BIDs, including those in Times Square and in the 23rd Street and 34th Street neighborhoods, have also become powerful and effective at promoting the interests of the businesses they represent.

One of the key services many BIDs offer is security, and one of the key goals of many BIDs is removing homeless people from the district, and keeping them out. In pursuit of the goal, many BIDs fund or operate social services, but they also work closely with police to encourage zealous enforcement of Quality of Life laws within the district.

But BIDs represent only the interests of businesses, and as they stray farther and farther into the realm of what have traditionally been government functions, particularly as they become the enforcers of public order, real questions about accountability arise. The potential for abuse when BIDs take on what are traditionally police functions was clearly illustrated in 1995, when the *New York Times* exposed a scandal at the Grand Central Partnership.[37]

The partnership had developed a broad array of social services, including a shelter, food distribution to the homeless, and a team offering outreach to homeless people within the district. In April 1995, four former partnership outreach workers went public, telling the

Times that they had regularly beaten homeless people to get them to leave the district, and that they had done so with the implicit authorization of their partnership supervisors. The four men said that they, and others, had been specifically chosen by the BID's associate director of social services to form special outreach teams that the administrator referred to as "goon squads."[38] One worker said he was chosen for the outreach team after the associate director saw him beat up two people. "[The associate director] told me I had a good left hand and a nasty temper which would make me very helpful on outreach," the worker said.[39]

The four former partnership workers described throwing the belongings of homeless people into gutters, tearing up cardboard shelters, shoving, punching, and kicking homeless people, and bludgeoning them with the walkie-talkies that the workers carried. Sometimes after beating a homeless person, they said, they would call 911 and tell police that the homeless person had attacked them.[40] They also explained that they intentionally chased homeless people from areas controlled by businesses with which the partnership had contracted (for example, banks that paid the Partnership to keep ATM vestibules clear) to other sites not under contract. "They were herding the homeless around like cattle, using them to get business," said James Gray, one of the four workers who spoke to the *New York Times*.[41]

The trouble with the Grand Central Partnership is the most notorious of the problems associated with New York City's BIDs, but BIDs have played a key role in moving homeless people out of many parts of Manhattan. Whether BIDs have brought this about through intimidation, through harassment, through assisting police in targeting quality-of-life offenses, or through helping people get services and shelter is unclear, but their claim to "improving" New York City is linked to their active role in relocating homeless populations.

Where have the once-so-visible homeless gone? One thing is certain: their disappearance is not the result of having somewhere to live. They have not gone to the shelter system either; the census for that system has not increased. Some are in New York/New York housing, but many more have moved to the far edges of the city, under bridges and in tunnels, where they are safe from police and security forces, but also more vulnerable and disenfranchised than ever. Others are in jail.

Community Courts

Another development in New York City's movement toward an ever-harsher criminal justice system was the development of community courts. The city's first, the Midtown Community Court, opened in 1993, just as Giuliani became mayor. Another community court, in Red Hook, Brooklyn, has since opened. Both projects were spearheaded by a private not-for-profit organization called the Center for Court Innovation.

Midtown Community Court was formed in response to many of the same public order concerns that led to the creation of New York's BIDs.[42] Community members in the Hell's Kitchen area, both residents and business owners, were frustrated to see the same petty drug dealers, prostitutes, and homeless people being arrested repeatedly only to return to the neighborhood a few days later. They felt that the criminal court downtown, where these defendants were prosecuted and sentenced, was not responsive to the needs of their community and did not take these minor offenses seriously enough.

The Midtown Community Court was built primarily with private funding and now has jurisdiction over all misdemeanor arrests west of Lexington Avenue between 14th and 59th Streets, as well as prostitution arrests throughout Manhattan. Designers of the court intended to provide "restorative justice" by making the defendants *and* the court accountable to the community. In practice, this meant harsher sentences; at Midtown, there is no such thing as the "time served" disposition that minor offenses often merit at the regular court downtown. Community service is very frequently the sentence at Midtown, compelling defendants to work on projects such as cleaning up graffiti or parks in the neighborhood. Defendants who fail to comply are jailed. Large computer screens in the courtroom inform the audience of the defendant's name, charges, and history.

The court's presence has encouraged far stricter enforcement in Midtown of laws prohibiting petty offenses. During the first year of operation, the largest proportion (38%) of the cases handled by the Midtown Community Court concerned theft of services—people jumping subway turnstiles.[43] The other main offenses were illegal vending, petty larceny, and prostitution. Some might question the need for an expensive new court to prosecute fare evaders.

The central paradox of the Midtown Community Court is that its mission encompasses both punishing people more and helping them. The tougher sentences are accompanied by social services' responses to defendants' behavior; the court offers defendants access to health services, mental health services, vocational counseling, housing referrals, and services targeted specifically at helping prostitutes get off the street. The court sends outreach workers to talk to homeless people and to encourage them to come to the court and access these services voluntarily—without being arrested first. These outreach workers go out in two-person teams with community policing officers from the Midtown North precinct, located next door to the court.[44]

The one outreach worker/one police officer team is a good metaphor for the entire Midtown Community Court phenomenon. In this "odd couple," and in the court as a whole, there is a pronounced merging of social service and law enforcement functions. The message seems to be, "We're here to help you—or else." Many people in the community do not understand what the Midtown Community Court does. Almost inevitably, when you mention the court, people say, "Oh, they divert people to services, don't they?" The truth is the opposite: what the Midtown Community Court does is punish people *more* and *then* offer social services. Defendants who in the regular court would have been sentenced to time served are instead ordered to perform community service. However much the social services at Midtown Community Court are helping some people, the main impact of the court has been to widen the net of persons subject to arrest and to provide harsher punishment for minor offenses.

Society has always grappled with how to cope with people who make choices that are not typically classified as criminal, but upset or annoy other people. The question of what to do with annoying people is further complicated as we develop more sophisticated techniques to treat socially unacceptable behaviors like substance abuse and some of the more disruptive symptoms of mental illness. The question of how much freedom society should allow people to make bad choices is particularly central in the area of mental health, where a long-standing debate rages between civil libertarians and treatment advocates (many of them family members of mentally ill people) over when it is permissible to confine people and force them to get treatment that they do not want.

In New York City at the turn of the twenty-first century, we may have arrived at an "orderly" but frightening solution to the eternal problem of annoying people. New Yorkers, most vocally the BIDs, have demanded that annoying people be removed from their neighborhoods. The mayor, with public support, has encouraged the police to arrest everyone who breaks any law, even laws targeting very minor offenses that had virtually become dead letters from disuse.

Suddenly, annoying behavior is, for the most part, truly illegal in New York City. Felony crime rates have plummeted, but the courts, probation officers, community service programs, and jails have maintained their workloads, saving jobs and funding, by replacing "serious" criminals with annoying "criminals." New York City's consistent and rapid movement during recent years toward ever more punitive responses to minor crimes has collided head-on with the collapse of the city and state's mental health systems and, in doing so, has drastically changed what is expected of New York City police.

THE COLLISION OF NEW YORK CITY'S MENTAL HEALTH AND CRIMINAL JUSTICE SYSTEMS

As New York's mental health system contracts and its criminal justice system expands, functions that were once primarily the purview of the mental health system—crisis intervention, assessment, and treatment—have increasingly become the responsibility of criminal justice agencies. One issue frequently neglected in discussions about the incarcerated mentally ill is the fact that every mentally ill inmate began his incarceration through an encounter with police—an encounter where the officer was forced to make swift decisions and exercise considerable discretion without the benefit of clinical expertise. This section details some of the ways that "criminalization" has affected New Yorkers with mental illness as a backdrop for assessing how the NYPD's role has changed with respect to dealing with mentally ill New Yorkers.

Staggering Numbers of Mentally Ill New Yorkers Are in Jails and Prisons

On any given day, there are approximately 7,680 mentally ill inmates in New York State's jails and prisons.[45] At least 2,850 of those are in the New York City jail system, making Rikers Island, de facto, the state's largest in-patient psychiatric facility.[46] Fifteen to 20 percent of New York City jail inmates are mentally ill.[47] In 1997, 15,000 New York City jail inmates were treated for *serious* mental disorders.[48] Twenty-five percent of New York City jail inmates receive some sort of mental health services—a total of about 33,325 people per year.[49]

These problems are not unique to New York City or New York State. Nationwide, attention is finally being drawn to the problem researchers describe as "the criminalization of mental illness" and "transinstitutionalization"—the movement of people with serious mental illnesses from community psychiatric hospitals into jails and prisons.[50] A federal Department of Justice study released in July 1999 found that nationwide, approximately 16 percent of jail and prison inmates were mentally ill—for a total of 283,800 mentally ill inmates.[51] This was an increase from a 1995 finding by the National Institute of Justice that reckoned as many as 13 percent of the nation's jail inmates suffer from severe mental disabilities.[52] In prisons, the situation is the same—an estimated 10 percent of all prisoners in state and federal facilities, a total of about 122,000 people, are seriously mentally ill.[53] This issue has received significant national attention recently, but is still largely uncharted territory when it comes to thoughtful solutions.[54]

Police, courts, jails, and prisons are not adequately prepared to deal with a woman who stands in traffic yelling at voices she hears in her head, or a man who stalks a famous person because he believes she is his wife. Police are much more likely to arrest the mentally ill than the non–mentally ill.[55] Once arrested, mentally ill people in New York State are incarcerated for longer and have less access to alternatives to incarceration than non–mentally ill offenders.[56] As a result, even mentally ill people charged with relatively minor misdemeanors often end up spending significant time in jail. While incarcerated, they receive very basic psychiatric care or none at all. Any psychiatric treatment they were receiving in the community is disrupted. When mentally ill inmates are released, they are generally not linked with mental health services or benefits or housing and, as a result, are likely to end up in trouble with the law again. This is the cycle that has criminalized mental illness and made jails and prisons New York's new psychiatric institutions.

Who Are New York's Mentally Ill Offenders?

Mentally ill people who are or have been incarcerated are perhaps the most disenfranchised people in New York City. They suffer the stigma and consequences of both mental illness and criminality, they are predominantly poor and of color, and they must often confront additional issues, including substance abuse, homelessness, and medical problems such as tuberculosis and HIV/AIDS. They are cut off from mental health services available to nonoffenders, and their psychiatric problems isolate them from advocates for "normal" defendants and prisoners.

Not surprisingly, people with mental illness in the city's jails are marginalized in many ways. They are overwhelmingly people of color: 50 percent African-American, 35 percent Latino.[57] They are disproportionately female: only 10 percent of the city jail population are women, but 17 percent of the inmates utilizing mental health services are female.[58] They are also likely to be unemployed: in a sample of seriously mentally ill inmates served by the NYC-LINK discharge planning program,[59] 28 percent had never been employed and only 10 percent were employed at the time of incarceration.[60] Fully 39 percent received SSI or SSD (social security disability benefits), 25 percent received public assistance, and 16 percent had no income.[61] Only 2 percent had private insurance, while the vast majority of patients in the sample relied on Medicaid (63%) or had no insurance (30%).[62]

People with mental illness in city jails are also likely to have histories of psychiatric treatment and of substance use. In a Health and Hospitals Corporation Office of Correctional Health Services study conducted in November 1997, 68 percent of inmates in the sample had had contact with the mental health system prior to their incarceration.[63] While more than half (54%) admitted to histories of substance use,[64] this figure is almost certainly low. Prevalence of substance use among the general New York City jail population is estimated to be 75–80 percent,[65] and there is no reason to expect a lower prevalence among inmates with mental illness.

It is impossible to separate issues concerning people with mental illness in jail and prison from homelessness. In New York City, a 1992 study found that 20 percent of jail detainees were homeless.[66] In NYC-LINK's first year, 29 percent of its clients were homeless.[67] The higher rate of homelessness among NYC-LINK clients corroborates another finding of this study—a strong association between homelessness and mental illness. Subjects of this study who had histories of homelessness were *twice* as likely as the never homeless to show some indication of mental illness (50 percent versus 25 percent). A 1995 study in New York City found that 43 percent of defendants with mental disorders were homeless at the time of arrest.[68] These figures show that while jail is serving as emergency shelter for thousands of homeless New Yorkers, it is especially true for homeless people with mental illnesses. On any given day, there are approximately 3,800 homeless people in the city jails—more than half as many as the 7,100 in the city's shelters for homeless adults.[69] A rough estimate of the number of homeless people with mental illness in the city jail system would be over 1,000.[70]

Lack of Discharge Planning Creates a Revolving Door

When a person with a serious mental illness goes to Rikers Island or one of the city's other jails, she probably receives some form of basic mental health care, including psychotropic medications as an outpatient in the general population, or in one of the segregated Mental Observation Units. However, many of these people have no insurance or income at the time of arrest. Many more lose their Medicaid while they are incarcerated. Without insurance, there is no way for a person with a mental illness to leave jail and continue getting the medications he needs to remain stable. Inmates with mental illness finishing their sentences at Rikers Island are generally put on a bus with other prisoners being released that day. Most mentally ill inmates are not given medications or a prescription to take with them. They are driven to Queens Plaza and released between 2 a.m. and 7 a.m. with $1.50 in cash and a $3 Metrocard.[71]

Even if a person with a mental illness is sufficiently organized to go directly to the welfare office, there will still be at least a 45-day wait for benefits and, more important, Medicaid. Temporary Medicaid benefits are theoretically available to qualified applicants immediately, but in practice the red tape involved in getting a temporary Medicaid card is daunting to even the most experienced social worker and all but impossible for a disorganized person with a mental illness in a crisis situation. Finally, a person with a mental illness who is resourceful and persistent enough to get a temporary Medicaid card is likely to be unable to find a pharmacy willing to honor a temporary card.

Without Medicaid or other insurance there is no access to treatment, and the inevitable happens: the mentally ill ex-offender decompensates,[72] acts out, and ends up in a hospital if lucky, but more likely back in jail.

The vast majority of mentally ill people in the criminal justice system are not dangerous or frightening, and are not incarcerated for long. Many of them are charged with relatively minor misdemeanors, and with increased enforcement of laws prohibiting quality-of-life crimes, as described above, more mentally ill people than ever, particularly the homeless mentally ill, fall into this category.[73] These people spend days, weeks, or perhaps months in jail;[74] then they return to New York City communities and neighborhoods where they need help reintegrating into society, remaining psychiatrically stable, and staying out of trouble.

Mentally ill people sentenced to upstate prison terms are not gone forever, either. Only 29 percent of inmates entering New York State prisons in 1996 were sentenced for violent felonies.[75] Almost everyone eventually gets out of prison, and 70 percent of state prisoners return to New York City when they get out. Each year, in New York City alone, 25,000 people who are mentally ill leave the criminal justice system and return to the community.[76]

Although the movement of people with serious mental illnesses from hospitals and community programs into jails and prisons is a national concern, this problem is particularly acute in New York City. The deterioration of New York's mental health systems has intersected with the increasing severity of the city's criminal justice system in a way that is terribly damaging for both the rights and the treatment needs of homeless mentally ill New Yorkers. As responsibility for dealing with the mental health needs of poor people has increasingly shifted from the mental health system to the criminal justice system, the New York City Police Department has been forced to take on new responsibilities that it is ill-prepared to handle.

The Impact on Police

NYPD officers, in addition to their already broad job description, have new and growing responsibilities in regard to dealing with mentally ill New Yorkers, particularly those who are homeless. Today, New York City police officers respond annually to a staggering 60,000 EDP (police lingo for "emotionally disturbed person") 911 calls,[77] making the NYPD perhaps the largest and busiest psychiatric crisis response team in the world. Officers also report that they often arrive at calls that have not been identified as EDP only to find that the problem involves a person experiencing a psychiatric emergency. These new responsibilities are not the product of a reasoned policy decision regarding what is best for the community, or a determination that police are qualified for such a task. Instead, they are the unintended by-product of concurrent policies making mental health treatment more inaccessible and defining "criminal" behavior more broadly.

The NYPD is in an untenable position. The department has near total responsibility for dealing with mental health emergencies, and the number of emergencies keeps rising. NYPD officers do not have the training or resources to do a competent job of responding to these psychiatric crises, and when tragedies happen it is not the mental health system or the mayor or the governor that is blamed, it is typically the police.[78]

Lack of Alternatives to Police Involvement

The NYPD's 40,000 officers are virtually always the first to respond to any crisis involving a person with mental illness. Even when a 911 caller specifically requests just an ambulance, the police are mobilized as well. If the ambulance arrives first, the emergency medical technicians generally wait outside until the police come when the situation involves an EDP.

The alternatives to calling the police when a person in New York City is facing a psychiatric emergency are limited and desperately inadequate. The city funds a number of psychiatric mobile crisis teams whose task it is to assess people who are in crisis and to hospitalize them if necessary. Unfortunately, the guidelines for these teams require only that they respond to calls within 48 hours, and a lack of resources prevents them from providing more rapid responses. Because of these limitations, the city's mobile crisis teams are of no use in real crises, and are able to respond only to people who have a stable place to live, where they can be found for the next couple of days.

The only option other than the police for dealing with homeless people in psychiatric crisis is a group called Project HELP. Project HELP is a single team of mental health professionals, based in a Manhattan hospital, assigned the task of reaching out to and, when necessary, hospitalizing the estimated 12,000 mentally ill homeless people in New York City. Needless to say, the group is overwhelmed by the task, usually cannot respond very quickly, and is able to take very little burden from the police department.

The Consequences of the Lack of Crisis Intervention Training for Police

Consider the following tragic conclusions to encounters between the NYPD and mentally ill New Yorkers in crisis:

October 1984:Eleanor Bumpers, a seriously mentally ill 66-year-old woman, is shot twice by police and killed in her apartment in the Bronx.

December 1987: Juan Rodriguez, a mentally ill man, is shot to death by police on the street in Laurelton, Queens.[79]

September 1988: Jorge Delgado, a seriously mentally ill homeless man, is shot and killed by police in St. Patrick's Cathedral.

May 1992: Earl Black, a schizophrenic man, is shot to death by police in his mother's Brooklyn apartment. His mother is also injured.

June 1998: Sterling Robertson, a 69-year-old mentally ill man, is shot to death by police in a Manhattan YMCA.[80]

October 1998:Kevin Cerbelli, a schizophrenic man, is shot eight times and killed by police in a Queens precinct house after jabbing the desk sergeant with a screwdriver.

May 1999: Rodney Mason, a seriously mentally ill man, stabs Officer Stephen DeLuca and is shot to death by the officer's partner in Queens.

June 1999: Renato Mercado, a 63-year-old seriously mentally ill man, is shot to death by police on the Upper West Side of Manhattan while brandishing a machete.

August 1999: Gidone (Gary) Busch, a schizophrenic man, waves a hammer at police who shoot twelve times, killing him, in Borough Park, Brooklyn.

Faced with the responsibility of being New York City's sole mental health crisis service, the New York City Police Department has not risen to the occasion. After Eleanor Bumpers was shot to death by police in 1984, public outcry forced the department to institute new training and procedures regarding the handling of EDP calls. Rather than developing an effective training program for all officers, or designing a procedure that would permit specially trained officers to respond to all EDP calls, however, the department made changes that, in the end, were mostly cosmetic. It developed specialized training and made it available to all members of the department's Emergency Services Unit (ESU). A new policy was developed whereby every time an EDP call came in, 911 operators dispatched regular officers to the scene who were nearby, plus a sergeant *and* ESU.

The problem? ESU teams are centralized, which means that each team is responsible for an area encompassing several precincts. In addition, ESU has many other responsibilities that may take precedence over helping acutely mentally ill people. According to the department's web site, ESU "supplies specialized equipment, expertise and support to the various units within the NYPD. From auto accidents to building collapses to hostage situations, the ESU officers are called upon when the situation requires advanced equipment and expertise."[81]

The consequence is that ESU almost always arrives after the beat cops, as does the sergeant—often long after. The officers who are first on the scene assess the situation and, in most cases, decide that the situation is under control and cancel the ESU call. In other situations, though, when a real crisis is occurring, the inexperienced, untrained officers are forced to handle it without ESU's assistance. For many of the people listed above, this delay may have been fatal. In the case of Gidone Busch, for example, the entire incident, from the initial 911 call to the call for an ambulance after Busch was fatally shot, took just nine minutes—and ESU was nowhere to be seen.

If the NYPD sought to improve its interactions with people with mental illnesses, one solution would be obvious: train officers to do a better job. At present, non-ESU officers receive 16 hours of training on mental health issues while in the police academy, with no follow-up training, ever. Specialized programs teaching officers to deescalate crises involving people with mental illnesses have been successful in other parts of the country, as long as the specially trained officers are also the officers who actually arrive when a psychiatric emergency occurs.[82] The NYPD, in spite of the fact that its officers appear to be killing mentally ill people in greater numbers every year, has made no concrete efforts to stop these tragedies. The NYPD's current system for responding to EDPs, sending ESU, clearly almost never functions as intended; it is time for the department to notice there's a problem and look for legitimate solutions.

The Consequences of Lack of Options for Police Other Than Arrest

January 3, 1999: Kendra Webdale is pushed to her death from a Manhattan subway platform by Andrew Goldstein, a schizophrenic man with a long psychiatric history.

April 28, 1999: Edgar Rivera is pushed from a Manhattan subway platform, allegedly by Julio Perez, a seriously mentally ill man; Mr. Rivera loses both legs.

June 13, 1999: Olga Maisonet, a seriously mentally ill woman, allegedly walks up to a stranger on a Brooklyn street and stabs him to death.

All of these people had run-ins with the police before these incidents happened, as had many of the people listed earlier who were killed by police. Usually triggered by minor offenses, these encounters could have been used as opportunities to get these individuals psychiatric help that they desperately needed—but that's not how things work in New York City. Officers have the discretionary power not to arrest in misdemeanor cases and, to some extent, even in felonies; but pressures on, and policies within, the city's hospitals seriously curtail the use of that discretion to get help for mentally ill people rather than arrest them.

Olga Maisonet's case illustrates these lost opportunities in a particularly dramatic fashion. Ms. Maisonet was arrested less than a month prior to fatally stabbing a stranger; the charge: stabbing a different stranger. At the time of both arrests, Ms. Maisonet was acutely mentally ill, with no access to the medications she needed to control her schizophrenia: her case had been closed at the clinic she attended, apparently because of problems with Medicaid. In the three previous years, she had been arrested and passed through the Brooklyn courts on five other occasions, twice for fare evasion and three times for loitering for the purpose of prostitution. None of these six prior encounters with the police or the courts led to Ms. Maisonet's receiving any psychiatric assistance, although family and friends describe her as someone whose psychiatric symptoms were not well hidden. "She would talk to herself, curse at herself, sometimes scream in anger," her daughter's boyfriend said. "She really needed someone who would try and help her."[83]

When police arrest someone who is clearly psychotic and has committed a minor offense, the officers often feel that the best response is to hospitalize rather than arrest the person. Unfortunately, there are many incentives for police arrest. An officer attempting to hospitalize a mentally ill person can plan on an annoying experience but is not guaranteed that attempts to hospitalize will be successful. With the exception of one small program that has been mostly abandoned,[84] there is no agreement or program in place to facilitate police referral of acutely ill people to psychiatric emergency rooms.

An officer bringing a mentally ill person to an emergency room in New York City will have to wait with the person for three or four or five or eight hours. Much of the delay is caused by the requirement that the person be medically screened before he or she receives a psychiatric evaluation. The demands of triage push these people to the bottom of the list of those waiting to see the medical staff—below gunshot wounds, stabbings, heart attacks, etc. Once the medical screening is complete, the person must wait again to be seen by the mental health staff.

During all of this time, the officer who, had the person been arrested, would have spent an hour or two at the precinct writing up the arrest report and other paperwork is instead expected to sit with an acutely mentally ill person in custody in an emergency room full of other acutely mentally ill people. Needless to say, many officers prefer to avoid this experience. Worse yet, from the officer's perspective, after all this time and aggravation, the person may not be admitted. Acute-care psychiatric hospital beds are in such short supply in New York City, and hospitals so concerned about billing, that if a person is not clearly a danger to himself or others, especially if he has no insurance, the hospital is likely to tell the officer to take the person away.

Having been through this experience, or having heard about it from other officers, an officer faced with an acutely mentally ill misdemeanor offender is likely to arrest the person just for convenience and efficiency's sake, even if the officer feels uncomfortable with that disposition. One large step the department could take toward improving how it handles EDPs would be to develop agreements with specific hospitals or with the city's Health and Hospitals Corporation to expedite the assessment and admission of mentally ill people brought in by police.

CONCLUSION

As unfair as it may be, and as misguided, for the NYPD to have become the city's sole crisis service, the department deserves blame for failing to rise to the occasion. On a policy level, the commissioner and other high-level officials at the NYPD should have fought hard to prevent other agencies—specifically the Department of Mental Health, the Health and Hospitals Corporation, and the Human Resources Administration—from abdicating their responsibilities to people with mental illness.

The NYPD is among the more powerful of New York City's government agencies; its officials have more influence over the mayor than do the commissioners of any of the social service agencies. NYPD officials might have argued successfully for mental health system reforms, such as dramatic expansion of the mobile crisis teams or revitalization and reform of the Comprehensive Psychiatric Emergency Program. They also could have worked with mental health professionals to develop training for all officers in how to intervene with people in acute psychiatric states and defuse crisis situations. In the alternative, NYPD administrators could have taken the strategy of specialist officers, used so ineffectually with the Emergency Services Unit, and placed mental health specialist officers in every precinct. Instead, it appears that the leadership at the NYPD views dealing with mentally ill people as a nuisance not worth worrying about too much, except for once in awhile when a killing by the police makes big headlines.

Of course, the real problem is not the police—it is a political climate that makes it unpalatable to spend a dime on mental health services but endlessly desirable to build new prisons. The rising death toll in encounters between the NYPD and people with mental illness is only a symptom of two broader problems—the collapse of New York's mental health system, and the steady expansion of the city's criminal justice system. Before anything can change for the better, before we can even stop things from continuing to get worse, New Yorkers must tell the elected officials who implement these policies that it is unacceptable to have a mental health system composed of police and jails.

NOTES

1. James is a composite based on two people.

2. Robert Gearty and Dave Goldiner, "Gentle Soul Buried: 400 Mourn Man Shot by Officers," *New York Daily News* (September 3, 1999): 8.

3. John Marzulli, Mike Claffey, and Patrice O'Shaughnessy, "We Had to Shoot—Cops Say Hammer-Wielding Man Left Them No Other Option," *New York Daily News* (September 1, 1999): 2.

4. Helen Peterson, William K. Rashbaum, and Alice McQuillan, "Kin Cry Police Coverup in Killing," *New York Daily News* (October 5, 1999): 4.

5. Cathy Burke, "Busch Kin: Gary Was No Monster," *New York Post* (September 2, 1999): 5.

6. New York City Department of Mental Health, Mental Retardation and Alcoholism Services, 1998–2001, Local Government Plan for Adult Mental Health Services, 47.

7. Id.

8. Office of Correctional Health Services Testimony before the City Council Subcommittee on Mental Health, Mental Retardation, Alcoholism and Drug Abuse Services, April 22, 1998, 2 (hereinafter "Lynch testimony," on file with author); 25% × 133,300 jail inmates per year (133,300 was the total number of admissions in FY 1997) = 33,325.

9. New York City Department of Mental Health FY 1996 Local Government Plan for Adult Mental Health Services, 326.

10. Michael Winerip, "The Crisis of the Mentally Ill," *New York Times Magazine* (May 23, 1999): 42.

11. Kara Blond, "The Debate over Detention," *Newsday* (May 30, 1999): A57.

12. Winerip at 47.

13. Velmenette Montgomery, "Overhaul Proposed for Mental Health System," *Albany Times Union* (August 2, 1999): A6.

14. Alice Tully, "Aid for Mental Health Sought," *Albany Times Union* (April 8, 1998): B2.

15. Richard A. Leva, "Italy Proves Mentally Ill People Can Be Integrated into Society and Still Receive Excellent Care," *Buffalo News* (September 13, 1998): H2.

16. City of New York, Mayor's Management Report: Fiscal 1996 (Volume II—Agency and Citywide Indicators): 103. Mayor's Management Report: Prelim. FY 1998: 99.

17. Policy Research Associates, Inc., Final Report: Research Study of the New York City Involuntary Outpatient Commitment Pilot Program (Policy Research Associates, December 4, 1998).

18. Winerip at 42.

19. Id.

20. In November 1999, Andrew Goldstein's trial for the murder of Kendra Webdale ended in a mistrial after the jury was unable to agree on whether to accept or reject Goldstein's defense that he was not guilty by reason of insanity. His second trial ended in a swift conviction. He was sentenced to twenty-five years to life in state prison.

21. While BIDs are not explicitly part of New York's criminal justice system, crime enforcement is one of their key roles. By providing security patrols and collaborating closely with local precincts to target "quality-of-life" concerns in business communities, BIDs have created a niche for themselves in New York City's criminal justice system.

22. Although this section discusses only quality-of-life crime enforcement, BIDs, and community courts, other signs that New York City is getting tougher and tougher on crime abound. For example, in the fall of 1999, the Brooklyn district attorney, Charles Hynes, instituted a policy of refusing to do any plea bargaining in cases where the defendant has ten or more prior convictions. While this might sound like a sensible-enough policy, the results can be extreme. For example, I first heard of this policy when I went to the Brooklyn House of Detention for Men to interview a homeless man who had for thirty-four years been treated for chronic paranoid schizophrenia. He had a long history of misdemeanor offenses and had been to prison several times for nonviolent offenses related to his drug use. When I asked about his current case, he told me that he was charged with jumping over a turnstile in the subway, and the district attorney's office wanted him to plead guilty and to be sentenced to a year at Riker's Island. I thought he must be lying or mistaken, that no one could possibly want a defendant to serve a year in jail (at a cost of $69,000 to taxpayers) for cheating the Metropolitan Transit Authority out of $1.50. His defense attorney confirmed the story, however, explaining that, since a one-year sentence is the maximum sentence for "theft of services," the formal charge for subway fare evasion, that was the DA's offer.

23. Judith A. Greene, "Zero Tolerance: A Case Study of Police Policies and Practices in New York City," *Crime and Delinquency* 45 (2): 171.

24. Nat Hentoff, "Trampling on the Fourth Amendment," *Village Voice* (September 6, 1999).

25. Id.

26. Elisabeth Bumiller, "In Wake of Attack, Giuliani Cracks Down on Homeless," *New York Times* (November 20, 1999): A1.

27. Id.

28. David M. Herszenhorn, "Citywide Sweep Leads to 23 Arrests of the Homeless," *New York Times* (November 22, 1999): B1.

29. Thomas J. Lueck, "Giuliani Meets Clergy to Explain Homeless Policy and Is Asked to Add Housing," *New York Times* (December 31, 1999): B3.

30. David M. Herszenhorn, "1,000 in Park Denounce Giuliani on Homeless Arrest Policy," *New York Times* (December 6, 1999): B1.

31. Somini Sengupta, "Ten Arrested at Rally against Crackdown on Homeless," *New York Times* (December 7, 1999): B5.

32. Nina Bernstein, "Seeking to Label the Homeless, with Compassion or Contempt," *New York Times* (December 5, 1999).

33. John A. Barnes, "Business Improvement Districts: Doing What Government Doesn't," *Investor's Business Daily* (September 6, 1995): B1; Vivian S. Toy, "City, Districts Reject Calls for Oversight," *New York Times* (November 9, 1995): B5.

34. N.Y. Gen. Mun. Law §980-a-p.

35. Thomas J. Lueck, "Public Needs, Private Answers—A Special Report: Business Improvement Districts Grow, at Price of Accountability," *New York Times* (November 20, 1994): 1.

36. Barnes at 26.

37. Bruce Lambert, "Ex-Outreach Workers Say They Assaulted the Homeless," *New York Times* (April 14, 1995): B1.

38. Id.

39. Bill Alden, "Are Street People Treated Like Dirt?" *New York Newsday* (April 15, 1995): A4.

40. Lambert at 29.

41. Id.

42. Henry Goldman, "Court Giving a Lift to Times Square," *Pittsburgh Post-Gazette* (October 26, 1997): A8.

43. "In New York City, a 'Community Court' and a New Legal Culture," National Institute of Justice publication, Washington, D.C. (1995).

44. "Street Outreach Services," Bureau of Justice Assistance / Center for Court Innovation publication.

45. Based conservatively on 1994 estimates provided by the New York Health and Hospitals Corporation, Department of Mental Health, and State Office of Mental Health for use in FY 1996 Local Government Plan for Adult Mental Health Services. Calculation is as follows: approx. 19,000 NYC jail inmates at a time (the average in 1997 was 19,205) × 15% mentally ill (an estimated 15–20% of city inmates are mentally ill) = 2,850; approx. 69,000 state prisoners at a time × 7% mentally ill (an estimated 7–8% of state prisoners are mentally ill) = 4,830; 2,850 + 4,830 = 7,680. This estimate is also very conservative because it does not include mentally ill people in jails outside of New York City.

46. For calculation, see n. 45. This figure is conservative given that mentally ill people in NYC jails normally are incarcerated for longer than the non–mentally ill (see note 6 above).

47. New York City Department of Mental Health, Mental Retardation and

Alcoholism Services, New York City FY 1996 Local Government Plan for Adult Mental Health Services, 326.

48. Butterfield, "Prisons Replace Hospitals for the Nation's Mentally Ill," *New York Times* (March 5, 1998): A1, A26.

49. Lynch testimony; 25% × 133,300 jail inmates per year (133,300 was the total number of admissions in FY 1997) = 33,325.

50. See, generally, E. F. Torrey, J. Stieber, J. Ezekial, et al. "Criminalizing the Seriously Mentally Ill: The Abuse of Jails as Mental Hospitals," *Innovations and Research* 2 (1993): 11–14.

51. Michael J. Sniffen, "Mentally Ill in Prison Put at 283,800 in New Report," *Buffalo News* (July 12, 1999): A3.

52. National Institute of Justice, "The Americans with Disabilities Act and Criminal Justice: Mental Disabilities and Corrections," NCJ publication no. 155061, 1995. (Washington, D.C.: U.S. Government Printing Office).

53. See Butterfield.

54. For example, the federal Substance Abuse and Mental Health Services Administration has recently spent several million dollars funding evaluations of existing criminal justice/mental health diversion programs in nine jurisdictions (including New York City) in an effort to determine what works and for whom.

55. L. A. Teplin, "Criminalizing Mental Disorder: The Comparative Arrest Rate of the Mentally Ill," *American Psychologist* 39 (1984): 794–803.

56. Marjorie A. Rock and Gerald S. Landsberg, "County Mental Health Directors' Perspectives on Forensic Mental Health Developments in New York State," *Administration and Policy in Mental Health* 25 (1996): 327. According to the New York City Health and Hospitals Corporation, the average length of stay in the New York City jail system for mentally ill inmates is 215 days, compared with a 42-day average stay for all inmates. See Butterfield.

57. Lynch testimony at 3.

58. Id. at 1, 3.

59. NYC-LINK is a program that provides discharge planning for a few of the mentally ill people in New York's jails and prisons.

60. NYC-LINK Pilot Project, Preliminary Data, Year One (on file with author).

61. Id.

62. Id.

63. Lynch testimony at 3.

64. Id.

65. Id. at 2.

66. David Michaels et al., "Homelessness and Indicators of Mental Illness among Inmates in New York City's Correctional System," *Hosp. & Community Psychiatry* 43 (1992): 150, 155.

67. NYC-LINK Pilot Project.

68. David A. Martell et al., "Base-Rate Estimates of Criminal Behavior by Homeless Mentally Ill Persons in New York City," *Psychiatric Services* 46 (1995): 596.

69. Calculation is as follows: 20% homeless (from the Michaels study, see note 66 above) × 19,000 jail inmates on any given day (the average for FY 1997 was 19,205) = 3,800. According to the Mayor's Management Report: Prelim. FY 1998, 125, the average number of persons lodged per night for FY 1997 by the Department of Homeless Services, Services for Adults, was 7,119.

70. There are several rough ways of calculating this based on the information available. First, 3,800 homeless people in jail (see n. 69) × 15% (DMH's estimate of the percentage of jail inmates who are mentally ill) × 2 (to account for Michaels' finding of the association between homelessness and mental illness) = 1,140. Alternately, 19,000 (the population of the jails) × 15% (the percentage mentally ill) × 29% (the percentage of NYC-LINK clients who were homeless in Year One) = 827. Finally, 19,000 (the population of the jails) × 15% (the percentage mentally ill) × 43% (the percentage homeless in the Martell study, note 68 above) = 1,226.

71. In August 1999, my agency (the Urban Justice Center) along with the law firm of Debevoise & Plimpton and another public interest organization, New York Lawyers for the Public Interest, filed a class action lawsuit on behalf of mentally ill inmates of the city's jail system challenging the discharge planning practices described above. The case, *Brad H. v. City of New York*, is pending. [Editors' note: On July 12, 2000, Justice Richard F. Braun of the State Supreme Court in Manhattan granted the plaintiffs a preliminary injunction in the lawsuit, ordering the City to undertake prerelease planning for the continued treatment of Rikers inmates who receive psychiatric care while they are incarcerated.]

72. "Decompensate" is a term of art used by mental health professionals to describe what happens when the psychiatric condition of a person with a mental illness deteriorates. Because many mental illnesses are not "curable," a person is said to have "compensated" when medication or other factors have controlled the symptoms of the illness; a return of the symptoms is a "decompensation."

73. For example, a 1996 study in Austin, Texas, found that 63 percent of public order offenses involved alcohol or substance abuse, a third of public order arrests were of repeat offenders, and two-thirds of repeat offenders were homeless. "Clearly, those who have no permanent residence and those suffering from addiction are particularly prone to commit these crimes, and to circulate in and out of the municipal justice system," the report concluded. See "Broken Windows and Broken Lives: Addressing Public Order Offending in Austin," Center for Criminology and Criminal Justice Research

at the University of Texas at Austin. Quoted in Patricia G. Barnes, "Safer Streets at What Cost?" *ABA Journal* (June 1998): 25.

74. The average length of stay in city jails is forty-six days for detainees and thirty-seven days for sentenced inmates. Lynch testimony.

75. Robert Gangi and David Leven, "Build No Prisons; Fix the Laws Instead," *Rochester Democrat and Chronicle* (December 1, 1997).

76. New York City FY 1996 Local Government Plan for Adult Mental Health Services: 326.

77. Elaine Rivera, "The Police and the EDPs: As Services for the Emotionally Disturbed Dwindle, Officers Fill the Gaps, Sometimes with Deadly Results," *Time* magazine 154 (September 13, 1999): 30.

78. For example, two of the recent shootings of people with mental illness by police (among those listed below) have resulted not only in media coverage critical of police, but also, at least potentially, in litigation against the department. In the case of Kevin Cerbelli, his mother recently filed suit against both the NYPD and several hospitals that treated Mr. Cerbelli. In the case of Gary (Gidone) Busch, his family has hired famed attorneys Johnnie Cochran, Barry Scheck, and Peter Neufeld, presumably in contemplation of a lawsuit against the NYPD.

79. "EDPs and Deadly Force: The Toll," *New York Daily News* (September 5, 1999): 35.

80. Id.

81. http://www.ci.nyc.ny.us/html/nypd/html/pct/esu.html.

82. A model developed in Memphis, Tennessee, known as CIT (Crisis Intervention Team) has been successful in reducing injuries to police and people with mental illness. The CIT model has been replicated around the country in places including Iowa, Oregon, and New Mexico.

83. Nina Bernstein, "After Stabbing, Earlier Case Questioned," *New York Times* (June 15, 1999): B3.

84. The Comprehensive Psychiatric Emergency Program, or CPEP, was based in a number of city hospital emergency rooms and had, among its priorities, the goal of making emergency psychiatric services more rapidly accessible to people brought in by police. The program seems to have met with some success initially but to have gradually disappeared almost completely, although the funding continues. Today, police have never heard of the program, and the hospitals receiving the funding seem no better at expediting admission of people brought in by police than any other hospital.

3

Giuliani Time

Urban Policing and Brooklyn South

Sasha Torres

I

This essay examines collisions between mass-mediated representation and the lived history of police brutality in black communities, particularly how such collisions shape politics and everyday life within contemporary American cities. I focus here on one such crash of the social with the representational, which occurred in 1997: the police assault, in August, on Abner Louima in Brooklyn's 70th Precinct house and the premiere, in late September, of a new police drama called *Brooklyn South*.

I am broadly concerned here with the question of how cultural representation generally, and television particularly, can help generate and sustain consensus around a set of public policies, like those of Mayor Rudolph Giuliani with respect to policing. It will be a fundamental assumption of my argument that these policies are both unjust and nonsensical, whether they are seen from the perspective of a progressive advocacy of social justice—which clearly holds no interest for Giuliani—or from a sense of efficacious policy or even political self-interest—which clearly hold more than a little interest for him. How does a large, diverse, and sophisticated population carry on urban business as usual, as if Giuliani's consistent, aggressive defense of indefensible police actions makes sense?

The suggestion that television—and entertainment television at that—plays an important role in the conversion of *nonsense* to common sense is clearly not a wildly original one. And it would be a serious methodological and political error to elevate the effects of *Brooklyn South* over the ordinarily pervasive structures of racism and classism that go a long way toward explaining Giuliani's success. Nor do I mean to dismiss the importance of lower crime rates in modulating public concern about police brutality and corruption.[1] Nonetheless, *Brooklyn South* is worth examining for two reasons. Specifically, the temporal proximity of its premiere to the attack on Louima suggests that the program's narratives may have served as a way in which viewers processed, both psychically and politically, the assault and its aftershocks. The text of *Brooklyn South* reimagined Louima (or, more precisely, the Louima-function, the black man assaulted by police) as a homicidal maniac, and Brooklyn police officers as generally presenting a unified front against police abuse. Such processing of the social through the representational tends to contain the disruptive challenges to police and mayoral authority posed by the savagery of the officers involved.

More generally, any extended consideration of contemporary policing must take the cop show into account as a key ideological technology in the production of disciplined, lawful subjects whose primary point of entry into narratives about crime will be their identification with the police. As I hope to demonstrate, all of the elements of *Brooklyn South*'s text—its narrative structure, its camera work and editing, its use of sound—are finely calibrated to encourage this identification.

II

Co-produced by Steven Bochco and CBS, *Brooklyn South* is set in Brooklyn's 74th Precinct. Reviewers have noted its envelope-pushing realism: the first nine minutes of the pilot episode—which I will discuss at length below—were unprecedentedly violent, making *Brooklyn South* an instant poster child for the new television ratings system; in addition, the "cop talk" is so thickly "authentic" that the dialogue—and thus the plots—in the first few episodes were extremely hard to follow. (CBS actually provided a glossary on the show's Web page.) Well before the pilot aired on September 22, though, industry watchers in the popular press were struck by further evidence of the show's "authenticity": the fact that the first few episodes of the series dealt with the death, in the station house, of a black suspect in police custody.[2]

Parallels to the Louima case were drawn immediately. Abner Louima was arrested in an altercation with police outside a Haitian club in Flatbush where his favorite singer was performing. He was beaten, he claims, on the way to the station, by four officers of the 70th Precinct and then was taken into the precinct bathroom, where he was sodomized by one of the officers, Justin Volpe, with the wooden handle of a mop.[3] Volpe then forced the handle into his mouth. Police then declined for 90 minutes to provide a police escort to the ambulance that arrived to take Louima, with life-threatening injuries to his colon and bladder, to the hospital; when he finally got there, he was held under guard, handcuffed to his bed, and denied visitors.[4] Officers explained his injuries by saying they had been sustained in a homosexual encounter. After he was treated, a hospital worker reported the incident in a phone call to the Internal Affairs Bureau, a call which was neither logged nor followed up. Relatives of Louima's who went to the precinct to file a complaint were told to "go home."[5]

In public discourse, the assault on Abner Louima was immediately temporalized, linked to the particular period of Rudolph Giuliani's mayoral administration. Immediately after the attack Louima claimed that his assailant had admonished him during the beating to respect the police because "this is Giuliani time, not Dinkins time."[6] Louima later recanted this reference to New York City's current and former mayors, and testified at the officers' trial that "he had begun falsely reporting it at the urging of a supporter—a brother-in-law of a nurse at Coney Island Hospital, where he was then being treated—who told him he was an auxiliary police officer and frequently heard police officers make such statements."[7] But whether or not the slogan represents authentic evidence of the internal culture of the NYPD these days, the fact remains that the phrase "Giuliani Time" has proved for many New Yorkers a durable and evocative descriptor of the meeting point of politics and everyday life during the city's current "boom."

It is impossible to understand the events in the Louima case without considering more broadly the urban temporality of Giuliani Time. Giuliani Time is a fantastical temporality, energized by a vision of the city with a Starbucks on every corner, Gapified, Disneyfied, and washed clean of undesirable elements like public sex and poor people. Indeed, in a moment refreshing in its candor, a top Giuliani aide looked forward to the day when New York's poor would simply *leave the city* because they realized that it's better to be homeless in warmer climates.[8] The capital of this imaginary New York is, of course, the "new" Times Square.[9]

Most often, Giuliani Time is marked out by battles in a low-intensity war between hizzoner and the unruly masses of New Yorkers who continually and frustratingly refuse to conduct themselves according to the desires of their mayor. During recent memory, Giuliani has engaged in well-publicized skirmishes with Midtown pedestrians, city cabbies, local hot dog vendors, and, perhaps most famously, the Brooklyn Museum. But the mayor is not content to confine his efforts to micromanaging everyday life. He has waged a sustained economic and social battle against the city's poor (via welfare "reform" and new policies on homelessness) and on sexual subcultures. At the same time, Giuliani has showered public resources and mayoral approbation on a police force which to many seems to be spinning dangerously out of control.

In New York in Giuliani Time, "safety" is paramount, and, indeed, the overall crime rate in New York has dropped significantly.[10] But it is a particular kind of safety, designed for a particular class of persons, and purchased at a high price: as Samuel Delany noted recently, the person for whom the new Times Square is supposed to be safe is the middle-class tourist from the suburbs.[11] Other kinds of persons, though, may find ourselves dramatically *less* safe. In Giuliani Time, under the mayor's celebrated "zero tolerance" policies, entire classes of persons—"squeegee guys," youth of color, sex workers, and the poor—have been effectively criminalized as the agents of what the current mayoral administration has dubbed "quality-of-life" offenses. As a result, charges of police brutality and misconduct have increased significantly over the final year of the Dinkins administration, and a vastly disproportionate number of the victims of police abuses are people of color.[12] In Giuliani Time, as Amnesty International reported in a 1996 study, "it is rare for NYPD officers to be criminally prosecuted for on-duty excessive force and even rarer for convictions to be obtained."[13] In Giuliani Time, the city of New York spent just over $29 million settling cases of police abuse in 1997 alone, and by the end of 1997 had spent a total of $98 million settling them since Giuliani took office.[14] In Giuliani Time, many of the debates about the mayor's stewardship of the department have revolved around the question of how best to "police the police," and more particularly around the question of independent monitoring of cases of abuse and corruption. A short history of those debates will provide a context for the rest of my discussion.

On March 27, 1998, a *New York Times* front-page headline announced "Giuliani Dismisses Police Proposals by His Task Force," while a subhead noted, "Mayor's Tone Is Caustic." The accompanying article detailed the latest phase in Giuliani's ongoing resistance to police reform, noting that he had greeted the report of his own "Task Force on Police and Community Relations" with "insult" and "sarcasm," and dismissed most of its recommendations.[15] For followers of Giuliani's bizarre approach to public relations, the *Times*'s subhead echoed countless earlier headlines for stories specifying the mayor's penchant for treating those with whom he disagrees with a combination of arrogance and petulance. For followers of his relations with the New York Police Department, the headline echoed countless earlier titles for stories about his repudiation of proposals made by the Mollen Commission to Investigate Police Corruption, the New York City Council, and, occasionally, police department insiders.

The Mollen Commission was appointed in 1992 by Giuliani's predecessor, David Dinkins, after Michael Dowd, a Brooklyn cop, was arrested by Suffolk County police on drug charges.[16] After a two-year investigation, the commission's final report documented that, in certain black and Hispanic neighborhoods, groups of rogue cops had organized into criminal "crews" much like street gangs and were dealing drugs, using departmental equipment in break-ins, skimming cash recovered from crime scenes, and "terrorizing" residents.[17] The report also identified what it called "willful blindness" to corruption pervasive among precinct commanders and departmental investigators, reluctance on the part of honest officers to report corrupt colleagues, willingness on the part of police union officials to tip off cops under investigation, and resistance to investigating corrupt cops for fear that negative publicity might be damaging to the department's reputation.[18]

The commission proposed a number of strategies to reduce police corruption, including raising the minimum age of recruits from twenty to twenty-two, increasing random drug testing, and expanding Internal Affairs' use of undercover agents.[19] But debates about the commission's recommendations quickly crystallized around the question of how to police the police. The commission, citing what its chairman, Milton Mollen, called "the shocking . . . incompetence and inadequacy of the police department to police itself," called for the creation of an independent "Police Commission" with investigative and subpoena power.[20] Giuliani, who was elected to his first term as mayor in 1993—

thanks, in part, to the endorsement of the Patrolmen's Benevolent Association—was faced with the task of reconciling the commission's endorsement of a monitoring body with the resistance of various sectors of law enforcement. He has managed this assignment with an aplomb both admirable and alarming: for several years he has claimed consistently both to support external oversight of the force while engineering just as consistently the impossibility of such oversight.

Immediately after his election, for example, Giuliani stated that he supported the establishment of a special prosecutor's office rather than the five-member panel recommended by the Commission, to investigate charges of corruption and brutality.[21] A casual observer might at the time have reasonably accepted the mayor-elect's claim that such an entity would be "even more independent" and thus even more effective in combating police malfeasance.[22] But a clue to the fact that Giuliani might not be telling the whole story was provided early on by the *New York Times*: "Last week, aides to Mr. Giuliani, who spoke only on the condition of anonymity, said it was unlikely that he would fully accept the proposals of a commission that in effect is a lame-duck group appointed by a lame-duck Mayor."[23] A closer examination of Giuliani's proposal reveals a crucial loophole. As *Newsday* reported on November 19, 1993, "Commission members were also troubled when Giuliani publicly recommended the formation of a special prosecutor's office to fight police wrongdoing. Although the commission hasn't yet issued its final proposal, a special prosecutor's office is considered a dead issue because Gov. Mario Cuomo's top law-enforcement officials say the state won't pay for it."[24] Indeed, Giuliani continued to champion the idea of a special prosecutor until August 1994, just two and a half months before Cuomo was defeated by George Pataki.[25]

At the same time, though, during the period from April through August 1994, the administration continued to float other proposals. At the end of April, *Newsday* quoted a Giuliani aide as saying that the mayor "has been extremely supportive of the commission, even backing off his campaign endorsement of a special state prosecutor to investigate police corruption until he hears what type of independent oversight the commission will recommend."[26] The next day, *Newsday* reported that the mayor was waffling on the question of whether the group would have "the power to conduct its own investigations," a power that was a crucial element of the Mollen recommendation.[27] Nine weeks later, after the commission released its final report, the

Times reported that "in recent months, [the mayor] has indicated that he leans toward giving the outside monitoring powers to the city's Department of Investigation," which is charged with monitoring public corruption citywide, rather than to a group dedicated specifically to investigating police.[28]

Finally, on August 20, the *Times* related that "Mayor Giuliani said for the first time that he favored creating an independent agency to monitor corruption in New York City's Police Department, and he said he would try to reach agreement with the City Council on what powers to give it."[29] The same day, *Newsday* noted that "Giuliani said he wants the panel to be created by the City Council rather than by a mayoral executive order." When the City Council passed a bill that did just that, by a vote of 39 to 9 in October, Giuliani immediately announced his plans to veto the bill, claiming that the council had arrogated to itself powers properly belonging to the mayor, and objecting to the council's plan that the panel have subpoena and investigative powers.[30] The veto finally came in December; when the council overrode the veto a month later, the mayor replied that he would "ignore" the vote. In February 1995, as Internal Affairs was uncovering a major corruption scandal in the Bronx's 48th Precinct (which eventually resulted in the indictment of sixteen of the precinct's officers), he announced plans to create his own panel by executive order.[31] The mayor's panel would be appointed entirely by hizzoner, and would have investigative and subpoena power to be used only at his discretion (or, in the *Times*'s words, "at the Mayor's pleasure").[32] By the end of the month, Giuliani's panel was in place, and the mayor was threatening to sue the City Council "within a week if Speaker Peter Vallone (D-Queens) does not agree on a new format giving the mayor power to appoint all commission members."[33] The mayor filed this suit in April 1994.

In June, while the courts adjudicated the mayor's conflict with the council, the debate over police monitoring shifted. Members of the NYPD, in Washington D.C. to attend a memorial for slain police officers, went on a drunken rampage in their hotels. Officers, "some in uniform and some naked, groped at women, shot off fire extinguishers, and caused extensive damage in hotel corridors."[34] In the wake of this scandal, Giuliani announced sweeping new anticorruption measures. In the process, he appropriated many of the Mollen Commission's recommendations for his own political gain, even as he shifted the burden of investigating charges against police from the Internal Affairs Bureau to individual precinct commanders.[35] At the end of the month, State Supreme Court Justice Beatrice Shainswit ruled with Giuliani that the City Council "overstepped its authority" in creating the police monitoring panel.[36]

In less than two years, in other words, Giuliani had managed to turn oversight (a term whose double sense I invoke advisedly) of the police over to the department itself, all the while claiming that he supported independent superintendence of the force. It is shocking, though hardly surprising, then, that Giuliani's panel, the "Commission to Combat Police Corruption," issued its first report praising "'significant improvements' in the New York City Police Department's anti-corruption efforts," or that the *Times* eventually reported that "a meddling City Hall and an uncooperative Police Department have rendered [the mayor's panel] largely irrelevant."[37]

So determined has the mayor's resistance to independent police review been that the struggle between the City Council and the mayor's office over police monitoring was reenacted almost to the letter in the wake of the Louima scandal. In a chain of events beginning in September 1997, the City Council again tried to create an independent police review board in revised legislation that granted the mayor the right to approve all the board's members. Giuliani again vetoed the council's proposal, the council again overrode the veto, and the mayor again sued the council to block formation of the board.[38] This time, though, the suit was unsuccessful, although the mayor's office vowed to appeal State Supreme Court Justice Richard F. Braun's ruling. The outrageousness of the mayor's opposition to police review, given the excesses of the Louima case, was neatly smoke-screened by the administration's grudging concession, in mid-September, to increase the budget of the city's Civilian Complaint Review Board—the drastically underfunded 98-pound weakling of NYPD oversight—by a measly $1.5 million.[39]

Giuliani's opposition to any genuinely independent entity empowered to investigate—much less to discipline—criminal officers of the New York Police Department has thus persisted through outside investigations by Amnesty International and the federal government. It has endured numerous department scandals involving corruption and brutality, unwavering in the wake of the assault on Abner Louima, the shooting of Amadou Diallo, and the shooting of Gidone Busch and Patrick Dorismond, to name only the best-publicized recent incidents.

It has persevered as the city's costs to settle lawsuits against the department have skyrocketed.

But the costs of Giuliani's consistency, and the police abuse that accompanies it, are garnered not only from the city budget, but also from the bodies and spirits of its citizens. This price is often extracted as the commission paid in the conversion of different denominations of masculine capital. In other words, the circulation of particular masculinities through historically and racially specific communities frequently requires the extraction of these surcharges, in the form, too often, of literal pounds of flesh from racially or sexually othered bodies. It is as if majoritarian culture, noting the othered body's superabundance to the rationally disembodied public sphere, tries violently to cut it to size.[40] I will track these exchanges through a set of representations depicting white police officers in brutal transactions with their others. On, then, to the fortunes of race and sexuality as currencies in a ruthless marketplace of identity, *Brooklyn South*.

III

Given its appearance during Giuliani Time, it is crucial to specify *Brooklyn South*'s central ideological project: to encourage its audience's identification with the police, to locate its viewers inside the "house" (the police station) and not as members of either "the community"—which the show depicts as violent, foolish, and irrational—or the Internal Affairs Bureau, which the show depicts as predatory and overzealous. The extent to which the series will go in this regard was borne out paratextually by its official CBS-sponsored Web page. Visitors were granted entry to the site by answering correctly one of the questions on the New York Police Academy entrance exam. Once admitted, they found, along with the standard cast bios and episode summaries, an audio link allowing them to listen "live" to Brooklyn police scanners; an up-to-date listing, complete with photos and vital statistics, race prominent among them, of "Brooklyn's [real life] Most Wanted," and the aforementioned "Cop Talk" glossary.

On a number of levels, the text of *Brooklyn South* is itself structured to encourage identification with its protagonists by providing viewers with ample scenes of their private lives, immersing them in police-procedural details, and granting them privileged access to the inner sancta of police life: locker rooms, interrogation rooms, "cop bars," and the like. These elements of the series are unsurprising. More remarkable, though, are the lengths to which the series goes to foreclose spectators' resistant, oppositional, or disidentificatory readings. It is crucial to note that, in this way, the series is a marked departure from the currently dominant narrative conventions for prime-time drama, conventions Bochco himself pioneered in series such as *Hill Street Blues* and *L. A. Law*. These series, and most of the dramatic series that followed them, are carefully organized to maximize ratings by allowing multiple—and sometimes conflicting—possibilities for viewer engagement across political, economic, and social locations. Unlike its generic predecessors, and its predecessors within Bochco's oeuvre, *Brooklyn South* actively works to render the viewers' engagement with the white male officers' various "others" at least unappealing and at worst actively dangerous.

The opening of the series' pilot episode provides a concise example of how *Brooklyn South* deploys narrative and visual elements to structure viewer identification. Critics who reviewed the pilot focused on the considerable violence, extreme even for its genre, that earned this episode television's first "TV-MA" rating (mature audiences). I am interested less in the fact of the violence than in the ways that violence is organized and rendered systematic by the sequence's editing.

The sequence opens with a minor car accident between a retired cop and the Asian woman who rear-ends him. Marking the Brooklyn streetscape as one organized, if not riven, by racial conflict, the former cop accuses the woman of "driving while Oriental." When she refuses to leave her car, he flags down two uniformed officers, telling them that the woman is behaving "as though I'm after her for Pearl Harbor or something." Meanwhile, back at the station, officers in roll call are being briefed on conditions in the precinct. Patrol Sergeant Frank Donovan (Jon Tenney) alerts his officers to be on the lookout for "this asshole, Deshawn Hopkins," as he points to a picture of a black man plastered to the front of the podium behind which he is speaking. A cut takes us back out to the street, where we see Hopkins, unprovoked, punching a white man on the street, then kicking in the headlight of a passing car before coming up behind one of the officers involved in the traffic stop and shooting him, execution style, in the back of the head. During the next six minutes, Hopkins continues to kill police officers, despite being shot several times himself, until he is finally apprehended by Officer Jimmy Doyle (Dylan Walsh), and brought into custody.

There are a couple of remarkable things about the editing of this sequence, in that it breaks two rules generally held dear by television editors: it contains two jump cuts and at least two significant continuity errors. In both cases, these transgressions of standard television editing practices are thematically linked.

A jump cut joins two shots in which the camera in the second shot is positioned less than 30 degrees away from where it was positioned in the first shot; because the camera positions for the two shots are so close together, the shots look very similar. Thus the jump cut has the effect of repeating the image with only a slight difference. Editors of U.S. commercial television generally avoid jump cuts because they are considered overly obtrusive, calling attention to the editing itself rather than the content of the two shots joined by the cut. In *Brooklyn South*, both jump cuts join two shots of cops leaving the safety of their cars to engage Hopkins; they thus double and insist on the counterintuitive and courageous determination of the officers to enter the fray.

Continuity errors are violations of the system of editing, perfected by Hollywood and inherited by television, designed to minimize the disruption of the cut in favor of maintaining continuous narrative action by matching the direction, movement, and position of figures from shot to shot. The continuity errors in the sequence I've described have to do with the perpetrator, Hopkins, and the virtually magical appearances of his guns. There is a moment as Hopkins is described on the soundtrack as a cocaine addict, just after he slugs the innocent bystander who has the misfortune to bump into him, which suggests that Hopkins has a gun tucked into the front of his pants, under his sweatshirt. The appearance of a gun held behind his back seven shots later is thus difficult to explain, given that the editor seems to have passed up an opportunity to build suspense by displaying Hopkins readying his weapon. When, later in this sequence, Hopkins suddenly appears and begins firing *two* guns where before he had only one, these rhyming narrative omissions—the text's refusal to explain where these guns come from—seem self-conscious enough (or perhaps *un*-self-conscious enough) to establish *Brooklyn South*'s insistence on Hopkins's virtually supernatural powers. With his maniacal-yet-glazed expression and uncanny calm, Hopkins seems able to conjure weapons from nowhere.

If this sequence is willing to flout some of the conventions of realist editing, though, it is also scrupulous in its observation of other such conventions, notably the manipulation of point of view (POV) in producing viewer identification. In particular, the editing here is extremely careful to align the spectator's view of what transpires with that of the police's. Hopkins is given only one point-of-view shot in the entire sequence; the police are assigned at least six. In addition, certain key shots that are not assigned to individual characters' POV are allied with the gaze of the police. Consider, for example, the mug shot to which Donovan gestures at roll call, and which serves as a kind of establishing shot for what follows; or the overhead shot of the slain body of the first officer Hopkins shoots. While this shot was most likely made with a crane, the extreme high angle suggests another trope of contemporary police narrative: the surveilling view from a police helicopter.

But if the cops are afforded, directly or indirectly, much of the power of the controlling gaze here, the tension in the sequence is produced by the menacing gaze of Hopkins, frequently represented as coterminous with his magically lethal firearms. Hopkins *looks* in order to *take aim*. And the sequence deliberately confuses the question of at whom Hopkins is aiming; it painstakingly conflates its spectators' position with that of the police/victims by the astonishing number of shots (twelve to be exact) that depict Hopkins moving menacingly or actually firing directly toward the camera. The spectator of this sequence, then, is carefully located in such a way as to experience both the police officer's power and his vulnerability.

Both textually and paratextually, then, *Brooklyn South* participates in the us-versus-them epistemology of Giuliani Time. In the process, it does its best to align its audience with the deeply pernicious racism and classism that currently organize the nation's most important urban spaces. Clearly, the series understands this "us" to be white and male, despite the token inclusion, among *Brooklyn South*'s characters, of two women officers (one white, one African American) and a male Latino officer. The series' algebraic arrangement of racial and sexual difference renders the terms "police," "white," and "male" equivalent to one another in a way that would make women and Latinos irrelevant, and male African American cops impossible. This tendency allowed a miscalculation simultaneously bizarre and utterly predictable: as originally cast, the show included no black male officers. Indeed, the entire pilot was reshot during the summer of 1997 after producer David Milch "noticed" that this omission might imply "a racial statement which was utterly unintended, a sense of 'us vs. them.'"[41] He went on to note "the paradox is, I didn't think in racial categories, which, of course, is the ultimate goal of our society."[42]

IV

Brooklyn South bifurcates the Louima incident into two separate plot lines, one involving the death of Hopkins while in police custody and one involving a gay-bashing by cops. With the verb "bifurcates," I am not claiming that the producers of the series intended explicitly to rewrite the Louima narrative in the particular ways they did (we know that at least the pilot was in the can before the attack on Louima). I am rather pointing out the temporal coexistence of these narratives within a larger social discourse about race and policing, and insisting that these narratives function within those discourses as at least mutually inflecting, facilitating conscious and unconscious identifications with the police.

To pick up the first plot after the clip I've described, Hopkins is dragged into the station house, where some of the surviving officers briefly consider leaving him where he can't get medical attention. He then dies, to the satisfaction of several of the cops. Internal Affairs (IAB), however, isn't so satisfied. Armed with an autopsy report saying that Hopkins died of a punctured lung from compression fractures to the chest, and that he sustained these injuries "after he was in the house," IAB lieutenant Sam Jonas (James B. Sikking) commences investigating the issue of how the police "comported themselves" during the incident, causing Donovan to remark bitterly, "Psycho killing people on the streets, and they'll look to make us wrong."

The story unfolds over several episodes, complete with unreasonable and overzealous African American community leaders holding premature rallies and press conferences. The IAB investigation focuses on Officer Jack Lowery (Titus Welliver), who was seen to slap Hopkins while subduing him. The audience, however, knows that the real culprit may be Officer Ann-Marie Kersey (Yancy Butler), whose fiancé, another cop, was killed in the incident and who admits to Donovan that she kicked Hopkins in the back and thus possibly dealt the deadly blow herself. Later, however, after a grand jury refuses to indict Lowery, and

Donovan inexplicably persuades Kersey not to come forward, all is for-given: the medical examiner issues yet another report saying that Hop-kins died of his gunshot wounds after all.

The second brutality plot line appears in episode 7, "Love Hurts," in which officers are called to the scene of a fight between two white men outside a gay bar. They find an enraged older man beating his pas-sive and pathetic lover, claiming he has made a pass at another man, a black man. The cuckolded lover (who has quite a mouth on him) calls this figure "Paul Robeson" and "Jackie Robinson," but he actually serves as a figure for Abner Louima, who was, after all, arrested outside a club in which, according at least to his assailants, abusive gay sex took place. Into the breach of this mélange of conflicting masculine styles—straight machismo, butch gay male, snap queen, gay milquetoast—se-ries regulars, Officers Roussakoff (Michael de Luise) and Villanueva (Adam Rodriguez) leap to take the batterer into custody. But when Roussakoff is hit in the head with a bottle and needs Villanueva to take him to the hospital, they hand off the arrest to two episodic characters, Officers Heagan and Pitterino. Suspicions are roused immediately at the precinct when Heagan and Pitterino arrive with the men, the older of whom has been badly beaten on the way into the house. They claim that his lover inflicted the damage; for his part, the lover claims that one of the officers has run his partner's head into a dumpster. During the rest of the episode, the 74th Precinct is letter perfect in its investigation of the brutality charge: Roussakoff and Villanueva serve, not as a blue wall of silence, but as champions of "the truth." Another cop, who wit-nessed the beating while off duty, appears unprompted to give Sergeant Santoro the number of the patrol car driven by the offending officers. The plot winds down with Heagan, who actually administered the beating, vociferously blaming "those fags" for ruining his life before he breaks down in tears asking, "Oh, my god, what did I do?"

In Brooklyn's 74th Precinct, then, as opposed to the 70th, police bru-tality is the product, not of a widespread culture of lawlessness among men who reasonably expect not to be punished for criminal activity, but rather of grief, extreme stress, or gender trouble; its perpetrators, fur-thermore, are genuinely *sorry* for what they have done. Investigations into misconduct are ardently pursued by IAB—no missing phone calls here—even when the victims are black cop killers or extremely bitchy queens. Fellow officers (with the singular exception of Donovan's pro-tection of Kersey, who is, after all, female and thus relatively harmless) consistently place their commitment to the truth before their commitment to their colleagues. Mistakes are made; highly charged situations sometimes get out of hand, but the disciplinary systems internal to the department are entirely adequate to correct those mistakes, to ease those situations. Independent police review of the sort that Giuliani has stonewalled would be superfluous here.

The identification with "good cops" that these narratives encourage is further supported by *Brooklyn South's* relentless effort to divide and conquer the overlapping and conflictual kinds of otherness that characterize the Louima case and, for that matter, everyday life in major U.S. urban centers these days. The series disentangles the strands of the story of Louima's violation. It is a complicated story of the anal rape of a Haitian immigrant arrested in front of a Haitian club the police claim was also a gay club, by a putatively heterosexual white male police officer engaged to marry an African American woman. *Brooklyn South* reconstitutes this story into two palatable prime-time narratives. The first is the story of a black man who killed cops and who was thus despised and maybe even assaulted by cops, but who turns out to have died of entirely justifiable gunshot wounds. The second is the story of a white mouthy gay batterer brutalized in what the show, at least, understands to be a nonsexual way by a white police officer who is promptly brought up on charges with the help of his partner and virtually every regular character on the series. In the process, the us vs. them clarity of *Brooklyn South* renders its others simple, clear, and easy to stigmatize, and plays its consensus-forming part in ensuring that our futures may be marked out in Giuliani Time.

NOTES

For their comments and suggestions, I am indebted to José Esteban Muñoz, Phillip Brian Harper, and to audiences at the 1997 Modern Language Association Convention, Dartmouth College and the University of California—Berkeley.

1. See, for example, John Tierney, "The Big City: No One Wants to See Crime in a Tradeoff," *New York Times*, March 25, 1999, B1; and Frank Bruni, "Ideas & Trends: Crimes of the War on Crime," *New York Times*, February 21, 1999, sec. 4, p. 1. Bruni notes: "Many Americans have tacitly blessed a more vigorous, invasive, belligerent brand of policing."

2. On the show's (and particularly the pilot's) violence, see Bill Carter, "TV

Notes," *New York Times*, July 16, 1997, C18; Gail Shister, "Reshoot of Bochco's 'Brooklyn South' Pilot Will Add a Black Officer," *Philadelphia Inquirer*, July 16, 1997; Monica Collins, "'Brooklyn' Accents True—Bochco Touch Equals Quality," *Boston Herald*, September 22, 1997, 34; Dennis Byrne, "Stereotypical Reality," *Chicago Sun-Times*, September 24, 1997, 43; Matthew Gilbert, "Another Badge of Honor: 'Brooklyn South' Engaging, Gimmickless," *Boston Globe*, September 22, 1997, C6; Caryn James, "When the Thin Blue Line Becomes Unstrung," *New York Times*, September 22, 1997, E1; Eric Mink, "A Rookie Explodes onto the Scene," *Daily News*, September 22, 1997, 64; Virginia Rohan, "Into the Wild Blue Yonder: Bochco's New Cop Drama, Brooklyn South, Takes TV Violence to the Limit," *Bergen Record*, September 22, 1997, Y1. On its "authenticity," see Collins and Verne Gay, "A Serious Shoot-Em Up," *Newsday*, September 22, 1997, B6. On the echoes of the Louima case, see Gilbert, James, and Rohan articles cited in this note and Greg Braxton and Jane Hall, "Too Close to Reality?" *Los Angeles Times*, August 21, 1997, F50.

3. The officers alleged to have been involved only in the beating on the way to the station house, Thomas Wiese and Thomas Bruder, were acquitted, though in March 2000 they were convicted of federal charges of obstruction of justice. After several fellow officers testified against him, Justin Volpe pleaded guilty to violating Louima's civil rights. Charles Schwarz was also found guilty.

4. Dan Barry, "Charges of Brutality: The Overview," *New York Times*, August 15, 1997, A1; ABC News, *Nightline*, "The Blue Wall," August 22, 1997.

5. *Nightline*, "The Blue Wall."

6. Dan Barry, "Charges of Brutality: The Overview," *New York Times*, August 15, 1997, A1.

7. John Kifner, "Louima Says His Attackers Did Not Yell 'Giuliani Time,'" *New York Times*, January 15, 1998, B3; Joseph P. Fried, "In Louima's First Day on Stand, He Tells of Brutal Police Assault," *New York Times*, May 7, 1999, A1.

8. Wayne Barrett, "50 Reasons to Loathe Your Mayor," *Village Voice*, November 4, 1997. Reason #1:

> Saying it would be "a good thing" if poor people left the city, RG said in response to questions about the effect of his welfare cuts: "That's not an unspoken part of our strategy. That is our strategy." Though this comment was reported by the news director of the city's own television station, the mayor corrected it, saying an exodus "could be a natural consequence," though "not the intention of our policy." The mayor's favorite newspaper, the *Post*, cited one of RG's "chief policy architects" as saying: "The poor will eventually figure out that it's a lot easier to be homeless where it's warm."

9. My thinking about the politics of the new Times Square is indebted to

Samuel R. Delany, *Times Square Red, Times Square Blue* (New York: New York University Press, 1999).

10. See David Kocieniewski, "The 1997 Elections: Crime; Mayor Gets Credit for a Safer City, but Wider Trends Play a Role," *New York Times*, October 28, 1997, B4.

11. Delany, *Times Square Red, Times Square Blue*, 158ff.

12. Wayne Barrett, "Beating the Cops," *Village Voice*, December 23, 1997, 36; Nat Hentoff, "Jim Crow in Blue: Eighty Per Cent of Civilian Complaints Are from Nonwhites," *Village Voice*, September 23, 1997; Deborah Sontag and Dan Barry, "Challenge to Authority: A Special Report," *New York Times*, November 19, 1997, A1.

13. The Amnesty International Report, "Police Brutality and Excessive Force in the New York City Police Department," can be found on the World Wide Web at http://www.amnesty.org/ailib/aipub/1996/AMR/25103696.htm. For press coverage of the report, see Clifford Krauss, "Rights Group Finds Abuse of Suspects by City Police," *New York Times*, June 26, 1996, B4, and Ellis Henican, "Please and May I Joining the Finest," *Newsday*, June 27, 1996, A2.

14. Deborah Sontag and Dan Barry, "The Price of Brutality: A Special Report," *New York Times*, September 17, 1997, A1; Deborah Sontag and Dan Barry, "Challenge to Authority: A Special Report," *New York Times*, November 19, 1997, A1; Wayne Barrett, "Beating the Cops," *Village Voice*, December 23, 1997, 36; Kevin Flynn, "How to Sue the Police (and Win): Lawyers Share Trade Secrets of a Growth Industry," *New York Times*, October 2, 1999, B1.

15. Dan Barry, "Giuliani Dismisses Police Proposals by His Task Force," *New York Times*, March 27, 1998, A1. The group's recommendations included instituting residency requirements for police officers and tougher entrance requirements for the police academy, and ending the "48 hour rule," which forces investigators to wait 48 hours before questioning officers who may have committed a crime. See also Barry, "Giuliani Sneers, and Even Friends Bridle," *New York Times*, March 28, 1998, A1; and "Giuliani Concedes He Could Have Been More Gracious," *New York Times*, April 2, 1998, B5.

16. Alison Mitchell, "Corruption in Uniform: The Mayor," *New York Times*, July 8, 1994, A1.

17. Clifford Krauss, "Corruption in Uniform: The Overview," *New York Times*, July 7, 1994, A1.

18. Ibid.

19. David Kocieniewski, "Giuliani Cool to Independent Police Monitors," *Newsday*, July 8, 1994, A20.

20. Selwyn Raab, "New York's Police Allow Corruption, Mollen Panel Says," *New York Times*, December 29, 1993, A1.

21. David Kocieniewski, "Corruption Panel Courts Giuliani," *Newsday*, November 19, 1993, 38.

22. Jonathan Larsen, "Prescription for Police Corruption Draws Controversy," United Press International, December 28, 1993.

23. Selwyn Raab, "Mollen Panel to Recommend Permanent Corruption Body," New York Times, December 29, 1993, B1.

24. David Kocieniewski, "Corruption Panel Courts Giuliani," Newsday, November 19, 1993, 38.

25. David Kocieniewski, "Giuliani Cool to Independent Police Monitors," Newsday, July 8, 1994, A20: "Giuliani, a former federal prosecutor who tried several cases against corrupt officers during the Knapp Commission scandal, said he will urge Gov. Mario Cuomo to revive the Special State Prosecutor's Office disbanded in 1990. Giuliani conceded it was 'highly unlikely' Cuomo would make such a move during an election year." See also Bob Liff and David Kocieniewski, "Rudy Backs New Cop Monitor," Newsday, August 20, 1994, A06: "Although Giuliani favors the creation of a legislatively mandated special prosecutor's office to investigate and try crooked officers, Gov. Mario Cuomo has indicated that he wouldn't authorize such a move."

26. Patricia Cohen, "Surprise! Rudy Backs the Panel," Newsday, April 21, 1994, A04.

27. David Kocieniewski and George E. Jordan, "Giuliani's Police Monitor: Will Watchdog Have Teeth?" Newsday, April 29, 1994, A06.

28. Alison Mitchell, "Corruption in Uniform: The Mayor," New York Times, July 8, 1994, A1.

29. "Giuliani Supports Police Monitor," New York Times, August 20, 1994, A1.

30. See John Shanahan, "Independent Police Review Nears Reality," Bergen Record, October 27, 1994, C14; Jonathan P. Hicks, "2 Council Committees Pass Bill to Create Police Agency," New York Times, October 27, 1994, B3; Hicks, "Giuliani Expected to Veto Police Monitor Bill," New York Times, December 12, 1994, B3; and Bob Liff, "Rudy's Power Play: He Starts Own Corruption Panel," Newsday, February 28, 1995, A17.

31. See Clifford Krauss, "Police Investigating Corruption Charges at Bronx Precinct," New York Times, February 2, 1995, A1; Krauss and Adam Nositter, "Crossing the Line—A Special Report: Bronx Abuse Stirs Crackdown on Police," New York Times, May 2, 1995, A1; Krauss, "16 Police Officers Are Indicted in Bronx Precinct Graft Inquiry," New York Times, May 3, 1995, A1; and Krauss, "16 Officers Indicted in a Pattern of Brutality in a Bronx Precinct," New York Times, May 4, 1995.

32. Jonathan P. Hicks, "Giuliani Considers Creating Own Police-Monitor Panel," New York Times, February 1, 1995, B3: "Paul A. Crotty, the Mayor's Corporation Counsel, said the administration was drawing up plans for an agency to serve at the Mayor's pleasure."

33. Bob Liff, "Rudy's Power Play: He Starts Own Corruption Panel," News-

day, February 28, 1995, A17. See also Jonathan P. Hicks, "Giuliani Names His Own Panel to Monitor Police Corruption," *New York Times*, February 28, 1995, B1. The mayor's legal action against the Council was eventually upheld by the state Supreme Court. See Daniel Wise, "City Council's Board on Police Invalidated: Mayor Wins Clear Victory in Power Struggle," *New York Law Journal*, July 29, 1995, 1.

34. Steven Lee Myers, "Police Study of Rampage Shifts Focus," *New York Times*, May 21, 1995, sec. 1, p. 37.

35. William K. Rashbaum, "Getting Back in Line: Rudy Unveils Plan to Stem Cop Corruption," *Newsday*, June 15, 1995, 5; George James, "New York Calls for Precincts to Control Police Monitoring," *New York Times*, June 15, 1995, A1.

36. Jonathan P. Hicks, "Judge Invalidates Creation of Police Corruption Panel," *New York Times*, June 29, 1995, B3. This decision was upheld on appeal; see Clifford J. Levy, "Mayor's Veto of New Panel on Police Is Upheld," *New York Times*, January 11, 1997, sec. 1, p. 29.

37. George James, "Mayoral Commission Offers Qualified Praise on Police Anti-Corruption Drive," *New York Times*, March 30, 1996, sec. 1, p. 26; David Kocieniewski, "Mayor's Panel on Corruption Faces Scrutiny," *New York Times*, September 22, 1997, B1. Kocieniewski quotes a commission staff member as saying that "[the commission's reports] are so sanitized by the Mayor's office it's got to be a joke."

38. Vivian S. Toy, "Council Backs a New Police Review Board," *New York Times*, October 1, 1997, B2; Toy, "Giuliani Again Vetoes Bill for Outside Police Monitor," *New York Times*, October 31, 1997, B3; Toy, "Veto of Police Board Overridden," *New York Times*, November 26, 1997, B3; Norimitsu Onishi, "Giuliani Sues to Block Police Board," *New York Times*, March 26, 1998, B7. The City Council's veto was eventually upheld by the New York State Supreme Court. See David Rohde, "Judge Rules for New Board to Fight Police Corruption," *New York Times*, September 1, 1999, B3.

39. Michael Cooper, "Mayor to Help Police Monitor He Had Fought," *New York Times*, September 17, 1997, B1.

40. My thinking here is indebted to the work of Lauren Berlant and Michael Warner. See, in particular, Berlant's "National Brands/National Body: *Imitation of Life*," and Warner's "The Mass Public and the Mass Subject," both in Bruce Robbins, ed., *The Phantom Public Sphere* (Minneapolis: University of Minnesota Press, 1993).

41. Gail Shister, "Reshoot of Bochco's 'Brooklyn South' Pilot Will Add a Black Officer," *Philadelphia Inquirer*, July 16, 1997.

42. Ibid.

PART II

THE POLICE

4

Can Zero Tolerance Last?

Voices from inside the Precinct

Jennifer R. Wynn

I was given a ticket for going through a red light—on my bicycle. I was infuriated. The next day I was lugging my bike up a staircase and a cop offered to carry it. I let him, but I thought twice about thanking him.

> —A 38-year-old woman from Brooklyn

I conduct research on inner-city drug use and come into contact with a lot of dealers and addicts. My brother-in-law is a street narcotics cop. He begs me for leads of people he can arrest. He's that desperate to make arrests.

> —A criminologist at John Jay College of Criminal Justice

I think we've gone overboard with zero tolerance. Cops are being held to unrealistic expectations to arrest people, and the result is that the community now sees us as occupiers, not problem solvers.

> —An NYPD captain with twenty years on the job

THE DROP IN New York City crime has made for tantalizing sound bites and boosted civic pride among the most cynical urban dwellers. But often lost from the commentary are the voices and experiences of uniformed officers charged with enforcing "zero tolerance" policing, the intensified law enforcement as well as style of management that holds law enforcement officials accountable for achieving acceptable results. This chapter, based on interviews with police officers, sergeants, and captains within the NYPD—all of whom requested anonymity for fear of reprisal—explores how zero tolerance plays out on the street, and what toll it has taken on its enforcers and targets alike. We will also examine how the city's other law enforcement agency, the Department of Correction, has successfully adapted elements of zero-tolerance policing to the city's sprawling jail complex on Rikers Island, producing a 90 percent decline in inmate violence since 1995.

Echoing the sentiments of every police officer interviewed, an NYPD sergeant with eleven years on the job described morale among police officers as "lower than [his] shoe." He cited insufficient salary, unflattering media coverage, and an anti-NYPD sentiment that has pervaded public thinking. Undeniably, the NYPD has driven down crime substantially over the past five years, but its success has been marred by a number of high-profile police brutality cases and aggressive police tactics that have changed—or ended—the lives of ordinary citizens. In responding to the current swell of public backlash directed at the NYPD, the sergeant noted that "perps consider harassment from cops as an occupational hazard. It's when the more mainstream, law-abiding citizens get busted for low-level infractions that the outrage begins."

New York City police feel their efforts as crime fighters have gone unrewarded, both internally and externally. Although city and union officials spent two years negotiating the current labor contract under which the NYPD's 39,000 employees work, "all we got were zeros," said the sergeant. The five-year contract gave police no raise for the first two years (and therefore no retroactive pay, which the cops had been counting on), and increases of 3 percent for the third year, 3 percent for the fourth year, and 6 percent for the fifth year. "Some people said 12 percent is a good raise," continued the sergeant, "but inflation is what, 3.5 percent? Over a five-year period that's almost 18 percent, so we actually lost ground. And we're underpaid to begin with. That's our thanks for fighting crime."

The sergeant pointed out that when Mayor Rudolph Giuliani negotiated with other city agencies, he stressed that any increases in pay would be based on productivity. "When we tried to bring productivity into the equation, he didn't want to hear it. What really happened is that the union and the mayor didn't hit it off. They had some disagreements, and Giuliani did his usual routine when he's pissed, which is basically, 'That's it—Stick 'em in the tail.'" What is implied in the sergeant's observations is that the morale problem over compensation may under-mine enforcement of zero tolerance—more effectively, perhaps, than a steady barrage of criticism from community activists and civil rights groups. At the same time, the implications of successfully negotiating a "productivity" raise are disturbing: creating financial incentives to en-force zero tolerance intensifies the pressure to apply it.

The fact that NYPD Commissioner Howard Safir did not get a raise for his troops deepened police officers' perception that, unlike his pred-ecessor, the swashbuckling, crime-fighting hero, William Bratton, Com-missioner Safir would not play hardball with the mayor. Safir stated publicly that he believed the police are underpaid and that their salaries should not be restricted to the limits set in pattern bargaining with other municipal unions,[1] but his resolve was soon tested. The city's chief labor negotiator went on record in favor of pattern bargaining over other approaches that might benefit more powerful unions such as the Patrolmen's Benevolent Association (PBA).[2]

Before leading the police department, Howard Safir was commis-sioner of the fire department, and most cops considered him an out-sider. Safir's close working relationship with the mayor and his use of police officers for personal matters further alienated him from the force. In April 1999, for the first time in its 105-year history, the PBA gave the commissioner a vote of no confidence and called for his resignation. Union officials criticized him for taking a free trip to the Oscars, send-ing cops to investigate a woman who ran into his wife's car, and having detectives chauffeur his daughter's wedding party. Though the PBA's move was purely political—only the mayor can remove the commis-sioner—former PBA president James Savage, quoted in the *Daily News*, insisted that the commissioner has an ethical "double standard—one for our members and one for himself."[3]

When asked how the police felt about Safir, a seasoned patrol offi-cer insisted on anonymity, then struggled to answer:

> I can't say what they think, but I can say what I think, or what I think they think. And that is . . . put it this way, the difference be-tween Safir and Bratton is that you knew Bratton would go to the mat for you. You had confidence that if you were doing your job right, and if you had the right intentions, that politics would not enter the picture. Mistakes of the heart would not be punished. If you made a mistake of the head, you would be punished as needed

and you'd be retrained. But mistakes of the heart were just mistakes of the heart. With this administration, you make *any* mistake, and that's it.

The officer was on a roll:

> What's frustrating is that we haven't been rewarded anywhere, not internally, not externally, not financially. I mean, you just keep getting hit every time you turn around, by the public, by your supervisors, by the press. In other jobs, if you make a mistake, the most that can happen is you lose your job. For us, we can be indicted and jailed; now that's a whole new way of looking at things. We come to the job *knowing* there's a chance we can get hurt, maybe even killed. But no one comes to the job expecting the kind of resistance we get from the public and also internally. You go out there trying to be a nice guy, do your job, fight crime, but once you start you see there are a lot of obstacles, very few rewards, the dirty little pay, and it becomes real frustrating, real quick. People wonder why morale is low, why officers' perceptions of their jobs change, and how that breeds corruption. You wonder how a cop can graduate at the top of his class and in four years he's an overweight, I-don't-care, disenchanted officer? Lemme tell you how—easy!"

The officer's critique raises questions that are central to the current debate over creating an oversight mechanism to ensure that officers will be accountable for their actions. What is disturbing in his comment is the implication that officers are exceptional, that they should not have to answer for their conduct. The prospect that officers will be called to account for actions that entail the exercise of judgment and some exposure to risk may be demoralizing, but the alternative is hardly an option: tolerating a double standard in which the police are not answerable for misconduct to the same extent and according to the same standards as civilians.

ZERO TOLERANCE—THE EARLY YEARS

When William Bratton came to the NYPD in January 1994, he was already familiar with the system. As head of the Transit Police Department (TPD), a formerly independent police department of some 4,000 officers, Bratton had the opportunity and managerial know-how to launch an aggressive, large-scale effort to "reclaim" the subway system. In less than four years, he produced steep declines in felony subway crime. Bratton brought the same police tactics, organizational strategies, and administrative processes to the NYPD.[4] More important, Bratton had the funding and the resources he needed to get the job done. Former mayor David Dinkins's "Safe Streets, Safe City" program had brought nearly 6,000 new police officers to the department. According to the Citizens Budget Commission, the number of uniformed officers grew by nearly half (47.4%), from 25,909 in 1990 to 38,201 in 1997. During the same period, the NYPD's annual operating expenditures rose by about a third (32%), from $2.5 billion in 1990 to $3.3 billion in 1997.[5] Buoyed by this windfall and his success fighting subway crime, Bratton was well equipped to carry out the quality-of-life platform featured in Rudolph Giuliani's 1993 mayoral campaign. Candidate Giuliani targeted squeegee men, petty drug dealers, prostitutes, and graffiti taggers in his promise to reclaim the streets of New York for law-abiding citizens.[6] With these as the city's priorities, William Bratton was the man for the job.

A captain who worked in Times Square when Bratton came onboard recalled officers' reactions to the new commissioner. "When Bratton came in, morale shot through the roof. The cops loved him. Now they could really be cops," he said. "I give Dinkins credit for getting the money to expand the force, but the real police strategies came in under Bratton. Dinkins got the cops, but even if Dinkins had been running the city then, we would've gone nowhere. We would've had all these extra cops and it wouldn't have meant dick. Dinkins wasn't mobilizing the police properly," he explained, emphasizing the importance of strategic patrol deployment.

"It's not the number of cops that controls crime, it's what you do with them. And when Bratton came in, he made the cops proactive instead of reactive. He told 'em, 'You're not just hanging out. Go find someone doin' something.'"

"As in, feel free to arrest someone for drinking a beer on the street?" I asked. "Feel free? Are you crazy? It was more like, you *better* arrest somebody for drinking in public." Bratton wanted to know where arrests were being made and who was making them, the captain added.

"And what he found was that 10 percent of the cops were making 90 percent of the arrests. So he told us, 'This is nonsense—everyone has to make at least one arrest a year."

"Are you talking quotas?"

"Absolutely. Call them what you want, but that's how you measure productivity." He gave an example to make his point. "Say you're a supervisor and you've got a cop who writes no summonses. You'd think, 'What? This guy can't find one summons in this area?' That would tell you he's not working."

"How does giving out summonses reduce crime?"

"A lot of nonsense gets put to bed. In Times Square, for example, most of the people we arrested were already wanted on a warrant. So if we did a sweep on a Friday night, our crime stats would go down and we'd be almost crime-free till Monday or Tuesday when the perps started clearing the system."

He said an added benefit was that the physical presence and visibility of the police during the sweeps helped lower robberies. "The perps weren't as likely to stick someone up if they just saw the police come in and round everyone up."

POLICE RESPONSE TO PUBLIC BACKLASH

Certainly, for some cops zero tolerance seems to sanction more aggressive policing. For others, the pressure to enforce zero tolerance is acceptable as long as the city compensates them for their stepped-up efforts. As evidence of disappointed expectations translates into a looming labor relations question, the possibility increases that disgruntled officers will withdraw support from the city's crime policies.[7] This possibility became apparent at a conference at New York City's John Jay College of Criminal Justice on October 7, 1999, where leading criminologists from across the country convened to debate the question: "Are America's get-tough policies responsible for the drop in crime?" The heavyweight champions of criminology posited a number of explanations. George Kelling, father of the "broken windows" theory,[8] spoke of restoring social order and the power of community policing to produce drops in crime. Fundamentally, the "broken windows" theory suggests that when a broken window is left unrepaired, it sends a message that nobody cares and leads to more severe property damage, resulting in citizen fear of crime and the downward spiral of urban decay. Criminologist James Alan Fox spoke of the effect of demographics on crime, stating that 10 percent of the crime decrease between 1990 and 1997 was the result of demographics alone, meaning that the smaller pool of people in their crime-prone years had driven down crime. Stanford professor John Donohue suggested that twenty-six years of legalized abortion was largely responsible for the nation's crime decline. The precipitous drop that began in 1992, he noted, can be attributed in part to *Roe v. Wade*, which essentially deprived the nation of a group of young people whose parentage and circumstances of birth could have made them more likely to engage in criminal activity as they came of age during the 1990s.[9]

In the last five minutes of the conference, the otherwise civilized discussion unraveled. Accusations of "dirty data" were hurled about, and the previously articulate panel became embroiled in bickering. The most strenuous attack was unleashed by then NYPD Deputy Commissioner Edward Norris, overseer of the city's crime-fighting strategies. Norris, who has since left the NYPD for a high-ranking position in the Baltimore Police Department, blamed the media for the recent rise in murders which had increased 10 percent as of October 31, 1999, compared with the previous year. He singled out the *New York Times* for its anti-NYPD coverage and the demoralizing effect it has had on police officers. "Every time a police officer gets involved in something, he is convicted in the media the next day," Norris said. Less than forty-eight hours later, the *New York Times* reported his comments in a half-page article. Media coverage, "particularly in the *Times*," noted Norris, his voice rising in anger, "has led people to believe that we are a brutal, horrible agency that is stopping crime by stomping on people's rights."[10]

Norris pointed to recent changes in the productivity of the elite Street Crime Unit, whose mission is to get guns off the street, and he cited a stunning statistic: "The Street Crime Unit represents only 10 percent of the police department (*editors' note:* 10 percent of street searches) but it's taken 40 percent of the guns off the street. We relied on the Street Crime Unit, but now they're doing less. We are not stopping people and being as assertive as we were, and that is why we are seeing the street shootings we had not seen for years."

On face value alone, Norris's comments were striking. His statement implied that the press influences not only public thinking but also actual policing, and therefore crime itself. What he did not mention was that of the 45,000 stops reported by the Street Crime Unit in 1997 and 1998, only about 9,500 resulted in arrests.[11] In a November 1999 report of an investigation of these stop-and-frisk practices, the office of New York attorney general Eliot Spitzer concluded that blacks and Hispanics were far more likely than whites to be stopped by police. On a citywide basis, Hispanics were stopped 39 percent more often than whites, and blacks 23 percent more often.[12]

While zero tolerance has made for titillating sound bites, it has been difficult to define with any precision. With its emphasis on cracking down on low-level offenses in order to prevent more serious crime, zero tolerance is an outgrowth of the broken-windows theory. The Giuliani administration's poster child for zero-tolerance policing was John Royster, whom police arrested for jumping a subway turnstile in the summer of 1996. Once police entered his data in the system, they realized Royster had attacked a woman jogging in Central Park several months earlier. Had zero tolerance not been in place when Royster jumped the turnstile, the police argue, he would likely have been issued a Desk Appearance Ticket and remained on the street.

For everyday New Yorkers, however, zero tolerance, as endorsed by the Giuliani administration, means that no disorder, offensive behavior, or criminal activity of any type will be tolerated anywhere, any time. It's difficult to avoid concluding that the administration's encouragement of aggressive policing created a climate in which the savage police assault on Abner Louima, the killing of Amadou Diallo, and the shooting death of mentally impaired Gidone Busch could occur. The larger problem is that zero tolerance is impossible to enforce—totally or uniformly. As long as human nature is what it is, crime will exist on some level. Attempts to eradicate all forms of deviant behavior are questionable at best. At worst, they make for selective law enforcement. Those people who break the law most obviously—people who drink on the street because they are homeless or cannot afford to drink at a bar— will be the ones who get caught most often. Foot patrol officers can apprehend the person who buys marijuana on the street far more easily than the person who hires a drug delivery service.

Critics of zero tolerance also say that "get tough" policing destroys the fabric of community-police relations. In fact, Rutgers University professor George Kelling, who, along with James Q. Wilson, introduced the idea of disorder-to-crime, has called the current practice of zero tolerance policing "the bastard child" of the broken-windows theory.

Kelling lamented that "people equate what I have written to zero tolerance and do so without any reference to the elaboration of that idea into policy. It gets frustrating for me when people don't give credit to the extent to which we wrestled with legal, constitutional and moral issues at great length when we implemented these policies."[13]

ZERO TOLERANCE ON THE STREET

Clearly, much has been lost in the translation of the mayor's call for zero tolerance, the strategies police officers use to accomplish it, and the ways in which their success as crime fighters is evaluated. "You're judged by the number of collars you make," says a captain with twenty years on the job. "It's part of your performance evaluation; it's how supervisors measure success. There's no other way to do it. Say you're a commanding officer and you have a vacancy on the midnight shift and three of your officers want it and you really don't know any of them. Who are you going to give it to? The guy who made two arrests in the past month or the guy who made six?"

The same captain acknowledged the mess that has been created by political pressure to drive down crime.

> I think we've gone overboard with zero tolerance. I mean, before we went overboard with DATs [Desk Appearance Tickets]. We called them "disappearance tickets" because you'd never see the perp again. But with zero tolerance, we have to give summonses for things that in the past we could basically *solve* on the spot. If a person was carrying an open container, we could just tell him to put it away and move along. Today, if you have a beer, you're going in. In the past, there would have to be some kind of trigger for us to lock a guy up.

The captain's use of the word "solve" is worth noting. Solving problems is a key strategy of community policing; it requires community interaction and skillful negotiation. Eradicating problems, on the other hand, is a cornerstone of zero tolerance, which boils down to getting the "perp" off the street and into the "joint," and doing this again and again until he learns his lesson. The steep rise in the number of New Yorkers arrested for low-level offenses—misdemeanor arrests shot up 69 percent between 1992 and 1997[14]—shows that the nature of both policing and punishment is changing. "This increase can be attributed to the crackdown on minor quality-of-life infractions under Mayor Giuliani's direction," said Michael Jacobson, former commissioner of the New York City Department of Correction and now a professor at John Jay College. "Clearly, arrests for minor offenses were not a high priority for the New York City police under Mayor Dinkins, who instead emphasized community problem solving police strategies." A foot patrol cop explained why community policing and zero tolerance make poor bedfellows. Community policing is social work; it is messy and time consuming. "Today, cops are under pressure to make more arrests, so they don't have the kind of time they used to have, and they need, to solve anything. A lot of them also don't want to be responsible for solving the problem, and many times they can't. So they're going to adjudicate it in the most expeditious way they can—arrest."

Raymond Manus, a recently retired NYPD lieutenant with three decades on the job—many of which were spent crunching statistics and formulating policy in the department's Policy Analysis and Management unit—wrote a trenchant article about problems of politically driven police initiatives. He began with a bold condemnation of politicians, whom he believes have misused federal funds under the guise of community policing. "Community policing has been a fraud perpetrated upon the public by pandering politicians," he stated. "In their haste to distribute Federal dollars to their home districts, Congressmen neglected their duty to check the power of the Executive Branch." He noted that "despite the record of abuse by police—who are, after all, agents of the executive branch of government—the legislative branch chose to fund additional police without considering the potential additional abuses. . . . Policies rewarding 'zero tolerance' produce quite different police actions than policies promoting partnerships."[15]

The following account by a narcotics officer trained on the Lower East Side illustrates not only the difficulty and danger of foot patrol work generally, but also how easy it is for problem solvers to become, or to be considered, problem creators.

> I'd been watching a dealer in action for well over an hour. We'd arrested two of his buyers several blocks away. So enough is enough. I go up to the guy and tell him I gotta take him in. That was my first mistake. It taught me never to give a criminal a warning again. He punched me in the face so hard I thought he broke my jaw and my

nose. I've never been punched that hard. I hit the ground; I was dazed. I got up because I knew I had to catch him. I couldn't let him punch me out and just lie there. I'd have no respect. So I managed to get up and run after him. I keep running. My gun belt weighs 30 pounds and I wasn't used to it yet, so it wasn't easy running. I chased him a couple blocks and I caught him. So there I was, tryin' to cuff him and naturally he resists. He swings at me, lands a couple more. So yeah, I punched him. I'm pissed. My heart is poundin' and my face is fuckin' killin' me. And now I got seven civilian complaints that will never come off my record because of that one account.

He added an interesting twist to the story.

The people who made those complaints didn't see that this guy had been selling drugs to their entire neighborhood all afternoon. They didn't see him punch me so hard I thought he'd broken my face. They didn't see that because that happened five blocks away. All they saw was me nab him and take him down and hit him back. The reason so many complaints are unwarranted is because the community residents aren't watching all the time, not that they should be, they got better things to do. But let me tell you, some people actually *do* see the perps dealing all day and they make complaints anyway. Why? Because in some of these families, the dealer is the breadwinner. They got a stake in what he's doing, so yeah, whether or not they see a use of force, they're making a complaint. That's why these complaints need to be looked at extremely carefully. . . . But the cop who stands on the corner and does dick all day, he's the one with no complaints on his record.

Evidence of public hostility toward police and the increasing rate of police misconduct are borne out in the rise in civilian complaints since zero tolerance was introduced. The filings of civil rights claims against the police for abusive conduct increased by 75 percent between 1994 and 1998, according to a New York City civil rights attorney.[16] Furthermore, the number of citizen complaints filed annually with the Civilian Complaint Review Board, the independent panel that reviews police misconduct, increased more than 60 percent between 1992 and 1996 and increased again in 1998.[17] The other side of the narcotics officer's criticism of civilian complaints is that suspected and adjudicated offenders have civil rights, and that a large number of complaints found justified by the Civilian Complaint Review Board are never acted upon by the NYPD. In fact, officers are not disciplined in half of the cases in which their conduct has been ruled improper by the board, mostly because police investigators reinvestigate and then throw out the cases for insufficient evidence.[18] During the summer of 1999, reports began to surface that, after a nearly two-year-long inquiry into the NYPD, investigators from the U.S. Attorney's Office for the Eastern District of New York were about to issue a report that the department's failure to discipline officers created an atmosphere that fostered brutality. A possible outcome of this investigation is a suit by the United States Attorney General against the NYPD.[19] A recent departmental development, which some claim is simply a ploy to placate the federal investigators, mandates that police officials will no longer reinvestigate misconduct complaints. Under the new system, when the department finds fault with a misconduct case forwarded by the Civilian Complaint Review Board, the department must send it back to the board's investigators for further review and to prepare the case for trial.[20] However, the decision to discipline an officer still rests with the department. Essentially, the police department still polices itself.

A black street cop who was born and raised in the inner city illustrated how zero tolerance plays out on the street, and how it encourages police misconduct and the creation of crime statistics. He began by defining the various levels of summonses:

COP: There are A, B, and C summonses. A's are for parking violations. B's are for moving violations, and C's are for violations like drinking in public that you have to answer in criminal court. As a foot cop, I have control of a certain area, and there are *a lot* of drug dealers in my area. I don't want to see them out there, not when I'm working. And they know they shouldn't be out there. So if they are, just on sight alone, I'm gonna give them a summons.

AUTHOR: For what? You're saying you'll make something up?

COP: Sure. I'll make up anything, like: 'You just ran that red light, here, take this summons for running a red light. Yeah, I know you're not in your car, it doesn't matter. Here's another summons for not wearing your seat belt.' You're looking at me strange. . . . Now, I'm not going to court by the way. Because I have nothing to testify for. But *he's* gotta go to court. When I don't show up, he'll just win, which is fine.

AUTHOR: So you've hassled him.

COP: It's not simply a matter of hassling. It's that now he's spending his time in the court system instead of selling drugs. And more important than that, most drug dealers don't show up in court. They don't answer summonses 'cause it takes too much time away from dealing.

AUTHOR: But then he's got a warrant out for his arrest, right?

COP: Bingo. Now you understand what I'm talking about? So now, when I turn that corner, all the knuckleheads got somewhere to go, because all of 'em got summonses on them. I don't need an excuse to take them off the street. All they gotta do is look at me funny and I can take 'em off the street. So guess what? Drug trafficking for that day is nonexistent. The kids can come out and play because all the knuckleheads are off the block. All I care about is that the people who work hard can walk outside and feel safe, and that the kids who wanna play can be outside and play. The block belongs to them, not the drug dealers. I'm gonna clear the dealers out any way I can. So if I gotta give you a summons, deserved or not, I don't care. And if it's not deserved, I'm not going to court—you won't have me fightin' you in court and perjuring myself—so you're going to win.

AUTHOR: So basically you're saying the ends justify the means.

COP: What I'm saying is that I don't want any shootings, any drug dealing. If I gotta give you a summons you don't deserve, so be it. The dealers know they shouldn't be there. It's my block for the day, not theirs.

AUTHOR: What if the guy is just standing there? Maybe he's not dealing.

COP: When you're a street cop you *know* who the dealers are, and the dealers *never* just stand there. They are working, controlling traffic, looking for buyers. They're in business 24-7. The dealer also usually doesn't live on the block he's working. When he's there, he's dealing. So when I get there, he can't be there. Because I'm not one of those soft guys. I'm a worker.

Being a "worker" and enforcing zero tolerance is made possible through Compstat, short for "compare stats" (actually the name of a computer file),[21] which pinpoints the types and frequency of crime in the city's seventy-six precincts. It has become synonymous with a proactive style of policing that allows an agency to identify spikes in crime and respond effectively. The deployment of foot patrol and special narcotics officers to high-crime areas relies on the use of Compstat. During weekly 7:00 a.m. Compstat meetings, precinct commanders are held accountable for crime in their areas and are grilled about plans they have for reducing it.[22] Prior to Compstat, commanding officers operated in the dark. As John Jay College professor and NYPD guru Eli Silverman notes in his 1999 book, *NYPD Battles Crime*: "During the early months of his administration, Commissioner William Bratton called for a weekly, one-on-one current events briefing with a representative from each of the NYPD's eight bureaus. . . . A disturbing reality surfaced: The NYPD did not know its current crime statistics. There was a reporting time lag of three to six months."[23]

With its emphasis on accurate and timely intelligence, rapid deployment of personnel, effective tactics, and relentless follow-up, Compstat makes it difficult for both perps and police to hide.

ZERO TOLERANCE IN THE JAILS

Out on Rikers Island, six miles north of the Empire State Building, refugees of zero-tolerance policing are hidden from public view. In 1999, over 130,000 persons served time on Rikers Island. Two-thirds of Rikers detainees are people who have been arrested for a crime but not yet convicted. They are in jail mainly because they cannot make bail. According to the Citizens Budget Commission, more than 25 percent of Rikers detainees face bails of $500 or less. Other statistics are worth noting: over 90 percent of detainees are black or Hispanic. One in eight male inmates—and a staggering 25 percent of female inmates—are HIV positive. An estimated 85 percent have a history of substance abuse. Thirty percent were homeless prior to incarceration. Only 10 percent have high school or equivalency diplomas.[24]

On October 25, 1999, I asked a group of twenty male inmates, ranging in age from nineteen to forty-four, about their perceptions of zero-tolerance policing in their communities. Similar to the conference at John Jay, the discussion erupted into a cacophony of complaints and accusations. Police officers were referred to as "criminals in blue . . . no better than we are."

"I got a year for three blunts," said an inmate from Washington Heights.

"I'm afraid to go home," said another. "I can get busted just walkin' down the street. These cops always be rushin' up on me."

"I'm gonna move to Jersey when I get outta here," twenty-four-year-old Lorenzo offered.

A burst of laughter. "Jersey? What are you, crazy, man? Them cops are totally racist."

The difference, Lorenzo explained, adding that he didn't "wanna sound racist or nothin'" is that "people in Jersey have a different way with their drugs." He shifted uncomfortably and wiped his hands on his greens (jail uniform). "I mean, people in Jersey, they be buyin' their drugs from a delivery service, not out on the street. They do their drugs inside. They're private about it. They don't be walkin' down the street like we do with a blunt behind our ear, yellin' and smokin' and drawin' attention to ourselves."

The Department of Correction estimates that approximately 75 percent of the inmates will be back in less than a year. "Most of them are doing a life sentence—one six-month bid at a time," former warden James Kane was known to say.

Despite the grim demographics of the Rikers population, two developments in the city's jail system worth noting are related to the practice of zero tolerance. One is that violence among inmates has dropped to record lows, declining 91 percent since 1995.[25] Former commissioner Michael Jacobson developed a multilevel strategy to reduce jail violence by taking zero tolerance technology (Compstat) and reconfiguring it into TEAMS (Total Efficiency Accountability Management Systems). Both inmates and employees are held accountable for reducing violence and contraband, and for keeping an orderly jail. According to former New York City Department of Correction commissioner Bernard Kerik, who expanded and refined TEAMS, the department has over one hundred performance indicators to assess and improve agency operations, for which correction staff are held accountable in weekly TEAMS meetings. For inmates, zero tolerance means that if an inmate slashes another inmate, for example, he is charged with assault, which can carry a sentence of up to seven years in state prison. (In the past, he would have been sent to disciplinary housing and lost his good-time credit.)

Advocates from Amnesty International USA and the Legal Aid Society have challenged some of the mechanisms the correction department uses for maintaining order, primarily the use of pepper gas and stun devices, and question the rigor of the city's system for disciplining corrections officers charged with abusing inmates.[26] However, interviews with many Rikers inmates and correction officers suggest that the jails are far calmer today than they were in 1994, and inmates say they feel safer. "This place is like a kid's camp compared to what it used to be," said an inmate who has been to Rikers eight times in the past six years.

Another significant development on Rikers is the expansion of social services. When Jacobson was commissioner, he secured funding to double the number of drug treatment beds for inmates battling substance abuse. He brought in an array of vocational training and education programs and helped save the High Impact program, the nation's first urban boot camp, when cutbacks in inmate services were threatened. Commissioner Kerik authorized the printing of thousands of guides to community-based resources for ex-mates, which will be added to the jailhouse packets inmates receive at orientation. A lesson to be learned from Rikers is that social services were added *before* zero tolerance was introduced. "Balancing more rigorous security policies with expanded inmate services made sense," said Jacobson. "We would have had problems if we just added more controls."

In the locked-down world of jail, the combination of zero tolerance and expanded social services seems to be working. However, jail is not the real world. Violence and disorder are obviously easier to tackle in a closed community with tight controls and a captive population than on the streets of New York where, by comparison, some citizens enjoy far more rights and liberties. In New York City, some cops have stated that the inner cities are simply too broken, or too out of control for police officers to repair, nor should they be responsible for doing so. "That's what social workers are supposed to do," said a patrol officer. A look at data supplied by Michael Jacobson, who served as a budget official in the Office of Budget and Management during two mayoral administrations, shows that elected officials have been far more concerned with incarcerating people than with fixing communities and bolstering social services. Between 1979 and 1997, the spending increase for corrections was well over three times that of social services and more than twice that of education. Specifically, spending for both education and criminal justice increased by 258 percent, whereas spending for social services went up 164 percent. During the same time period, expenditures for corrections (New York City jails) rose by 582 percent.[27]

What these figures seem to suggest is that the growth in criminal justice, and particularly corrections, has helped produce the drop in New York City's crime. Not so, argues Jacobson in "Trends in Criminal Justice Spending, Employment and Workloads in New York City since the Late 1970s," a detailed analysis of changes in city expenditures under former mayors Ed Koch and David Dinkins, and the current mayor, Giuliani. Jacobson writes:

> The completely counter-intuitive answer is that over the last 20 years, crime has increased the most when the City has increased spending on criminal justice the most; crime has declined as City increases on criminal justice spending have slowed. During the three Koch administrations, the City increased criminal justice spending by 170%, yet crime rose by 25%. During the Dinkins administration, criminal justice spending rose by 19%, while crime declined by 16%. During the first Giuliani administration, spending only increased by 12%, while total reported crime declined by 41%.[28]

Jacobson shows that, at least in New York City during the past twenty years, more spending on crime has not led to greater public safety. For Jacobson, these statistics are persuasive evidence that the city needs to "move aggressively to severely limit further expansion of the criminal justice system, especially while there are such pressing needs in education and social services."[29]

Unless social services are increased, and the city's social service agencies are better run, it is unlikely that the criminal justice system will stop growing. Take the case of thirty-year-old James, released from Rikers Island two months ago. James applied for public assistance his first day out. "I had no money, absolutely none," he said. "I needed car fare to get to interviews, and money to buy a shirt and tie." James's plan was to use public assistance until he found a job. Fifty days had passed and the city's Office of Human Resources Administration (HRA) had not yet processed his public assistance application. Despite visits and calls to HRA, and attendance at job development classes, which HRA now requires of people on public assistance, James was still without a job and without public assistance. "Committing a crime is getting harder and harder to resist," he said. "I've borrowed what little I can from my grandmother," he said, adding that her telephone service was recently disconnected, and he therefore has no way of being reached by potential employers.

Returning to the question posed at the beginning—Can zero tolerance last?—consider the following: crime is down, the police are weary, and the jails are full. The varied and often critical voices within the NYPD offer compelling reasons to confront the social costs and consequences of the city's seemingly mindless—or, rather, perhaps all too mindful—embrace of zero tolerance. As the data analyzed by Michael Jacobson show, increased spending on criminal justice has not led to greater public safety. If the current mayoral administration increased funding for social services and showed the same "zero tolerance" for inefficiency in agencies such as HRA, the drop in crime that New York City has enjoyed might endure, and the quality of life for all New Yorkers might well improve.

NOTES

1. "What Kind of Recruits Does $9 Million Buy?" *Law Enforcement News: A Publication of John Jay College of Criminal Justice/CUNY* (October 15, 1999): 6.

2. Steven Greenhouse, "City Unions Shift Strategy on Bargaining," *New York Times*, November 12, 1999: B1; Michael Cooper, "Citing Recruitment Lag, Police Union Leader Says Pay Is Too Low," *New York Times*, August 12, 1999: B6.

3. John Marzulli and William K. Rashbaum, "Cops' Rebellion against Safir," *Daily News*, April 14, 1999 (online edition).

4. George L. Kelling and William Bratton, "Declining Crime Rates: Insiders' Views of the New York City Story," *Journal of Criminal Law and Criminology* 88 (Summer 1998): 1217.

5. Dean Michael Mead, "The State of Municipal Services in the 1990s: The New York Police Department," *Citizens Budget Commission* 1 (May 1998).

6. Judith A. Greene, "Zero Tolerance: A Case Study of Police Policies and Practices in New York City," *Crime and Delinquency* 45 (April 1999): 171.

7. Jayson Blair, "Police Official Blames News Coverage for Murder Increase," *New York Times*, October 9, 1999: B5.

8. James Q. Wilson and George L. Kelling, "Broken Windows: The Police and Neighborhood Safety," *Atlantic Monthly* (March 1982): 29.

9. Anonymous, "Preventive Medicine? Study Links Crime Decrease to 1973 Abortion Decision," *Law Enforcement News: A Publication of John Jay College of Criminal Justice/CUNY* (September 30, 1999): 1.

10. Jayson Blair, "Police Official Blames News," B5; William K. Rashbaum, "New York's Top Police Strategist Is Joining the Force in Baltimore," *New York Times*, January 9, 2000: Metro 24. [Editors' note: The complex relationship between morale and law enforcement has remained a contested issue, particularly in the aftermath of Mayor Giuliani's withdrawal from the U.S. Senate race in New York, and after a few highly publicized episodes in which some observers claimed that the police were less vigilant, even "indifferent," in response to violations of law that occurred in public gatherings. See, e.g., Kevin Flynn, "Lower Morale, Yes. But Apathy?" *New York Times*, June 18, 2000: Metro 25. See also David Barstow, with C. J. Chivers, Juan Forero, Sarah Kershaw, and Nina Siegal, "View From New York Streets: No Retreat by Police," *New York Times*, June 25, 2000, sec. 1, p. 1.

When, in connection with these June 2000 incidents, some police officers and supervisors later faced disciplinary charges for failing to respond appropriately to reports from several women and a youth that they had been sexually abused, police union representatives complained that the charged officers had been made "scapegoats" and political "victims." See Kevin Flynn, "9 Officers Facing Discipline in Park Attacks," *New York Times*, July 4, 2000: A1; C. J. Chivers, "Suspension Cites Lax Response to Groping," *New York Times*, June 27, 2000: B1.]

11. Kit R. Roane, "Spitzer Threatens Subpoena on Frisk Data," *New York Times*, May 16, 1999: 39.

12. Kevin Flynn, "Racial Bias Shown in Police Searches, State Report Asserts," *New York Times*, December 1, 1999: A1.

13. "A *Law Enforcement News* Interview with Professor George Kelling," *Law Enforcement News: A Publication of John Jay College of Criminal Justice /CUNY* (May15/30, 1999): 6.

14. New York State Department of Criminal Justice Services, *Computerized Criminal History System and Indictment Statistical System, 1998.*

15. Raymond Manus, "100,000 Police = Politics and Poor Planning," *Law Enforcement News: A Publication of John Jay College of Criminal Justice/CUNY* (October 15 1999): 8.

16. Judith A. Greene, "Zero Tolerance: A Case Study of Police Policies and Practices in New York City," *Crime and Delinquency* 45 (April 1999): 171.

17. Id.; *New York City Civilian Complaint Review Board Report for 1998*, 3, 13.

18. Kevin Flynn, "Police Accept Civilian Panel's Inquiry in Misconduct Cases," *New York Times*, October 8, 1999: B3.

19. Jodi Wilgoren, "Federal Inquiry of Police Draws Mixed Reaction," *New York Times*, July 11, 1999: 23.

20. Editorial, "A Stronger Civilian Review Board," *New York Times*, August 13, 1999: A20.

21. Eli B. Silverman, *NYPD Battles Crime* (Boston: Northeastern University Press, 1999), 98.

22. Id.

23. Id. at 99.

24. Citizens Budget Commission.

25. Christopher Drew, "An Iron Hand at Rikers Island Drastically Reduces Violence," *New York Times*, November 8, 1999: A1.

26. Id.

27. Michael Jacobson, "Trends in Criminal Justice Spending, Employment, and Workloads in New York City since the Late 1970's," *Crime and Justice in New York City*, ed. Andrew Karmen (New York: McGraw-Hill, Primus Custom Publishing, 1998), 240–241.

28. Id. at 254.

29. Id.

5

girlz in blue

Women Policing Violence in the NYPD

Amy S. Green

I WISH I had a dollar for each time I've been asked, "You teach *theater* at John Jay College of *Criminal Justice*?" To the many incredulous posers of this query, it has apparently seemed odd that a college that prepares students for careers in law enforcement could have the slightest use for theater. When I joined the faculty of the Department of Speech and Theatre in the fall of 1995, I had had little personal contact with the police. I knew them mostly through media accounts. My ideas about the police came from the news, TV shows, and movies, and what I learned there wasn't always pretty, or accurate, as I would soon find out. I quickly realized that my images of cops were based on facile stereotypes, and as a member of the John Jay community, I felt obliged to get a more accurate picture.

One of my biggest misconceptions involved women officers. I was always surprised when female students identified themselves as police officers. Out of uniform, they just didn't look like cops to me. I'm not sure what I expected. Tough talkin' babes with broad shoulders and short haircuts, maybe? Or lithe blondes with flowing, layered curls, à la Charlie's Angels? Whatever. The women officers in my classes defied any stereotype. They were a diverse group. Some dressed in heels and skirts; others wore jeans and T-shirts. They came from many ethnic and religious backgrounds and lived in different parts of the metropolitan area. Several told me they were mothers, a few lesbians, and at least one was a lesbian mother. I was fascinated. I wondered what had attracted these women to policing, what was it like for them to serve in a predominantly male organization, whether they brought a particularly feminist practice or perspective to their work, and why were they so hidden from public view?

It was obvious that I had a lot to learn, and my main mode of research and expression is theater. So, with the help of a research grant from the CUNY Professional Staff Congress, I began to interview women officers in the New York City Police Department (NYPD) in order to gather raw material for an original play. I interviewed approximately two dozen women "on the job" with the NYPD. *girlz in blue*, a 90-minute, verbatim, documentary drama, was the result of my research. The play's six nameless characters are real people. The dialogue is lifted straight from my transcripts. *girlz* was first performed by a cast of John Jay students, at the college, in March 1999. Its audience included other students, faculty, staff, and administrators, as well as several dozen male and female NYPD officers. In addition to five performances of the play, we presented a "Symposium on Women in Policing: Agenda for the New Millennium," which featured women leaders from within the NYPD, its fraternal organizations, and other metropolitan police departments, and a workshop on "Careers for Women in Law Enforcement," for which alumnae returned to campus to counsel students.

I interviewed the subject officers during the summers of 1997 and 1998. The group included police officers, sergeants, detectives, and lieutenants and represented both precinct workers and those assigned to other NYPD agencies such as the Internal Affairs Bureau and other special investigative units. This small, voluntary group does not comprise a scientific sample, but they opened a hidden world to me and revealed a subculture whose example may offer the best hope for more humane policing in the city. The women with whom I spoke might bristle at being considered different professionally from their male colleagues. They do the job as well as the men, they say, and want no special consideration. But they often compared their on-the-job responses favorably to those of the guys and speculated that a male officer in the same situation would have resorted to physical force or the use of firearms when the women did not. They claimed not to regard a suspect's refusal to comply immediately as a threat to their own authority and said that they were willing to take the time to do what they were taught in the academy—to sort it out, be patient, and achieve "verbal compliance." They boasted about times their cool prevailed over a male partner's macho and confided about pressures to conform or keep quiet when things got "out of hand." They joked about the function of testosterone behind the badge. One thing all the women shared was a sense of humor.

Women bring varied backgrounds and experience to policing; they are not an undifferentiated group. Yet, if it is true that women officers are more likely to practice their profession according to the book, and that they are equally effective with fewer instances (or less intensity) of physical force, and if the NYPD now includes more than 6,000 women officers, what impact does or could their presence have on the style of policing in the city? Are these women developing a particularly "feminist" model of interaction with the public? Are they more likely to be injured or less likely to make arrests because of their reluctance to use force? And if all performance measures are equal, are the women having a positive influence on the city's police culture? If not, why not? Do such factors as isolation, intimidation, and the need to please male superiors impede women's opportunities to assert themselves within the department?

Ultimately, my theatrical ethnography raises many questions about the nonviolent strategies women officers use to gain cooperation from disorderly citizens. Whether or not these strategies are more prevalent among women, and how they might be adopted more generally among both male and female officers, remains to be seen. Increasing numbers of women will serve the NYPD in coming years, and their potential impact as mitigators of excessive force has yet to be unleashed.

WOMEN OFFICERS AND THE USE OF FORCE

The officers with whom I spoke talked about the use of physical force in similar terms: as a last resort, as the final recourse when reason, humor, and/or verbal coercion had failed. They differentiated themselves from their male colleagues in their readiness to use force and in their desire to engage individuals in respectful discourse to get the job of public safety done. One of the younger officers I interviewed, a woman with seven years on the job, was quite clear about how her gender shaped her professional identity and style:

> I have a regular partner. She's a female. We got partnered, I think, by
> sheer luck. I really don't know why. But we have the same work ethic,

how we want to approach people, how we want people to deal with us. One of the first reactions we get is "Two women in the car! How cool! We never see two women in a car." And I'm, like, "Well, here we are!" I think it makes people a little easier. Sometimes I think it makes people push more, because they see there's no male in the car. They'll try and get over. They think we won't be as forceful as a man. And then when we come out, we are forceful. Catch them by surprise. Totally. Surprise, surprise. When I say forceful, I don't mean hands-on, physical. Forceful in the way we carry ourselves. How we communicate. You know exactly what I mean when I say it.

She and her partner have not only adapted to the baggage that comes with being a female police officer but managed to marshal it to their advantage. Their conscious use of body language and tone of voice to gain authority reminded me of how I use these elements of acting in front of my classroom. Like teaching, police work is itself a genre of performance, part genuine interaction, part histrionic display. Because women are still not considered typecast in the role of police officer, it takes a little more imagination from them, their coworkers, and the public to forge the identity of female officer.

Many of the women I interviewed boasted about attaining verbal compliance from tough customers. They attributed their ability to calm volatile situations to the fact that, unlike many male colleagues, they do not interpret a distressed or unruly citizen's hostility as a personal attack. They claimed to look upon resistance as inevitable, especially in a climate of public distrust of the police. More than one officer proudly described difficult situations they had settled with patient dialogue and then speculated that the outcome might have been more explosive "had it been a man" who responded to the call. The story told by one lieutenant who began her career on Transit patrol provides a good example:

> I had an emotionally disturbed person on a southbound D train, going over the bridge to DeKalb Avenue. . . . I look into the conductor's car, and I see that the guy is hitting people with a broom. So I get half the crowd out, and then I lock one side. The conductor gets everyone else out. So, now it's me, him, and the conductor. I take my hat off. I start talking to the guy. He starts breaking glass. I'm trying to calm "Henry" down as I'm calling for backup. In 8 minutes, we arrive. We call an ambulance. About a hundred cops. One door is opened up. We all get

him. We all take him out. He's under control. Nobody's hurt. A few glass plates are broken. End of story. Had it been a male cop, there probably would've been a shootout, or there woulda been a beating. That's my opinion. I didn't take it personal. This guy was a *nut*. A lot of men look at it as ego vs. ego, but a lot of women look at it as "How can I get myself out of this situation without getting myself or anyone else in my vicinity hurt?"

I must stress that these women are not pacifists, philosophically opposed to the use of force in the line of duty. They understand that violence can be a part of police work. They carry weapons and are confident that they are as well trained and competent in their use as their male counterparts. One woman in the group was behind a barrel, first in the line of fire, during a famous Emergency Services Unit operation in the 1980s. She was prepared to shoot if necessary but never did because the suspect opened fire before the unit came through the door. She was one of six officers shot. The other five were men. The difference between men's and women's inclination to use force, the women say, is that some men feel justified to do so at a much earlier stage of conflict than most women.

In fact, the women's testimony suggests that both male and female officers experience a desire to use force but differ in terms of the point at which that impulse crosses over into action. The same lieutenant who calmed "Henry" down recalled another incident when she had to resist the adrenaline rush to strike back:

I had a guy hit me square in the face. I'll never forget, Delancey Street on the F train. Knocked me right in the face. I threw him against the wall. He put his hand in his pocket. I went down there fishing. Here I am fishing in his pants. "Give me your fucking hand." I don't care what I pull out, but he's getting cuffed. Some woman said that I did not effect the arrest properly. Here I am, bleeding from the mouth in the scuffle. I wanted to free him and throw her in front of a moving train! But this it what you deal with, and you go on.

Not that the women are angels. This self-restrained lieutenant smiled when she told me the story's punchline. "The justice of it all," she said, "is that he had a minor accident in jail and got killed."

Nor are the women of the NYPD invulnerable to their own brand of sexist prejudice. One dialogue exchange reflected their impatience with the trigger-happy men in the department:

DET. 2: You would think by now there would be no more attitudes like that. Where do they learn that? I've concluded that it's a genetic thing. It's gotta be some kinda genetic damage. A failing in the Y chromosome.

DET. 5: That shield. That uniform, you put it on . . .

LT. 3: Cops today . . .

DET. 5: Arrogance.

LT. 3: . . . chiefs tomorrow.

DET. 5: Arrogance.

It seems that these female officers are in fact vulnerable to sexism and provocation. They are also ready and willing to use force, but only when they have run out of alternatives and must resort to what they consider their weakest professional tool.

IS THERE SUCH A THING AS "FEMINIST" POLICING?

Despite the substance of the testimony, in which women officers distinguished their tactics and techniques from those of male officers, the women tended not to claim (or admit) that they were part of a developing practice of "feminist" policing. I imagine that most of them would reject both the term and the concept. Self-identified feminists—individuals who consciously and conspicuously oppose the political, economic, and social subordination of women—are reportedly rare among female officers of the NYPD. As an activist lesbian officer told me, "I was twenty-eight when I came on this job. I had been to college and majored in women's history. I was a feminist, which is unusual for a woman in this job. They might be feminists, but they don't know how to say that." Women who break rank to speak out or assert a feminist stance place themselves in social, political, and/or physical jeopardy among their mostly male colleagues. I got the sense that an early feminist claim that men and women are essentially the same still dominates departmental ideology among those who accept women as full-status police officers. Feminist thinking has progressed in the intervening years, however, to the point where such theorists in the 1980s and 1990s have identified gender differences in cognitive and emotional patterns and responses, for example, without fear that doing so diminishes women's equal cultural, economic, and social status.[1] The women with whom I spoke willingly and proudly detailed the ways their work style differs from that of males, but they were reluctant to suggest that they are not, in fact, "the same" as the men, even if the differences make them better at their jobs.

A brief historical review sheds some light on why this 1970s mentality persists. Prior to the Federal Crime Control Act of 1973, which mandated that agencies could be eligible for its benefits only if they were in compliance with the 1972 Equal Employment Opportunity Act, women in the New York City Police Department could be deprived of professional and wage equity because technically they held a different job than the men. "Police women didn't go out on patrol," a now-retired sergeant, one of the original females on patrol in 1974, explained to me. "You went to the Youth Division. Some of them did detective work. Cells. Matrons. It was `Policewoman.' That was the title. `Police Man,' `Police Woman.' Two different tests. Two different lists. Separate training." As long as the job titles differed, there was no need to worry about gender equity.

Once women were sworn in as "Police Officers," the same newly coined, unisex title as the men, they were expected to live up to the prevailing reform concept that women deserved equal pay and opportunity because they could do their jobs just like the men. Proving themselves in the NYPD meant conforming to male police models, or at least paying lip service to them. Given the contemporary gender-political climate, it is not surprising that the department held women officers to a preexisting male standard rather than redefining the now-gender-neutral job, taking the best of the prior, separate, male and female titles. Instead, the values and virtues of what had been traditionally women's work were discounted, superseded by male imperatives.

Despite the dissolution of official gender differentiation, I was told that women are still frequently assigned to traditionally female posts. One detective who told me that she had joined the NYPD because she "saw a highway cop riding his Harley Davidson, and said, 'That's what I wanna do,'" found herself unhappily assigned to a stereotypically female job:

I was dumped into the kiddie cases, from newborn to under-eleven. I did it every day. It was a horror. From all the sex crimes to serious assaults, which was burns, beatings, broken bones. I could tolerate that, but the sex crimes was really, really horrifying. Every day. I had no expertise in that. You do find a lot more female officers in sex crimes, in the kiddie cases. Some of them are there by choice, because they have that social worker instinct. They relate to the kids. A lot of them have kids. I don't have any kids. I didn't wanna be there. I had absolutely no choice.

If female police officers are not content to assume the tasks that have traditionally been women's work in the police department, yet they do not necessarily want to do "men's work" men's way, what, exactly, is feminist policing? The closest thing I can offer to a definition, other than the preference for verbal over physical tactics, are the responses I got when I asked my interviewees, "What's a good cop?" Typically, their answers were peppered with humorous jabs at men, but they were also filled with references to empathy and compassion and conspicuously free of references to physical strength or bravado as the hallmarks of good policing. A veteran detective who works in an anti–organized crime unit offered the following: "What's a good cop? A good female cop or a good male cop? To me, a good male anything is someone who basically keeps his mouth shut and does what he's told. All women cops are good cops. I haven't met any that aren't. You have to do 200 percent to their 50 percent all through this career. Good cop? I have to think about that. Somebody who can be a little empathetic to my problem. Somebody who will listen." What I found most interesting about her definition is her emphasis on the emotional dynamics of working with people in trouble. She places primary importance on providing a sense of caring, demonstrating compassion for the person in need, rather than coming in as an omnipotent authority figure and solving the problem. Perhaps her point is that officers who have relinquished the power and pressure of the latter posture are better able to deflect hostility, not to "take it personal."

Another officer defined a good cop with a statement that reminded me of the way my stay-at-home mother used to describe her job. This officer recited an inventory of the multiple roles she plays in the course of a day's tour:

> A good cop? That's a loaded question. A good cop? Gosh. The typical statement is "a police officer's job is to protect and serve." That's it. "Protect and serve." Quote, unquote. Then you've got "a police officer's job is to: serve the public, be a mother, be a parent, be a psychiatrist. Make sure rules and regulations aren't broken. Be a teacher. Be an aide. Be a comforter. You walk in the door, see what's goin' on. To an old person who's just been robbed, you have to be their sister, their son, their daughter. To a parent, you have to be their parent. You just never know what role you're gonna get into. You are an actress, an actor. You're a lot of different things.

Here again, the emphasis is on responding to the needs of others, which requires considerable mental and emotional flexibility. Does her point of view reflect a viable alternative to the duality of good cop/bad criminal? Is the ability to switch gears frequently and/or the willingness to define oneself by multiple, simultaneous, labels something that women are more likely to cultivate or that is culturally gendered? Is this something that some male officers also do—or that more male officers could learn to do? Her description may sound a lot like motherhood (even including the disciplinary function), but unlike mothering, this style of police work bears no connection to women's biological sex role. Just as we now include fathers in the semantic shift to "parenting" and "nurturing," can we reenvision policing according to a blended-gender model? How much would male officers have to modify their professional values and behavior (and how willing would they be to do so) were they to adopt more of what has traditionally been considered a female approach?

Of course, the majority of male officers do use their academy training to handle most situations with nonviolent techniques. Otherwise, the incidence of brutality allegations would be astronomically higher than it is. It is false and irresponsible to tar all male police officers with the same dirty brush. In fact, it was one of my staunchest pro-feminists who carefully avoided gendered prepositions when she defined a good cop as "probably someone who doesn't get involved emotionally in things. Somebody that does the right thing." She went as far as to grudgingly acknowledge that not all of her male coworkers are perpetrators of brutality when she agreed that "there's some of them out there that have integrity."

So, if a "feminist" approach to police work offers hope of reduced brutality because it values verbal techniques, disparages official violence, and stresses empathy over authority, and if these techniques are not, in fact, available only to, nor practiced exclusively by, women officers, why has police brutality persisted, perhaps even grown worse, during the same period when more women are serving on the streets of New York? In other words, why haven't women officers had more of a positive impact on the departmental culture of violence? The beginnings of an answer can be detected in the reports I heard about the harassment, intimidation, and suppression of women officers as individuals and in groups.

WHY HAVE THE APPROACHES TO POLICING PROFESSED BY MY INTERVIEWEES AND OTHER WOMEN OFFICERS HAD SO LITTLE IMPACT ON THE LARGER CULTURE OF POLICING OF THE NYPD?

With nearly 6,000 women on the job in New York in 1999 out of a total force of more than 38,000, that is to say nearly 16 percent of uniformed officers, it would be reasonable to expect that approaches to police work that may be more prevalent among women—such as verbally oriented problem solving—would have an influence on the approaches to policing throughout the city. If brutality allegations are an indication, the persistently high level of complaints suggest otherwise. The Civilian Complaint Review Board has documented a stunning disparity between the relative percentages of complaints lodged against men and women officers. Women comprise nearly 16 percent of the NYPD, but the board's statistics show a consistent annual pattern of more than 90 percent of complaints lodged against male officers, compared to less than 10 percent against females. CCRB's *Semiannual Report* for January–June 1998 said the board could "offer no reason for this."[2] Clearly, further study is warranted of the attitudes and behaviors of women officers to come up with an explanation.

The relationship between the numbers of women on the NYPD and statistics on official misconduct is, of course, far more complex and subtle than I can begin to explain. For example, are there proportionately more women working desk duty in jobs that are far less likely to put them in situations that tend to provoke males to violence? Do the men actively keep their female partners and coworkers away from nasty skirmishes, out of either a protective instinct or fear that the women might report what they see? Does the presence of women in partnerships, teams, units, or task forces actually reduce the likelihood of abusive behavior among their male colleagues? These and other potentially significant factors are well deserving of further inquiry.

What I heard from the women I interviewed, however, offers some clues as to how the department has become so prone to misconduct against civilians. I heard dozens of stories that document departmental tolerance for internal intimidation, humiliation, and the kind of simple rudeness that creates a hostile and potentially explosive environment. The women recounted tales of verbal and physical harassment, threats, and a litany of daily torments they endured from male officers that went either unpunished or, frequently, unreported because the women feared reprisals or a lack of respect for not being able to "take it like a man."

In a job where physical safety, sometimes life or death, depends on the support of your coworkers, being disliked, unpopular, or outright ostracized can have dire consequences. The threat of being considered less than collegial forces many women to put up with intimidation and harassment. The abuse may be as annoying as being called names, or as terrifying as being abandoned in a dangerous situation. This story illustrates how a simple playground taunt can make life miserable for a woman in the department and lead to more dangerous forms of isolation:

> My first partner was a straight woman. Of course, they thought we were sleeping together. It's unfortunate, but that's what they're gonna think. We had to fight for them to let us be together. Two females! They called us, um, you're gonna laugh. I laugh now. "Tuna Patrol." I didn't appreciate it then, because when we called for help, they'd key us out. You know what that means? They would key us out, break up the signal. And they would call us "Tuna Patrol."

Another detective provided a similarly harrowing example of how petty precinct pranks, if unchecked, can escalate into life-threatening abuse:

My ex-lover, she used to work in the 7-2 Precinct, which is in Sunset
Park. She was the youth officer. They wrote all over her walls
"dyke" and all this other stuff. They cut up photographs of her and
some kids. They took files and threw them all over the room. She
complained about it, and they retaliated, and they wouldn't answer
her calls for help. She was on patrol by herself. She went to a school
where there was a fight, and some guy started to assault her. And
the people in her precinct jammed the radio. It took a while for them
to get to her. And, you know, she could've been severely hurt. So
this stuff is there. It's reality.

The women reported that few men were willing to stand up to their
misbehaving comrades, and women who seek help from supervisors
are more likely to end up being labeled a problem themselves than in
having the harassment stopped. Some women choose to take matters
into their own hands:

I remember there was one guy in the lounge, and he'd take off his gun
belt, and he'd fix his pants, and he'd practically take his pants off. I
confronted him about it, and he started screaming at me. I complained
that it was inappropriate for him to fix his pants in a lunchroom, and
he told me that women didn't belong in this job, and if I had a problem with it, I should leave the room. He used to make sexual remarks.
The guys would laugh. They used to think it was funny. There used to
be pornography in the lounge. The guys used to go in there and watch.
Videotape. Video-type. . . . You know, men with animals—bestiality. I
complained. Well, they stopped the tapes, but they were all pissed at
me because they couldn't watch pornography anymore.

Social discomfort is among the milder forms of injury the women
reported to me. Male officers who challenge their female colleagues'
physical readiness for the job can inflict physical damage as well. The
following story illustrates not only the extent to which male-to-female
officer abuse is perpetrated and tolerated, but that there is a gap in perception between men's and women's definitions of the job:

I had a problem with some guy in the gym. He was a small guy, so
they made him my partner. He useta overcompensate, you know,
the psychological term, when you're not too bright in one way, so

you kinda excel in other ways? He wound up getting 100 in the gym! He'd hurt me. In fact, I was injured during a judo throw. He threw me on his instep, and I had a back injury. I spoke to him after I came back from the hospital. I started screaming at him "What's wrong with you? I'm not the enemy." He said, "Well, you know, you have to be able to do this now. You're a cop." I said, "Yeah, but you're treating me like a perp. I'm not a perp. I'm a peer. There's a difference." And he was enraged that I challenged him. I think it had to do with the fact that he didn't think women belonged on the job. He thought they were somehow inferior, and he had to prove that by beatin' me up. And my thing is that's not what this job is about. This job is not about physical statue [sic]. In fact, the guy wouldn't've been hired if they hadn't dropped the height require-ment, `cause the guy was only 5'4". So, it's interesting how he made his own decision as to who belonged on the job and who didn't.

The price of speaking up officially can be equally devastating. Even when she is not defending herself, a woman may pay a heavy social price for going public:

Nobody would talk to me, nobody would work with me, because I had backed up an allegation another female officer had made regard-ing race discrimination. I went as a witness. I was the only officer who didn't have a "memory lapse," and because of the fact that I'd testified against two cops and a lieutenant, they ostracized me. I'd walk into the kitchen, they'd all walk out. This one guy . . . used to make blatant racist remarks. His wife had a miscarriage, and he made a comment about how people in the ghetto would put out babies like baby ma-chines. And there were African-American police officers in the room. Nobody would stop him. But eventually our charges were "unsub-stantiated," or did they make it "unfounded"? They said that there was no discrimination. I thought that was really interesting. Even though I testified on this woman's behalf, and she testified on my be-half, somehow it was "unsubstantiated."[3]

Clearly, women on the job feel a lot of pressure to keep their mouths shut, to put up with verbal and physical abuse on a daily basis. The oc-casional big-money harassment lawsuit makes its way into the head-lines and public debate, but we are rarely privy to the more insidious,

everyday incidents of intimidation and humiliation. Examples less blatant than those mentioned above suggest just how deeply ingrained
and subtle the forms of discrimination can be. Women rookies can find
themselves at a double disadvantage in a work place notorious for subjecting its newcomers to intense hazing and initiation rites: "When I
came into the police department, they sent me directly to Harlem. I
went into anti-crime, plainclothes, jeans and sweatshirts. Of course, I
had to do late tours for 6 months because they didn't want any 'girls' in
the day unit." Occasionally, abuse comes cloaked in acceptance. This
seasoned detective didn't seem to pick up on the sexist attitude that be-
lied her earliest patrol experience: "I think my first partner picked me.
I was the only woman on the late tours, and I could hold my own, so I
didn't have too much problems. No one didn't want to work with me
or anything. The man never got outta the car. Got outta the car to eat
and go home. That was it. Every job we went on, he sat in the car. I went.
Whether it was the 6th floor or the basement."

It does not strain credulity to imagine that this sedentary veteran
would not have expected a male rookie to accommodate his disinclina-
tion to leave the patrol car. Did the older officer in fact choose a female
partner because he believed she would accept his unfair terms without
complaint? Why was he willing to risk the mistakes that her inexperience might cause, no less place her personal safety in jeopardy? Was this
really a vote of confidence in her or an abdication of his professional responsibility to teach a beginner the ropes? Typically, the female officer
who told me this story resourcefully turned the situation to her advantage: "I had a lot of adventures, though. I did have a lot of adventures.
Foot chases, car chases. The wrong way up the Harlem River Drive. But
it worked out. He answered all my questions, which is more that I can
say for a lotta guys on this job. He was honest and fair. Pretty legit. So I
learned a lot. I was lucky."

One of the saddest results of the barrage of harassment leveled at
females in the NYPD is that many women become afraid to ally themselves with other female officers for fear of further alienation. This is especially true when they believe that such alliances might prompt accusations of lesbianism. In order not to provoke the men further, in order
to avoid being labeled a lesbian, many women forgo the social and emotional support and the political power that could be generated through
unity. At times, the women's "fraternal" organization has suffered
drops in enrollment due to this prejudice: "A lot of women wouldn't

participate in the Policewomen's Endowment Association because the president was a lesbian. And the assumption is that most of the women there are lesbian, and they don't want to be affiliated. You're guilty by association. Unfortunately, there's a stigma that the women are helping to perpetuate. That it's not okay to be with other women, because then you might be branded as a lesbian, which is something bad."

If it seems as though gay women are doubly disadvantaged by being twice removed from the straight, male standard, straight women complain that they are even worse off. Increasing numbers of lesbian women are out on the job now and unafraid to be identified as lesbian. They are not worried about the label and so are more likely to join female support groups, clubs, and organizations. On the other hand, straight women who do not wish to be considered lesbian shy away from such affiliations and are left feeling much more isolated and politically disadvantaged. "I think the gay women on this job have a lot more support for each other than the heterosexual women," I was told by a rueful, straight lieutenant. "I think there is a stronger bonding. There is a stronger networking. They are a little bit more supportive to each other."

Given the extent of male-to-female officer harassment, the intensity of the women's fear of reprisal, and the sense of isolation it engenders in so many women officers, it is a wonder that so many women resist the pressure to emulate the more aggressive behaviors of some of their male colleagues. Another area ripe for further investigation is to document the coping mechanisms that enable these women to remain true to their personal values in the face of such pressure to conform. Many of my subjects talked about how women in policing cope with job stress, thereby avoiding the siege mentality that they believe leads some men to lash out inappropriately.

One woman speculated that while many men become wholly engrossed in and identified with their police jobs, the career fits differently into the totality of women's lives. The same family responsibilities that can make a woman officer's life infinitely more hectic and complex than that of a man with a wife who is able, and perhaps expected, to take on much of the family care taking can also help keep her on an even keel.

A lot of women on this job are mothers. They have to juggle child care and work around a chart. This is not easy. To be able to do a job like this, that's physically and emotionally demanding, an unbelievable level of stress at times, then go home and care for children and a house, and the husband who doesn't take out the garbage. I give them a lot of credit. . . . A lot of things happen to [male] cops. Drug problems, drinking problems, marital problems, problems with their kids. Women just don't have time for that shit.

Just gotta cope. That's what women do, yes? Women cope.

As before, it is necessary to point out that the officer is referring to a stereotype when she describes male officers who spend their off-duty hours drinking too much and taking the pressures out on their families. Neither she nor I would disagree that plenty of male cops are devoted husbands and fathers who cope without abusing alcohol. Her portrait of the pragmatic female officer who is too busy taking care of loved ones to hang out with other off-duty cops or wallow in self-pity does, however, have a certain appeal.

One of my favorite stories came from the detective who wanted to ride the Harley but ended up working with sexually abused kids. She talked about how hard it was to get up in the morning to face her excruciating daily task until she found relief in a soothing second job.

What relieved my stress? You're gonna laugh. Of course, you're not gonna hold me to this: I worked in a flower shop. On the weekend and at nights, after work I'd go to the flower shop. I knew this Korean woman over in Bayside. She had a flower shop, and she let me work there. She taught me all about the flowers, how to make arrangements, how to clean the flowers when they came in. The thing that really relaxed me the most . . . take the carnations. When they come in, they're closed. You have to sit there and massage them. You take your thumbs and open them. I would just sit on the floor with this big bucket. It was soooo relaxing. I did that five days a week.

This particular woman has no spouse/partner or children to come home to. Instead, she sought comfort in a gentle and constructive pastime that allowed her to leave the pain of her workday safely behind each evening. I retain a vivid visual image of her as she told me about her secret moonlighting career. Years after the fact, her shoulders still softened, her head fell back gently, and her breathing pattern slowed as she mimed the carnation-massaging gesture. At the same time, she seemed slightly embarrassed by the almost guilty pleasure she took in her serene respite. I wondered, sadly, if her unconsciously internalized image of the good-cop-as-tough-guy still battled her self-image of good-cop-as-compassionate-woman.

Here again, scholars of policing could come up with more definitive answers to whether or not these strategies for resisting peer pressure and coping with the stress of policing are more likely to be used by women and, if so, what steps would be necessary to encourage more male officers to adopt them as well. At a minimum, my interviews suggest that women officers of the NYPD have additional strategies to offer the department as it continues to examine the problems and patterns of unacceptable police conduct. The experiences of these officers contain valuable information about attitudes and practices that are less likely to lead to abusive behavior. It would be a shame if the leadership of the NYPD did not avail itself of this treasure trove as it undertakes the internal review that must lead to reform of persistent problems of abuse and brutality.

CONCLUSION

As I researched, rehearsed, and mounted the John Jay College production of *girlz in blue*, I gained enormous respect and compassion for the women who have bravely taken the challenge to serve side by side with male police officers to maintain law and order on the sometimes daunting streets of New York City. Interviewing women officers and hearing their tales of internal harassment and personal courage opened my eyes to a hidden world of feminist struggle for respect and economic and civil rights. The student actors who played the characters went through a similar process of education and emotional identification. Tears were shed more than once as the actors worked to get under the skin of these feisty, often-beleaguered characters who never gave up or caved in. Some of the students questioned their own career plans, asking themselves if they had the stamina to persevere under hostile conditions, and wondering when things would get better for women on the job. What began as an artistic project inspired an intense personal, sociological, and political public conversation, first among the cast and crew, and later college-wide, about the status of women police officers. My students and I were proud to have stoked the controversy and championed the cause of our sisters in uniform.

It has been more than twenty-five years since women attained nominal equality within the NYPD. Their performance and contributions to the department have disproven the doubts of the wary and, in some cases, surpassed the expectations of their staunchest supporters. Clearly, women officers deserve more from the NYPD than its admission that they are not a liability. The approaches taken by the women officers I interviewed may in fact hold the key to transforming the NYPD into a less volatile, less violent police force. They are in a position to help pave the way toward a relationship with the public in which all officers face less public suspicion and resentment and enjoy more respect and cooperation on the streets. Yet the reality of many women officers' daily on-the-job experience is still fraught with disrespect and abuse from some of their male colleagues. I do not believe it is far-fetched to imagine that the department's willingness to turn a blind eye to instances of intramural cruelty, especially that perpetrated against female officers by males, may be interpreted by some officers as tacit forbearance of interpersonal aggression against civilians. If prejudice, discrimination, and abuse are tolerated within the ranks, it is not surprising that some officers feel justified—or at least unafraid of consequences—when they perpetrate similar acts on the streets. Likewise, when female officers are not lauded for their restraint in the uses of force and firearms in difficult situations, the department fails to reinforce its own academy teachings and so seems by default to endorse official misconduct.

So heavy are the weight of their success and the pressure not to complain when that success is impeded by any but the most blatant forms of abuse, that few women officers allow themselves outlets for their anger and frustration. *girlz* gave theatrical vent to their trials and triumphs. In the process of coaching student actors to play six of those women and to do their stories justice in front of an audience, the theatrical company engaged in an extended exploration into and debate about the plight of women officers of the NYPD and what could be done to liberate them as individuals and as a potential force for reform within a troubled department. The students and I were delighted by the support we seemed to rally for women members of the NYPD and by the feathers we seemed to ruffle among those stubborn skeptics who still remain unconvinced that women have much to contribute to the practice of humane policing in the city.

I am not finished with *girlz in blue*. As internal disrespect of women police officers continues despite official denials, the play merits a wider audience. It will be interesting to see how the voices are received in a non-criminal-justice-oriented environment. Will a strictly civilian audience be sympathetic to the women's plight, or will a general distaste for and distrust of the police cause these women to be identified with police power and its abuses, rather than to be seen as a less-than-fully-empowered subgroup? Will they be turned off by the women's anger and sarcasm? Will they become impatient with them for having fought their way into a tough field and then complained about its discomforts? Or will a popular audience be able to see past the organizational identity and accept the characters as complex individuals striking out as professional pioneers and demanding equality and respect?

Whatever the theatrical future of *girlz in blue*, the story of women in policing has a long way to go. Women are joining police forces around the country in greater numbers, and women who have served for a number of years are moving into supervisory and management positions in greater numbers. The city of New York stands at a critical moment in terms of the future of policing. In the midst of growing public dissatisfaction, we have enough experience to make significant observations about the positive role and efficacy of many of the department's women officers. Do we have the will and the courage to recognize and use the evidence in hand? It is overly simple to believe that all the department need do is ask its male officers to emulate their female colleagues, or to believe that all women work in the same way. Yet as it strives to combat the scourge of police brutality, the NYPD might do well to recognize, reward, and take some lessons from the substantial resources that exist already among the women in its ranks.

NOTES

1. See, e.g., Deborah Tannen, *Talking from 9 to 5: How Women's and Men's Conversation Styles Affect Who Gets Heard* (New York: William Morrow, 1994), and *You Just Don't Understand: Women and Men in Conversation* (New York: William Morrow, 1990); Daniel Evan Weiss, *The Great Divide: How Females and Males Really Differ* (New York: Poseidon Press, 1991); *Women and Men: New Perspectives on Gender Differences* (Washington, D.C.: American Psychiatric Press, 1991); and *Women, Men, and Gender: Ongoing Debates* (New Haven: Yale University Press, 1997).

2. *New York City Police Department Civilian Complaint Board: Semiannual*

Report, January–June 1998 22 (New York: Police Department, Bureau of Public Information).

3. *Editors' note*: In June 1998, the United States Government and the NYPD settled a lawsuit alleging that the NYPD had violated federal civil rights laws by sexually harassing women officers. In the settlement agreement, the NYPD agreed to take "all steps reasonably necessary to maintain a discrimination-free workplace including mandatory training on responses to gender discrimination and sexual harassment, changes in procedures for reporting, handling, investigation, and consideration of equal employment opportunity complaints, and revising departmental policy concerning display of sexually explicit materials." See, generally, Settlement Agreement, *United States of America v. New York City Police Department*, 96 Civ. 4217 (MBM) (THK), U.S. District Court for the Southern District of New York.

6

No Justice, No Peace

Andrea McArdle

SAFE CITY, MEAN STREETS

While New York City burnishes its reputation as a safe haven for developers, tourists, and affluent residents,[1] the iconic presence of Emma Lazarus's Statue of Liberty offers a more ambivalent welcome to the city's new immigrants.[2] Meanwhile, in the streets of the city, the claims of safety are tested daily. Young pedestrians and bike riders in the poorer neighborhoods are routinely stopped and questioned by police in the Giuliani administration's campaign to reduce drug-related crime. These confrontational investigative tactics have led community members to dread the police rather than welcome their presence.[3] In its declared war on guns and street crime, the NYPD dispatches scores of barely trained recruits into the Street Crime Unit where, in 1997 and 1998, NYPD data indicate that 45,000 people—primarily black and Latino males—were stopped and frisked, often for no reason other than the fact that they were black and Latino. Anecdotal information gathered from NYPD officers suggests that there is extensive underreporting of these encounters—perhaps only one in five stops—according to New York's attorney general, Eliot Spitzer.[4] At the same time, aggressive "quality-of-life" initiatives designed to promote public order and "protect" public spaces have targeted the homeless, sex workers, and gay men.[5]

In this narrative of a new economic order, police use of force is an accepted part of a campaign to pacify the city's more marginalized, less marketable communities. When the circumstances of a violent incident are contested, the mayoral establishment routinely supports police officers. Mayor Giuliani's remarks following the killing in April 1997 of sixteen-year-old Kevin Cedeno attest to this presumptive crediting of police officers' accounts of events "until and unless there are facts that are established that they acted improperly. That's how a decent, civilized and orderly society operates. You give the benefit of the doubt to the sworn police officers."[6] The mayor's hasty release of Patrick Dorismond's minor police record shortly after the unarmed Dorismond was killed in an altercation with undercover officers on March 16, 2000—as if to mitigate the damage, and deflect attention from the conduct of the officers involved—is another example of the presumptive bolstering of the police and discrediting of civilian casualties of police violence.

When evidence of police violence is more pronounced, police misconduct is framed as isolated and exceptional. Then Police Commissioner Howard Safir's characterization of the vicious assault on Abner Louima as a "criminal act," as distinguished from "police brutality,"[7] suggests that brutality, far from being viewed as criminal, is essentially tolerated and minimized in police culture. The extent to which police brutality is itself criminalized becomes a "measuring stick" for whether or not it is possible for the law to operate evenhandedly, to avoid a disenfranchising double standard.[8] Yet, city officials refuse to acknowledge that brutality, under any definition, is driving current dissatisfaction with the NYPD. Incredibly, Commissioner Safir editorialized that it is a lack of civility rather than the use of force that fuels the criticism.[9] In April 1999, the NYPD inaugurated refresher courses on basic politeness, issuing cheat cards that remind officers to use terms of respect such as "sir" and "ma'am," and to say "thank you."[10]

This continuing failure to acknowledge police criminality in all but the most egregious instances has led disconsolate family and community members to enact their grief and anger publicly. In the wake of the Amadou Diallo shooting, the NYPD is perhaps the most intensely scrutinized police force in the country. The New York State Attorney General's Office completed an investigation into the Street Crime Unit's stop-and-frisk practices late in 1999, and in that same year the NYPD was investigated for civil rights abuse by the United States Attorney's offices for the Eastern and Southern Districts of New York, the New York City Council, the New York City Public Advocate's Office, and the U.S. Civil Rights Commission.[11] In this context, the relative infrequency with which official New York registers the occurrence of police criminality hardly betokens a "civilized" society, however the mayor has appropriated the term.

THE GENDER AND RACIAL LIMITS OF
ENFRANCHISEMENT

In deciding when and against whom to carry out their assigned campaign of criminalization, police officers exercise an extraordinary amount of discretion.[12] As sociologists of law recognize, those who enforce legal rules apportion and apply power unevenly, in ways that are not admissible when the rules are being formulated.[13] Inevitably, the persons most likely to be marked as criminal not only tend to be among society's most disempowered but also the most vulnerable to police brutality during the course of law "enforcement." When the same officers who brutalize civilians are not held accountable for their criminal acts—either by the NYPD or by the legal system that enforces the criminal law—the resulting double standard deepens divisions between the police and people in the community, and disenfranchises these police victims. This lack of effective recourse is one manifestation of a pattern of discrimination against poor persons of color and, increasingly, women, in the application of criminal law—from the point of arrest to sentencing.[14]

I have chosen "enfranchisement" as a framework because, like the closely allied concept of citizenship, it involves a notion of membership, a sense of belonging to, and claiming rights under, a community. With its broader semantic scope, enfranchisement encompasses the claim of any person—whether or not a citizen in the formal legal sense—to the equal benefit of laws for the security of persons and property.[15] Recognizing the rhetorical and conceptual ties between enfranchisement and citizenship, I have drawn on the discourses of citizenship to analyze the way in which the city's failure to criminalize police brutality invokes inequalities historically inscribed in those discourses.

The idea of enfranchisement implicates what constitutional law scholar Christopher Eisgruber identifies in the context of birthright citizenship as the "responsiveness principle"—the idea that the legitimacy of government derives from its responsiveness to all persons who are subject to its general authority and police power.[16] In practice, the principle of equal responsiveness operates unevenly. The benefits of full participation and "standing," to use Judith Shklar's term,[17] are not uniformly available. Historically, the idea of citizenship has been bound up with white male political and social prerogative.[18] Even after the formal conception of citizenship was broadened, the identification of full citizenship with the privileged position of white men has been sustained by a web of law and customary practice.[19]

In practice, the formally inclusive discourses of citizenship have excluded from the benefits of social and civic standing those persons whose gender, race, sexuality, or poverty marks them as "other." A society's failure to acknowledge and redress the damage that police violence inflicts places all of us at risk. Yet the impact of tolerating that violence disproportionately affects persons seen as nonnormative and invokes the same patterns of exclusion that are linked with the (failed) idea of citizenship. Recognizing these gendered and racialized implications is critical to evaluating a legal infrastructure that often relegates the victims of police abuse to a space beyond the law's cognizance.

THE LEGAL FRAMEWORK FOR ASSESSING EXCESSIVE-FORCE CLAIMS

In New York City, an array of internal departmental rules, standards of liability in tort law, and penal code provisions circumscribe the use of force by police in effecting arrests, preventing escapes, and defending against imminent use of physical force. These rules generally bar the application of deadly force, coercive methods for eliciting confessions, and unnecessary physical force. Only under circumstances in which an officer can show a "reasonable belief" that the use of force was "necessary"[20] do these rules authorize the use of nondeadly and even deadly force. The rules are not identical in scope. In fact, the NYPD's internal regulation on deadly force is stricter than the standard under the state penal law.[21]

The existence of rules restricting police behavior should be distinguished from their enforceability. Egon Bittner has argued that police use of force remains largely unmoderated because the very concept of a "lawful" application of force is "practically meaningless."[22] In general, rules that define the outer limits of permissible force (outlawing use of deadly force against a fleeing, unarmed, nonviolent felon) or that impose a categorical ban on conduct (forbidding use of torture in extracting confessions)[23] are easier to apply than rules based on contextual, fact-bound standards that address the circumstances under which the police may be called upon to make "split-second judgments."[24] The difficulties of applying these rules aside, rules that are part of a system of noncriminal regulation (the police department's internal disciplinary provisions, tort remedies that often conclude with a negotiated out-of-court settlement to compensate individual victims)[25] do not allow a public airing of the circumstances of police use of force. Criminal prosecution of the police ensures that the adjudication of liability will be a public process.

CRIMINAL LAW AS DISCOURSE

As David Garland has shown, the set of practices and institutions that constitute penality operate as an authoritative, condemnatory discourse expressing the normative judgment of the community[26]—or at least of the political and economic elites whose values and interests tend to define the "norm."[27] The seriousness of this discourse is dramatized by the public, ritualized dimensions of imposing sanctions—the formal rendering of judgment in open court, the performative nuances of restraining freedom of movement, the lurid drama surrounding an execution.[28] The power to signify the stigma and opprobrium attached to criminal liability, and to reinforce the rigor of the rule that was breached,[29] offers a powerful explanation for the importance attached to criminal prosecution of police brutality in disempowered urban communities.

Within these communities, and especially among the families who have lost loved ones at the hands of the police, the lack of a consistently functioning model of criminal prosecution communicates the law's unresponsiveness to the victims of urban police violence. For their family members, a debilitating sense of frustration and disempowerment intensifies the experience of grief. When, for example, Washington Heights resident Kevin Cedeno died after being shot in the back by Officer Anthony Pellegrini, Kevin's grandmother, Joy Cedeno, said her family would "find no peace until the officer has been arrested, indicted, and convicted." When Manhattan district attorney Robert Morgenthau announced that a grand jury considering the Cedeno case had determined not to indict Pellegrini, members of Cedeno's family condemned the decision and renewed their commitment to seek "justice," hoping (without success) to launch a federal probe of the shooting.[30]

POLICE BRUTALITY AND THE CRIMINAL PROCESS

Before the 1970s, prosecutions for excessive force were uncommon in New York. Paul Chevigny, longtime commentator on the culture of police abuse in New York City, suggests that the growth of the civil-rights movement and a greater sense of political vulnerability among prosecutors in the 1970s shifted more attention and resources to police brutality cases.[31] At the same time, disclosures of widespread bribe taking among New York City police officers led to the creation of a state-level Special Prosecutor's Office charged with investigating and prosecuting police corruption.[32] In an era in which claims of police corruption and excessive force were treated as conceptually distinct, the limited mandate of the special prosecutor led to a division of labor in which prosecution of excessive-force cases fell to local district attorneys.[33]

In the past twenty-five years, there have been a limited number of successful excessive-force prosecutions against police officers in New York City—typically the more publicized cases of deadly force or torture.[34] However, with a few exceptions, the most prevalent form of physical violence against civilians—the routine, gratuitous use of force that accompanies arrests and street encounters[35]—generally goes unpunished, and often unrecognized. If the level of excessive-force complaints filed with the Civilian Complaint Review Board is any indication—an overall rise of 44 percent between 1993 and 1996, with some decline noted thereafter but a general rise in complaints during the second half of 1998[36]—the incidence of violent encounters has increased markedly under the Giuliani administration. In all probability, the actual level of police brutality is underrepresented in these statistics; the disincentives against officially registering episodes of police violence secure their invisibility. Among those charged with crimes, lack of medical corroboration for an injury, or the concern that asserting an excessive-force claim would complicate the progress of plea negotiations, may discourage victims from raising the issue.[37] Among immigrant groups, fear of disclosing an unregularized status, and procedural misunderstandings fueled by language differences, intensify feelings of vulnerability that can prevent a complaint from surfacing.[38] In much the same way, targets of the quality-of-life campaign such as homeless people and persons cited under the public lewdness law have been reluctant to come forward, deterred by a process that can be humiliating as well as intimidating. Furthermore, since few complaints result in serious disciplinary measures against the police, filing a complaint can be an exercise in futility.[39]

BARRIERS TO PROSECUTION

When excessive-force allegations come to the attention of prosecutors, institutional pressures—some structural, others informal—can work against successful prosecution. Most obviously, prosecutors rely on sources of evidence that police officers supply. Prosecutors also provide legal advice and instruction to police officers during criminal investigations.[40] As a practical matter, prosecuting these officers for misconduct jeopardizes that close working relationship.[41] Present and former prosecutors report that lack of cooperation in ongoing cases as well as browbeating of prosecutors by the police "gallery" during trials of other officers are commonplace.[42] Moreover, since the decision to prosecute in any case involves an exercise of discretion,[43] any failure to prosecute police violence will fuel a perception that prosecutorial discretion has been abused. The chief of the New York City Police Department's Internal Affairs Bureau has suggested that a decision not to prosecute a "minor" occurrence of violence may reflect a judgment that departmental discipline will be more severe than a criminal penalty.[44] Nonetheless, the structural basis of prosecutorial-police cooperation creates an "institutional conflict of interest."[45]

When local prosecutors do investigate police brutality, it is usually through the mechanism of the grand jury, an investigative body drawn from the local civilian population and controlled by the prosecutor who presents evidence in the case.[46] As the prosecutors I interviewed were quick to point out, all witnesses called to testify before a grand jury in the New York State court system enjoy "transactional" immunity—full immunity from prosecution for any conduct related to the transaction about which they have testified.[47] In excessive-force investigations, summoning police officers to testify about a violent episode in which they may be involved forecloses any possibility of prosecuting them for the incident in a New York State court.

Issues of immunity aside, since 1994 two New York City commissions called into existence to investigate police misconduct have documented that officers who witness violent encounters involving other officers not only are disinclined to incriminate them, but are prepared to lie to avoid doing so.[48] This closing of ranks is especially impenetrable in brutality cases because of the belief, apparently deeply ingrained among most police officers, that force is necessary to survive on the street.[49] The result is that criminally violent behavior is compounded by perjury or other crimes involving false statements.

Sessions of the grand jury are closed to the public; a victim of a crime under grand jury investigation has no right to participate in the proceedings and no access to the evidentiary record. When a grand jury fails to indict, the closed nature of the proceedings forecloses review of the amount and quality of evidence that the prosecutor presented.[50] The terse announcement of "no true bill" typically produces a sense of desolation within communities in which police violence occurs, and, increasingly, trenchant criticism about the prosecutorial process. In response, traditionally reticent prosecutors have begun to engage more directly with these communities, at least to the extent of preparing remarks about the grand jury process for public consumption.[51] For instance, prosecutors prepared reports concerning the grand jury's failure to indict officers accused in the shooting deaths of sixteen-year-old Yong Xin Huang,[52] twenty-three-year-old Aswan Watson, an unarmed man shot eighteen times by police officers in a precinct-based anticrime unit,[53] and sixteen-year-old Kevin Cedeno.[54] On rare occasions, a grand jury panel may issue a report recommending remedial action other than criminal prosecution, as a Brooklyn grand jury did in the Watson case, urging the NYPD to adopt improved selection criteria and training for anticrime officers.[55] With or without these communications, victims' families and communities continue to feel under siege by the police—and betrayed by a legal system that they experience as depersonalizing.

ADJUDICATING WITHIN THE CREDIBILITY GAP

The limited available data indicate that criminal charges in excessive-force cases are uncommon. There is virtually no empirical work that documents these prosecutions and their dispositions; the most comprehensive data source, based on responses from law enforcement agencies to a national survey conducted by the Police Foundation, noted a low response rate among enforcement agencies for this inquiry, and is confined to the year 1991.[56] No public agency makes data from New York City available in this form,[57] though on occasion local news media have attempted to document the record of prosecutions.[58] These media efforts, and a 1996 report prepared by Amnesty International concerning police brutality in the city, indicate that when a police officer is indicted on excessive-force charges, typically the officer waives the right to a jury trial and proceeds before a judge as trier of fact.[59]

Local prosecutors confirm this practice, noting that, in New York State courts, jury-trial waivers are virtually unmoderated, unlike the federal system in which prosecutorial consent is required.[60] Presumably, the defense preference for "bench" trials in police cases reflects a belief that a jury drawn from an alienated urban community will question the veracity of a police-officer defendant. There is ample evidence that officers frequently falsify reports and lie under oath to conceal the use of force and other abuses of authority.[61] In fact, in the relatively rare instances in which New York City police officers charged with serious felonies in the New York State court system opted for a jury trial, convictions followed.[62]

If urban juries are persuaded that police officers' propensity for truth telling is low, juries drawn from suburban communities may be more accepting of a police officer's version of events. In the Diallo case, the defense persuaded a panel of New York State appellate division judges to transfer the trial venue from Bronx to Albany County, a jurisdiction seen as friendly to law enforcement.[63] Given the demographics of the two counties (Albany's combined black and Latino population is 12 percent compared to the Bronx's 90 percent), and the jury's resounding acquittal of the officers on all counts, comparisons to the suburban Simi Valley, California, siting of the first Rodney King trial seem inevitable.[64] In urban bench trials, judges have shown themselves to have complicated responses to police witnesses that work to the advantage of officers charged with crimes. In 1997, for example, local prosecutors in the Bronx took a series of felony cases to trial involving a range of police misconduct, including deadly and excessive force. Virtually all of the cases resulted in acquittals.[65] In a 1998 Manhattan case, Detective Olga Vasquez and Officer Richard Thompson were acquitted in a bench trial of felony charges in connection with the assault of a narcotics suspect hospitalized for six days after suffering seven rib fractures. Criminal charges against the victim, Norman Batista, who allegedly had resisted arrest, and the principal prosecution witness, another narcotics suspect, had been dismissed before the start of the officers' trial.[66]

More recently, an off-duty police officer, Michael Meyer, was acquitted after a bench trial of felony assault and reckless endangerment charges in the Bronx shooting of Antoine Reed, an unarmed squeegee man. Reed had committed a quintessential Quality of Life offense: he had started to clean Officer Meyer's windshield while his car was stopped in traffic at a highway exit ramp. Witnesses testified that Meyer exited the car and advanced toward Reed, as he backed up across several lanes of traffic. Meyer fired his service revolver at Reed, who suffered a ruptured spleen, then claimed that he acted in self-defense. Acquitting Meyer, New York State Supreme Court Justice John Collins noted that the prosecution failed to disprove self-defense. The court also ruled inadmissible a half-dozen civilian excessive-force complaints that had been lodged against Meyer since 1984 and that prompted his reassignment to building-repair duty involving limited interaction with the public.[67] Although there are exceptions,[68] the outcomes in these cases suggest that in contests of credibility between a police officer and a civilian (particularly when the latter has a criminal record or is facing criminal charges in connection with the same episode), judges will be inclined to believe police witnesses.

Conversely, judges tend to discredit officers facing criminal charges who testify for the prosecution against other officers, apparently on the theory that any cooperating officer seeks favorable consideration from the prosecution and has an obvious motive to lie.[69] Since it is often assumed that the option to cooperate with prosecutors and negotiate a more favorable plea disposition is always available to officers whose own criminality has come to light, officers who do not cooperate but proceed to trial are more likely to be viewed as truthful.[70] Even when officers who testify on behalf of the prosecution are not cooperators, as in the trial of Francis Livoti for criminally negligent homicide, the credibility of police witnesses can assume central importance. In the state court prosecution of Livoti, a conflict among the prosecution's police witnesses about the circumstances of Livoti's application of a chokehold upon Anthony Baez, moved the trial judge to note that the testimony of the police was a "nest of perjury."[71] Acquitting Livoti, the court ultimately resolved that question of credibility in favor of the four male officers who corroborated Livoti over the testimony of Latina officer Daisy Boria, whose embattled position in the police department before and after the Livoti case became the subject of her own lawsuit against the NYPD that has since been settled.[72]

In the still relatively rare successful prosecution of on-duty officers for excessive-force charges, issues of credibility either have been more peripheral or otherwise were easier to resolve against the officer based on the evidence.[73] In the first federal civil rights prosecution in the Louima case, police officers corroborated Louima's testimony implicating Justin Volpe and Charles Schwarz in the station-house assault. The manslaughter conviction of transit police officer Paolo Colecchia in 1997 for the shooting of Nathaniel Levi Gaines, a fleeing, unarmed man suspected in a subway stalking, turned on the interpretation of the statute (authorizing a police officer to use deadly force only when the officer "reasonably believes" such force is necessary to prevent an escape of a person suspected of committing a violent felony).[74] In this case, the New York State Supreme Court accepted the Bronx district attorney's argument that the use of deadly force was not reasonable since there was no indication that, at the time of the shooting, the officer or anyone else was in danger.[75] Sentenced to a term of one and a half to four and a half years' imprisonment, Colecchia is one of only a handful of New York City police officers who have received prison sentences for on-duty homicides.[76] After working closely with the Gaines family during the investigation and trial, Norman Siegel of the New York Civil Liberties Union attested to the sense of vindication that the judgment produced among the many persons who contacted him following the verdict. He noted a willingness to imagine—laced with caution—that the legal system is capable of a fair result.[77] At Colecchia's sentencing, Gaines's father acknowledged the prison term as "important."[78]

THE SEMIOTICS OF SENTENCING

Beyond adjudicating guilt or innocence in nonjury trials, judges also impose sentences. In the state system, the legislature has established a penalty structure for offenses, including minimum and maximum penalties for certain felony-level convictions; within these limits, judges enjoy considerable latitude.[79] In the federal system, judges' discretion has been reined in by the adoption of sentencing guidelines that were

intended, among other things, to remove the variability in sentences between civilians and the police in assault cases and to authorize additional sanctions for civil rights violations.[80] Available data are limited
on sentencing patterns in cases in which police officers were criminally
convicted. The record of dispositions in a recent series of state and federal prosecutions of officers from the 30th Precinct in Manhattan on
charges including drug dealing, theft, and assault, for example, were
uneven at best. They often did not seem commensurate with the conduct involved,[81] in part perhaps because a number of officers cooper-
ated with authorities.

Though there are some indications that sentences under the federal
guidelines in police brutality cases are more stringent than in the
preguidelines era, they are still far more lenient than sentences for assault committed by civilians.[82] Moreover, as the United States Supreme
Court noted in its review of the sentences of Lawrence Powell and
Stacey Koon, officers convicted of federal civil-rights violations in the
assault of Rodney King after an acquittal in a state jury trial, only a limited number of factors are excluded categorically from consideration. A
court may either add to or subtract from the penalties prescribed under
the guidelines in a number of circumstances, subject to an appellate
standard of review of "substantial deference" to the sentencing court.[83]
Reviewing the sentencing court's application of the guidelines only for
evidence of an abuse of discretion, the Court in the Powell case upheld
a reduction from the guidelines based on the sentencing court's deter-
minations that King had provoked the initial phase of the beating, that
the officers were susceptible to violence in prison (considering the high
visibility of the case), and that Koon and Powell were being subjected
to the burden of successive prosecutions.[84] The Court ruled that the sentencing court had abused its discretion in reducing the guidelines-pre-
scribed penalties based on the officers' low likelihood of recidivism and
their loss of office following the convictions.[85]

The signifying power of the opinion should not be underesti-
mated. The Court placed its imprimatur on a district court ruling that
applied the guidelines in a way that accepts the prevailing justifica-
tions for police brutality.[86] The availability of a large number of officers who could have assisted in placing King in custody obviated any
imagined need for such an aggressive response.[87] By justifying, on the
ground of King's provocation, a reduction in the term of imprisonment prescribed for the officers' conduct, the Court seemed to aban-

don any pretense of reading the facts, even granting the deferential abuse-of-discretion standard. Rather, the opinion reproduced racial and gender stereotypes, invoking a long-familiar narrative within the criminal law that demonizes men of color[88] and recasts victims of state-sanctioned violence as aggressors. Additionally, as Justice David Souter pointed out in his separate opinion, treating successive state and federal prosecutions as a basis for reducing the sentence produced a "normatively obtuse" result: it allowed a defendant to benefit when the federal prosecution was necessary precisely because the trial in the state court failed to produce a just outcome.[89]

THE NEED FOR EVENHANDED CRIMINAL PROSECUTION

It would be misguided to suggest that the barriers to enforcing the criminal law against police brutality have been simply a dysfunction of the system of law. Legal institutions and the discourses that accompany them reflect and reinforce economic and political forces in the postindustrial city that produce deep structural inequalities. For this reason, to argue for an invigorated use of a legal process that is itself tied to a larger flawed system is to risk reproducing those very flaws, albeit with a different set of defendants. Yet, if more vigorous criminal prosecution is an imperfect response to the physical and psychic battering and harassment that have become a way of life for many people in the city, it is still an important ingredient in a coordinated antibrutality legal strategy. Prosecution of police criminality can have a deterrent effect and, perhaps more importantly, it enables people to invoke a process for recognizing and resolving public wrongs that for practical purposes has long been unavailable to them. The actual measure of a law, after all, is a citizen's experience of it—the ways in which it operates when people invoke and use it.[90]

At a minimum, modifications in criminal law and institutional practice are needed to improve the responsiveness of the legal system to victims of police violence. One option that has strong support in the civil-liberties community is a permanent special prosecutor's office with jurisdiction over both corruption and police brutality cases or the variant proposed by the U.S. Commission on Civil Rights.[91] By focusing only on police misconduct and maintaining its own investigative staff to develop evidence, a special prosecutor's office would not be in the position of cooperating with the police officers whom it prosecuted or be subject to the subtle (and sometimes none-too-subtle) intimidation tactics that police groups have employed to undermine local efforts to prosecute misconduct.[92]

Predictably, local prosecutors disagree. They argue that the resources available to prosecuting agencies in large cities, and the size of the prosecutors' staffs and the police force in New York City, reduce the likelihood of conflicts of interest and the concern that local district attorneys are unable to enforce the law vigorously against the police.[93] But the thin record of successful prosecutions in New York City does not bear out this optimism. One prosecutor acknowledged that a special prosecutor's office might be marginally better at developing a comprehensive database and at targeting resources but said it is "not inevitable" that a special-prosecutorial model is preferable.[94] (Federal prosecutors are somewhat insulated from the concerns generated by the need to interact with municipal police officers, in that they have less occasion, except in joint investigations, to work with these officers.) Of course, it bears emphasis that a special prosecutor's office will be effective only if police officers are willing to break ranks and testify against other officers, risking retribution and ostracism.[95]

Under either a special- or local-prosecutor model, additional reforms are needed at a minimum to counter institutional biases against conceptualizing police brutality as crime. Identifying improved methods for uncovering and documenting police violence is essential to ensuring that the magnitude of the problem is understood and exposed to critical scrutiny. Developing a comprehensive database that links law enforcement agencies throughout the city and across jurisdictions within the state would facilitate investigation and aggressive prosecution of brutality.[96] As noted, the state penal law's rule on the justified use of deadly force is not as strict as the NYPD's own regulation. Bringing the state rule into conformity with the more stringent departmental guidelines on deadly force is a step that should be taken both to reduce potential confusion concerning the applicable standard and deter unwarranted use of deadly force. Narrowing the scope of the immunity granted to witnesses who testify before state grand juries would facilitate investigation of brutality incidents without foreclosing the possibility of prosecuting the officers who testify. Requiring a grand jury to file reports in all cases in which it declines to indict may help to allay the frustration of communities in which law-enforcement efforts and police use of force have escalated.

REMEDIAL MECHANISMS OTHER THAN
CRIMINAL PROSECUTION

The view that criminal prosecution should play a central role in efforts to counter police brutality is grounded in the concern that tolerating aggressive police behavior in the name of crime control, the quality of life, or any other "salutary" social policy delegitimizes the rule of law that these programs at least implicitly invoke. The argument for the intensified use of the criminal process advocated here takes a differently nuanced position from other commentators on police brutality, most of whom accord criminal prosecution a more peripheral role in a remedial scheme. The Mollen Commission, for example, favored a comprehensive, preventive approach to the problem of police misconduct rather than a return to a special prosecutor model; it opted for internal anti-corruption structures and an external commission to audit the department's procedures and conduct independent inquiries, as needed.[97] Paul Chevigny has recommended criminal prosecution only for the "clearest" cases.[98] Jerome Skolnick and James Fyfe have argued that in the area of occupational crime, professional peers are better equipped than persons outside the field to address professional derelictions. Moreover, they conclude that to achieve justice for victims of professional wrongdoing, compensatory tort actions are preferable.[99] At a National Emergency Conference on Police Brutality and Misconduct held in New York City in April 1997, lawyers from the Center for Constitutional Rights advocated use of international law standards against excessive force and class actions to contest unreasonably dangerous police practices and technologies.[100] Amnesty International's 1996 report on police brutality in New York City, much maligned by city officials at the time, called for strong disciplinary measures, the creation of an independent oversight body to monitor brutality and corruption, and, where appropriate, criminal prosecution under international standards for abuse of force or firearms.[101]

Another potentially effective remedial mechanism that deserves consideration is the injunction action—a lawsuit seeking prospective and systemic relief by enjoining unlawful conduct and mandating institutional reform. One such suit brought by the National Congress for Puerto Rican Rights and six individual plaintiffs, pending in a federal district court in Manhattan as this was written, seeks to enjoin the NYPD's Street Crime Unit officers from the ongoing practice of stopping and frisking civilians without "reasonable articulable suspicion," to enjoin officers from basing stops on race and/or national origin, and to require improved training for SCU officers.[102] All of these proposals have merit, and any of them might be used effectively—in conjunction with criminal prosecution.

Since 1994, under Title XXI of the Violent Crime Control and Law Enforcement Act, the U.S. Attorney General has had the authority to bring a civil action against law enforcement agencies to enjoin a "pattern or practice" of conduct violating federal law. The Justice Department has instituted such actions against Steubenville, Ohio; Pittsburgh, Pennsylvania; and the state of New Jersey.[103] In these cases, the United States filed a complaint commencing a lawsuit simultaneously with a consent decree in which the local government defendant agreed to institute new procedures. For example, Pittsburgh, with a force of about 1,100 officers, agreed to the appointment of a federal monitor and to institute a computer tracking program to follow officers who are involved in multiple brutality complaints.[104] Recently, the Justice Department began litigation with Columbus, Ohio, after the city's police union would not agree to changes prescribed under a proposed consent decree.[105]

The "pattern or practice" lawsuit can be a powerful goad to reform the existing structures of police agencies. Presently, Justice Department attorneys are negotiating with officials of the city of New York, and police departments in Los Angeles, New Orleans, and Buffalo are all under investigation.[106] The discussions with the city of New York cap an investigation initiated in 1997 by Zachary Carter, then U.S. attorney for the Eastern District of New York, after the assault on Abner Louima came to light.[107] Leslie Cornfeld, deputy chief of the Civil Rights Division for the U.S. Attorney's Office in the Eastern District, and former deputy chief counsel to the Mollen Commission, has headed the inquiry. In March 1999, Mary Jo White, U.S. attorney for the Southern District of New York, joined the investigation, focusing the attention of her office on the operations of the Street Crime Unit.[108]

News reports have been circulating for months that the federal investigation has uncovered enough evidence of systemic problems (concerning the handling of excessive-force complaints and the failure to track officers who are most often complained about) to justify going forward with a lawsuit.[109] As of this writing, U.S. Attorneys were negotiating with the city over the terms of a consent decree.[110] Mayor Giuliani had gone on record at one point in the discussions as refusing to accept the kind of federal monitor that the cities of Pittsburgh and Steubenville agreed to in their consent decrees with the attorney general.[111] Should the long-anticipated suit against New York City go to trial rather than settle, there is no precedent, and no direct legislative history, to guide a court in determining whether the attorney general could prove a pattern or practice of misconduct under this statute. Case law interpreting similarly worded provisions in cognate civil rights statutes suggests, however, that the Justice Department could meet the "pattern or practice" standard in litigation against the city.[112] Still largely untested, the "pattern or practice" suit could prove a finely calibrated instrument for attacking systemic problems within local police agencies. At the same time, it is not a substitute for the signifying power of criminal law.

CONCLUSION

In a statement delivered after the officers in the Diallo case were arraigned, Bronx District Attorney Robert Johnson encapsulated the current preoccupation with crime control in New York City: "Troubling questions have been raised . . . regarding police/community relations, civil liberties and the issue of respect. Questions have also been raised about public safety. . . . Certainly we need law and order, but we should not have to sacrifice the freedoms they are designed to protect."[113]

In the end, it may be that the resistance to criminalizing police brutality is linked to a feared chilling effect on "successful" police work if formal rules and institutional practice governing police use of force are stringently applied. Legal institutions charged with responding to overzealous law enforcement are not insulated from an increasingly strident discourse that legitimates hyperaggressive measures in the name of crime control.[114] If, as Paul Chevigny has argued, the police serve as the "repository" of society's "illiberal impulses," there will be little incentive within these institutions to control or deter routine "acts of oppression" undertaken to maintain order and sanitize public space.[115] Additionally, there is a psychic cost to acknowledging that the guardians of the criminal law are themselves in violation of the law. Yet in disenfranchising persons of color, women, homeless persons, and gays and lesbians, the law's failure to respond consistently and even-handedly has its own inescapable cost.

For the targets of police brutality, institutions that fail to address police violence reproduce all-too-familiar patterns of exclusion within the legal order. Simply stated, the failure to apply law evenhandedly delegitimizes a presumed society of laws. It deprives victims of police crime of the appropriate expectation that invoking the law will be enough to control and deter criminality. Certainly, criminal prosecution should not be the only response to police brutality. A remedial system that emphasizes individual instances of past misconduct cannot get at the root of systemic racism or gender/sexuality bias. Yet the symbolic and deterrent effects of the criminal law are especially needed to begin to repair the damage done in communities where there has been no sense of justice and no occasion for peace.

NOTES

1. David M. Halbfinger, "New York Visitors Set a Record in '96," *New York Times* 3 July 1997: B5.

2. The reference is to Emma Lazarus's 1883 paean to the Statue of Liberty. See Dan Vogel, *Emma Lazarus* (Boston: Twayne Publishers, Div. of G. K. Hall and Co., 1980), 157–159, 202–203. See also "Bill Seeks to Protect Immigrant Workers," *New York Times* 2 July 1997: B4; Steven Greenhouse, "Bill Seeks to Make Sure Immigrants Get Paid," *New York Times* 30 June 1997: B4.

3. Jane H. Lii, "When the Saviors Are Seen as Sinners," *New York Times* 18 May 1997: sec. 13, 1; David Kocieniewski, "Policing Its Own," *New York Times* 11 January 1997: B3.

4. Kit R. Roane, "Spitzer Threatens Subpoena on Frisk Data," *New York Times* 16 May 1999: Metro 39.

5. See, e.g., essays by Erzen, Barr, and by Gore, Kang, and Jones in this collection.

6. David Firestone, "Benefit of the Doubt," *New York Times* 9 April 1997: B3. The mayor's response to the allegations in the Louima case was a departure from his customary stance. David Firestone, "Giuliani Police Quandary," *New York Times* 15 August 1997: A1 ff.

7. "The True Finest Will Come Forward," Editorial, *New York Daily News* 15 August 1997: 44.

8. The quoted language is from Norman Siegel, executive director of the

New York Civil Liberties Union, during the course of a telephone interview on 4 June 1997.

9. Howard Safir, "For Most, Brutality Isn't the Issue," *New York Times* 19 April 1999: A23.

10. See, e.g., Amy Waldman, "Safir Says Police Need to Deal Better with Public," *New York Times* 16 April 1999: B8; Michael Cooper, "Giuliani and Safir Try to Push Politeness Cards at a Roll-Call," *New York Times* 8 April 1999: B3.

11. See, e.g., Kevin Flynn, "Green's Criticism of Police Is Flawed, Giuliani Says," *New York Times* 16 September 1999: B1.

12. Paul Chevigny, *Edge of the Knife: Police Violence in the Americas* (New York: New Press, 1995), 80; Ted Robert Gurr in collaboration with others, *Rogues, Rebels, and Reformers: A Political History of Urban Crime and Conflict* (Beverly Hills and London: Sage Publications, 1976), 135, 164.

13. Roger Cotterrell, *The Sociology of Law: An Introduction*, 2d ed. (London, Dublin, Edinburgh: Butterworths, 1992), 272.

14. See the National Criminal Justice Commission, *The Real War on Crime: The Report of the National Criminal Justice Commission*, ed. Steven R. Donziger (New York: HarperPerennial, 1996), 107–121, 146–158; see also Monte Williams, "Study Shows Rise in Number of Women Jailed for Drugs," *New York Times* 1 December 1999: B18.

15. This principle is reflected in 42 U.S.C. Section 1981(a), which states that "[a]ll persons within the jurisdiction of the United States shall have the same right in every State and Territory to make and enforce contracts, to sue, be parties, give evidence, and to the full and equal benefit of all laws and proceedings for the security of persons and property as is enjoyed by white citizens, and shall be subject to like punishment, pains, penalties, taxes, licenses, and exactions of every kind, and no other."

16. Christopher L. Eisgruber, "Birthright Citizenship and the Constitution," 72 *N.Y.U.L. Rev.* 54, 72–73, 79 (1997). Eisgruber uses the responsiveness principle to identify a rule for birthright citizenship under the Fourteenth Amendment of the United States Constitution, concluding that all persons born in the United States—including the children of undocumented immigrants—should be treated in law as "subject to the jurisdiction" of the United States with a valid claim to share in its social, political, and economic benefits. Id. at 65, 72–85.

17. Judith N. Shklar, *American Citizenship: The Quest for Inclusion* (Cambridge, Mass., and London: Harvard University Press, 1991), 2–3, 14–22.

18. As Shklar argues, citizenship acquired value to the extent that it was unavailable to slaves, women, and some (propertyless) white men. Shklar 49–50. To this list of excluded persons should be added native Americans, infantilized in legal discourse as dependent and lacking agency, and denied citizenship status until 1924, see James H. Kettner, *The Development of American*

Citizenship, 1608–1870 (Chapel Hill: University of North Carolina Press, 1978), 293–300; Ian F. Haney Lopez, *White by Law: The Legal Construction of Race* (New York: New York University Press, 1996), 41; free blacks who, in the antebellum era, generally did not enjoy the right to vote or hold political office, Kettner 311–333; and non-white persons seeking to become naturalized citizens, who remained ineligible for citizenship under the naturalization laws until 1952. Haney Lopez 43. Persons of African ancestry were exempted from the racial bar to naturalization in 1870, however. Haney Lopez 43–44.

19. The conditioning of suffrage on literacy and payment of poll taxes, Eisgruber 57; Donald G. Nieman, *Promises to Keep: African-Americans and the Constitutional Order* (New York and Oxford: Oxford University Press, 1991), 106–108, and the institution of separate but nominally equal access to public services and economic opportunity, Nieman 104–113, 119–120, persisted into the mid-twentieth century, even after a sustained period of law reform offered an invigorated interpretation of the equal protection principle. See, generally, Nieman 169–188.

Neither did the acquisition of voting rights in 1920 constitute women as equal participants in the public order. Until 1934, the consequence of marriage to a man racially ineligible for American citizenship was loss of a woman's own status as a citizen. Linda K. Kerber, "A Constitutional Right to Be Treated Like American Ladies: Women and the Obligations of Citizenship," *U.S. History* as *Women's History*, ed. Linda K. Kerber, Alice Kessler-Harris, and Kathryn Kish Sklar (Chapel Hill and London: University of North Carolina Press, 1995), 27–28. It was not until the late twentieth century that a woman's right to privacy and bodily self-determination was recognized; Kerber 355. See, e.g., *Roe v. Wade*, 410 U.S. 113 (1973) (recognizing a woman's right to choose to terminate a pregnancy); *Planned Parenthood of Southeastern Pennsylvania v. Casey*, 505 U.S. 833 (1992) (invalidating statutory requirement that a woman notify her husband before obtaining an abortion).

20. New York Penal Law Section 35.30(1) authorizes use of physical force on a reasonable belief that such force is necessary to effect arrest, prevent escape, or defend against the use of physical force by a person suspected of committing an offense. This section also authorizes a police officer to use deadly force on a showing of a reasonable belief that such force is necessary to effect arrest, prevent escape, or defend against physical force involving a designated felony or a felony entailing use of physical force against another person; to effect arrest or prevent escape of an armed felon; to defend the officer or another person against the use of deadly force. See also Amnesty International, *United States of America: Police Brutality and Excessive Force in the New York City Police Department* (New York: Amnesty International USA, 1996), 37–38 ("Amnesty International Report") (noting that the New York City Police department guidelines, which state that "deadly force shall not be used to subdue a fleeing felon

who presents no threat of imminent death or serious physical injury to themselves or another person," are more stringent than Section 35.30[1]) and the constitutional rule in *Tennessee v. Garner*, 471 U.S. 1 (1985), which held that deadly force may not be used against an unarmed fleeing felony suspect. Judge-made rules have rendered inadmissible the fruits of a coerced confession. See Chevigny 132–133.

21. See Amnesty International Report 37–38.

22. Egon Bittner, *Aspects of Police Work* (Boston: Northeastern University Press, 1990), 119, 121–122.

23. See Chevigny 132.

24. *Graham v. Connor*, 490 U.S. 386, 396–397 (1989).

25. Victims of excessive force may institute civil-rights lawsuits to recover money damages against police officers and the municipalities that employ and train them. In fiscal year 1998, 1,686 of the 2,105 police action claims, and $27.3 of the $28.3 million disbursed by the city, involved allegations of police misconduct. In comparison to 1998 figures, the cost of all police claims was $27.5 million and $20.5 million in 1996. Although the dollar value of judgments and settlements increased, the 2,105 police claims of all types filed in 1998 decreased from 2,266 in fiscal year 1997. From fiscal years 1992 to 1998, police action cases have been the fourth most expensive category of claims. New York City Comptroller's Annual Report Fiscal Year 1998 5, 28 (August 1999). The Commission to Combat Police Corruption, an agency Mayor Giuliani established in 1995 in lieu of the independent monitor recommended by the Mollen Commission, has criticized the departmental disciplinary system—the other non-criminal process for adjudicating police misconduct claims—citing delays and inefficiency. See William K. Rashbaum, "Mayor's Panel Faults Police Sept. on Discipline System for Officers," *New York Times*, 29 June 2000: A1.

In theory, suits that result in a judgment or settlement should deter police misconduct, yet there is much evidence that neither police officers nor the police department is influenced by the outcomes of these actions. New York City, like most municipalities, usually indemnifies officers for damages awards so that officers have no economic incentive to modify their behavior. Alison L. Patton, "The Endless Cycle of Abuse: Why 42 U.S.C. Section 1983 is Ineffective in Deterring Police Brutality," 44 *Hastings L. J.* 753, 768, 771–772 (1993). Police departments do not monitor these suits, and tend to view their results as too variable and unreliable to be used as a basis for evaluating an officer's job performance. Telephone interview with Joel Berger. See also Patton 782–787. Charles Campisi, chief of the Internal Affairs Bureau for the New York City Police Department, acknowledged in an interview on 30 May 1997 that the police department did not consider itself bound by a jury determination of liability against a police officer, adding that it would depend on the "facts" of a case whether the department would pursue disciplinary measures against an officer found liable for civil-rights violations in a civil suit.

26. David Garland, *Punishment and Modern Society* (Chicago: University of Chicago Press, 1990), 191–193, 199, 251–260, 262, 264–265, 287, 292. See also Peter L. Davis, "Rodney King and the Decriminalization of Police Brutality in America: Direct and Judicial Access to the Grand Jury as Remedies for Victims of Police Brutality When the Prosecutor Declines to Prosecute," 53 *Maryland L. Rev.* 271, 288 (1994); Alexa P. Freeman, "Unscheduled Departures: The Circumvention of Just Sentencing for Police Brutality," 47 *Hastings L. J.* 677, 712–716 (1996).

27. Gurr 135, 175–178, 180.

28. Garland 253–254, 257.

29. Cotterrell 144.

30. Merle English, "A Move to Stop Brutal Cops," *Newsday* 26 April 1997: A07. *See also* Metro News Briefs: New York, "U.S. Ends Rights Case on Police Killing of Youth," *New York Times*, 12 December 1997: B6.

31. Chevigny 72, 100.

32. The City of New York Commission to Investigate Allegations of Police Corruption and the Anti-Corruption Procedures of the Police Department, *Anatomy of Failure: A Path for Success* (7 July 1994), 16–17 ("Mollen Commission Report").

33. Mollen Commission Report 44, 150.

34. Chevigny 73, 99.

35. Chevigny 73, 75–76; Amnesty International 9–10, 14; Davis 285–287. A case in point is the lawlessness of police officers in their effort to enforce a curfew in Tompkins Square Park in August 1988. That effort resulted in many beatings of civilians and over a hundred complaints to the Civilian Complaint Review Board as it was then constituted, though only a handful of arrests. Chevigny 74–77, 81–82.

36. The Civilian Complaint Review Board data indicate that the total number of complaints filed against NYPD officers in 1998 increased by 4.1 percent over the 1997 level. During this same time period, there was a 2.3 percent increase in the number of uniformed officers. *New York City Civilian Complaint Review Board Report* for 1998, 3. Although the peak year for complaints of excessive force was 1995, Lii 1, 12, there has been a general rise in complaints since the middle of 1998. *New York City Civilian Complaint Review Board Report* for 1998, 13.

37. Interview on 22 May 1997, with Steven Zeidman, then associate professor of clinical law, New York University School of Law. Prosecutors from the Brooklyn and Bronx district attorney's offices indicated that if a person charged with a crime does allege excessive force when arraigned on the criminal charge, prosecutors in a separate unit of their office will investigate the claim, effec-

tively freezing prosecution of the underlying charge in the interim. For the investigation to go forward, the defendant must be prepared to substantiate the allegations and waive provisions of law relating to the timing of a preliminary hearing and trial. If the investigation corroborates the defendant's claim, the district attorney's office will either pursue criminal charges against the officer or refer the matter to the Internal Affairs Bureau within the police department and, where warranted, may dismiss the underlying charge against the defendant-victim. Interview with Charles Guria, chief of Corruption Investigations Bureau, Kings County District Attorney's Office, 8 May 1997; interview with Thomas Leahy, chief of Rackets Bureau, 13 May 1997, and telephone interview, 30 May 1997.

38. See, e.g., Mae M. Cheng, "The New New Yorkers: Dispelling Myths, Educating the Public; Unit Aids Immigrants with Police Services," *Newsday* 3 April 1996: A25; Michele Parente, "Bias Crimes Down in the Bronx," *Newsday* 8 January 1992: 24 (noting that reports of bias underrepresent incidence of bias crimes among new immigrants vulnerable to legal or informal sanctions because of their undocumented status).

39. See Graham Rayman, "Arrested Progress/CCRB's Probes of Police Often Beset by Delays, Dead Ends," *Newsday* 30 April 2000: A5. See also Dan Barry, "Independent Agency Fails to Police the Police, Critics Charge," *New York Times* 13 July 1997: Metro 19. Although the quantum of proof required in Board cases is the "preponderance of the evidence" standard that applies in civil cases, Paul Chevigny states that the actual standard is more stringent, usually requiring independent corroboration of a complainant's testimony. Chevigny 94; Amnesty International Report 5–6, 55–60. Of the 4,962 complaints filed in 1998, 300 complaints were substantiated, 1,086 were unsubstantiated, 812 were either unfounded or the employee was exonerated, 323 were concluded through conciliation or mediation, 2,384 resulted in "truncated investigations" (e.g., witness/victim unavailable or uncooperative), and 21 were "administratively closed" (e.g., complainant is unavailable or fails to appear for interview). New York City Civilian Complaint Review Board Semiannual Status report January–December 1998, vol. 6, no. 2, pp. 28–30, 74. For years, the NYPD reinvestigated claims substantiated by the CCRB and then failed to bring disciplinary action against the officers under investigation. In a recent move, the NYPD announced that it would not reinvestigate CCRB investigations but instead would refer cases to the CCRB for additional investigation, if thought necessary. Editorial, "A Stronger Civilian Review Board," *New York Times* 13 August 1999: A20.

40. Martin Wallenstein, "Prosecution in New York City," 159, in John Jay Faculty, *Criminal Justice in New York City* (1999).

41. See, e.g., Davis 271, 290–291. Recently, two of New York City's five district attorneys (Charles Hynes in Brooklyn and William Murphy in Staten

Island) acknowledged this functional dependency on the police when they testified before an arbitration panel in support of the Patrolmen's Benevolent Association's effort to secure a larger wage increase than the city had offered the union. Steven Greenhouse, "2 Prosecutors Back Police on Pay Issue," *New York Times* 4 June 1997: B3. Yet practices differ among district attorneys. In Manhattan, for example, prosecution for many police misconduct cases (typically systemic, precinct-wide instances of corruption or excessive force) is handled by a separate unit of prosecutors who have no day-to-day dealings with local police. However, some brutality cases are investigated and prosecuted by trial division attorneys who do interact with the police on an ongoing basis. Interview with Ric Simmons, former assistant district attorney in Manhattan (New York County). July 3 and 5, 2000.

42. Interview with Charles Guria, Kings District Attorney's Office, 8 May 1997; telephone interview with Maryanne Harkins on 13 March 1997, formerly deputy bureau chief, Rackets Bureau, Westchester County District Attorney's Office. See also Robert D. McFadden, "Officer Got No Support from P.B.A., Lawyer Says," *New York Times* 31 May 1997: 23 (reporting general practice of police officers and Patrolmen's Benevolent Association to appear in court during trials of other officers).

43. Davis 292–295.

44. Interview with Charles Campisi, chief of Internal Affairs Bureau, New York City Police Department, 30 May 1997. Chief Campisi acknowledged that the police department does not make public the dispositions in departmental disciplinary proceedings, anticipating that the public would either conclude that the penalties imposed were too lenient or too severe. He also indicated that Police Commissioner Howard Safir had lobbied the state legislature for changes in the current law that would increase the severity of penalties imposed for violations of departmental rules.

45. Telephone interview with Norman Siegel, executive director of the New York Civil Liberties Union, 4 June 1997.

46. Davis 297–298. Davis notes that although currently prosecutors control the grand jury process, historically the grand jury exercised more independence; Davis 299–306. He argues that victims of police brutality should seek direct or judicial access to the grand jury when prosecutors do not prosecute; Davis 308–352. New York law does not authorize direct citizen access, see New York Criminal Procedure Law Article 190, though arguably a court could entertain an application to impanel a grand jury; Davis 352.

47. Interview of Charles Guria and Dennis Hawkins, deputy, Rackets Division, Kings County District Attorney's Office, 8 May 1997; interview of Anthony Girese, counsel to Bronx district attorney and Thomas Leahy, Bronx County District Attorney's Office, 13 May 1997. See New York Criminal Procedure Law sections 50.10(1), 190.40(2). If it can be established that an officer lied

to the grand jury, a prosecution for perjury is authorized. New York Criminal Procedure Law section 50.10(1).

48. Mollen Commission Report 36–43; the City of New York Commission to Combat Police Corruption, *The New York City Police Department's Disciplinary System: How the Department Disciplines Its Members Who Make False Statements* (12 December 1996), 9–30 ("Commission to Combat Police Corruption").

49. Telephone interview on 13 March 1997, with Maryanne Harkins.

50. New York Criminal Procedure Law section 190.25(3), (4)(a).

51. Interview with Anthony Girese, counsel to Bronx County district attorney, 13 May 1997.

52. The youth, the only son of Cantonese immigrants, had been playing with a pellet gun. Ellis Henican, "No More Games; Many Questions after Teen's Death," *Newsday* 26 March 1995: A08. The Brooklyn District Attorney's Office released a statement prepared independently from the evidence before the grand jury recapitulating the evidentiary facts, including the officer's claim that the weapon had fired accidentally. Amnesty International Report 46. Referring to this incident, which provoked many expressions of concern in the Asian community, Dennis Hawkins of the Kings County District Attorney's Office acknowledged that prosecutors had an obligation to try to educate the community about the reasons for a grand jury's failure to indict. Interview with Dennis Hawkins, 8 May 1997.

53. The same office issued a statement cataloguing its efforts to present the case, which included the testimony of forty witnesses. Joseph P. Fried, "Two Officers Are Cleared in a Killing," *New York Times* 3 May 1997: 25–26.

54. "Morgenthau Comments on the Fatal Shooting," B2. In another approach to keeping lines of communication open, the Bronx District Attorney's Office offers a mentoring program for area youth that is staffed by department employees, including District Attorney Johnson. Telephone interview with Thomas Leahy, Bronx District Attorney's Office, 10 August 1999.

55. Kit R. Roane, "Training of Some Officers Is Criticized by Grand Jury," *New York Times* 14 February 1998: B3.

56. Anthony M. Pate and Lorie A. Fridell, *Police Use of Force: Official Reports, Citizen Complaints, and Legal Consequences* (Washington, D.C.: Police Foundation, 1993), 52, 146–149, 157 (vol. 1), table B.41.1 (vol. 2). A federal statute adopted in 1994, Title XXI of the Violent Crime Control and Law Enforcement Act, requires the attorney general to publish a yearly summary of data about excessive use of force by law enforcement officers. 42 U.S.C. Sections 14141–14142. This provision is essentially an unfunded mandate. To date, no report has issued that directly addresses the provisions of the statute. Telephone interview with Robert Moossy, Special Litigation Section, Civil Rights Division, U.S. Department of Justice, 10 August 1999.

57. Neither the New York State Division of Criminal Justice Services, the

state's Office of Court Administration, nor the various district attorney's offices maintain records reflecting the number of excessive-force cases brought against police officers and their outcomes.

58. David Kocieniewski, "Sergeant in 30th Precinct Is Spared Prison Sentence," *New York Times* 18 April 1997: B3; Elaine Rivera, "Minorities Feel Singled Out; They Account for 92.6% of 1990 Killings," *Newsday* 12 March 1991: 8.

59. Amnesty International 60, 62.

60. Under New York law, there is no provision for prosecutorial objection. Assuming that a waiver is voluntarily made, the court must consent to it unless it determines that it is calculated to secure an "otherwise impermissible procedural advantage," e.g., a severance in a joint trial. New York Criminal Procedure Law Section 320.10(2).

61. Commission to Combat Police Corruption 9–11.

62. Indicted on second-degree manslaughter charges, housing officer Jonas Bright was convicted in 1995 of the lesser offense of criminally negligent homicide for fatally shooting 29-year-old Douglas Orfaly, an unarmed Latino man, during an investigative stop. William K. Rashbaum, "Ex-Cop Guilty in Man's Death," *Newsday* 23 April 1995: A30. More recently, Constantine Chronis was convicted by a Suffolk County jury of first-degree assault (with depraved indifference), menacing, and official misconduct, but was acquitted of intentional assault, in an off-duty, racially charged incident. In April 1999, Chronis was sentenced to four-to-eight years in prison. Robert Gearty, "Prison Term for Ex-Cop. 4 Yrs. in Racial Beating near Hamptons Disco," *New York Daily News* 20 April 1999: Suburban 6; John T. McQuiston, "An Ex-Officer Is Convicted in a Beating," *New York Times* 24 February 1999: B5. In October 1999, two off-duty Brooklyn detectives, Lloyd Barnaby and Mark Cooper, were convicted after a jury trial of various misdemeanor charges in connection with the assault of Reginald Bannerman, but acquitted of felony-level assault charges. Bannerman later died after he was hit by a subway train several blocks from the scene of the attack. A judge acquitted two other detectives of attempting to cover up the incident. Joseph P. Fried, "2 Officers Convicted of Assaulting Man Who Was Later Killed by Train," *New York Times* 2 October 1999: B4.

63. See Bob Herbert, "In America: A Whitewash in Albany," *New York Times* 27 December 1999: A23; Richard Perez-Pena, "Albany County Is Friendly Place for Police Officers on Trial," *New York Times* 18 December 1999: B1, B2.

64. See Jane Fritsch, "New Site for Trial Often Factor in Outcome," *New York Times* 17 December 1999: B12; Jane Fritsch, "Four Officers in Diallo Shooting Are Acquitted of All Charges," *New York Times* 26 February 2000: A1.

65. Lizette Alvarez, "Cases Crumble in Prosecution of Officers," *New York Times* 13 April 1997: 31–32.

66. Anonymous, "Two Officers Acquitted on Charges of Brutality," *New York Times* 6 November 1998: B5.

67. Michael Cooper, "Officer Acquitted in Squeegee Man's Shooting," *New York Times* 9 July 1999: B1, B6.

68. Alvarez, "Cases Crumble," 31–32. In an off-duty shooting incident, Bronx Supreme Court justice Steven L. Barrett convicted Officer Richard Molloy of second-degree manslaughter in the death of Irish immigrant Patrick Phelan, and sentenced Molloy to 4–12 years in prison. Amy Waldman, "Officer Sentenced to 4 to 12 Years In '96 Killing of Irish Immigrant," *New York Times* 13 May 1999: B2.

69. Alvarez, "Cases Crumble," 32. Thomas Leahy of the Bronx County District Attorney's Office confirmed the reluctance of local judges to convict on the strength of a cooperating police officer's testimony.

70. Telephone interview with David Dorfman, assistant professor of criminal law, Pace Law School, and former staff attorney with the Legal Aid Society, March 1997 (date approximate).

71. National Congress for Puerto Rican Rights, Trial Report, *Justicia* 4 October 1996; Kocieniewski, "Safir Dismisses Officer," 23.

72. *New York Law Journal* 8 October 1996: 27.

73. Charles Guria of the Kings County District Attorney's Office said that a judge is less likely to credit police testimony that is patently "bizarre," as in a case in which a defendant police officer charged with assaulting an Asian-American store owner testified that the store owner caused his own injuries by banging his head against a store counter.

74. New York Penal Law Section 35.30(1).

75. Nick Ravo, "Officer Guilty of Killing Unarmed Man in the Bronx," *New York Times* 30 May 1997: B3.

76. Randy Kennedy, "Prison Term for Officer Who Killed Unarmed Man," *New York Times* 22 July 1997: B1.

77. Telephone interview of Norman Siegel, 4 June 1997.

78. Kennedy B1.

79. New York Penal Law articles 55–85.

80. Freeman 681–682; Kate Stith and Jose A. Cabranes, *Fear of Judging: Sentencing Guidelines in the Federal Courts* (Chicago and London: University of Chicago Press, 1998) 3–8.

81. Kocieniewski, "Sergeant in 30th Precinct," B3. Given the reluctance of police officers to testify against their colleagues, prosecutors rely on the cooperation of officers with cases pending against them, in exchange for a more lenient sentence. John Sullivan, "Ex-Sergeant Is Sentenced in Police Corruption Case," *New York Times* 17 June 1997: B3.

82. Freeman 703 n. 104. Data maintained by the United States Department of Justice's Civil Rights Division reveal that for the period of nearly seven years (from 1987 to 1994) following adoption of the federal guidelines, there has been a higher proportion of adjudications of guilt, sentences of imprisonment, and

longer terms of imprisonment among law enforcement defendants than in the two-year period before the guidelines took effect; Freeman 733–738. However, there are also indications that law enforcement defendants receive shorter prison sentences than other persons convicted of civil rights violations; Freeman 739–740.

83. *Powell v. United States*, 518 U.S. 81, 98 (1996).

84. Id. at 105, 111–112.

85. Id. at 109–111.

86. Freeman 683.

87. Davis 277 n.19.

88. See, e.g., A. Leon Higginbotham, Jr., *Shades of Freedom: Racial Politics and Presumptions of the American Legal Process* (New York and Oxford: Oxford University Press, 1996), xxv–xxvii.

89. *Powell*, 518 U.S. at 118 (Souter, J., concurring in part and dissenting in part).

90. Cotterrell 270, 284–285.

91. Suggesting as a model the office headed by Charles Hynes in the late 1980s, Norman Siegel argues that a team of prosecutors headed by a highly visible, experienced trial lawyer and staffed by aggressive litigators, investigators, and community organizers could deter police criminality and restore accountability. Telephone conversation with author, 4 June 1997. More recently, Siegel, Margaret Fung, executive director of the Asian-American Legal Defense and Education Fund, and Michael Meyers, executive director of the New York Civil Rights Coalition, each a member of a task force created by Mayor Giuliani after information surfaced about the assault on Louima, filed a dissenting report that specifically called for the establishment of a special prosecutor's office for brutality cases. *Deflecting Blame: The Dissenting Report of the Mayor's Task Force on Police/Community Relations*, March 1998. In June 2000, the U.S. Commission on Civil Rights recommended that an independent agency pursue the most serious charges of brutality. See United States Commission on Civil Rights, *Police Practices and Civil Rights in New York City* 187–190 (June 2000).

92. Siegel recalled that thousands of police officers demonstrated outside the office of Kings County district attorney Elizabeth Holtzman when she created a Law Enforcement Investigations Unit to prosecute police misconduct, which he termed a "step in the right direction." According to Siegel, the unit was "never aggressive" after that episode. Telephone interview of Norman Siegel, 4 June 1997.

93. Interview with Dennis Hawkins, Kings County District Attorney's Office, 8 May 1997; interview with Anthony Girese, Bronx County District Attorney's Office, 13 May 1997.

94. Interview with Anthony Girese, 13 May 1997.

95. Siegel argues that, to date, police officers have seen only risks to them-

selves in cooperating in a largely unsuccessful process for prosecuting police misconduct. He predicts that officers would be more willing to provide incriminating evidence against other officers if there were a permanently funded office to launch aggressive initiatives against police criminality. Interview with Norman Siegel, 4 June 1997.

96. Interview with Anthony Girese, Bronx County District Attorney's Office, 13 May 1997.

97. Mollen Commission Report 150–154.

98. Paul Chevigny, *Edge of the Knife*, 98, 101.

99. Jerome H. Skolnick and James J. Fyfe, *Above the Law: Police and the Excessive Use of Force* (New York, London, Toronto, Sydney, Tokyo, Singapore: Free Press, 1993) 196–199.

100. Remarks of Michael Deutsch, former legal director of the Center for Constitutional Rights, Plenary Session: Models of Community Struggle and Police Accountability and Legal Workshop. National Emergency Conference on Police Brutality and Misconduct, 26 April 1997.

101. Amnesty International 65.

102. Amended Class Action Complaint for Declaratory and Injunctive Relief and Individual Damages, National Congress for Puerto Rican Rights v. The City of New York, 99 Civ. 1695 (SAS), paragraphs 78–88. See also Benjamin Weiser, "U.S. Judge Refuses to Halt Suit Seeking to Disband New York City's Street Crime Unit," *New York Times* 21 October 1999: B5.

103. See Debra Livingston, "Police Reform and the Department of Justice: An Essay on Accountability," 2 Buff. Crim. L. R. 815, 816, fn4. See also Jerry Gray, "New Jersey Plans to Forestall Suit on Race Profiling," *New York Times* 30 April 1999: A1.

104. Marshall Miller, "Police Brutality," at 186, 191. Telephone interview with Robert Moossy, Special Litigation Section, Civil Rights Division, U.S. Department of Justice, 10 August 1999.

105. Interview with Robert Moossy, id. See also Associated Press, "Ohio City's Police Union Fights U.S. in Brutality Case," *New York Times* 26 November 1999: A41.

106. Benjamin Weiser, "Federal Authorities Grow More Aggressive in Examining Police Nationwide," *New York Times* 28 March 1999: 46.

107. Miller, "Police Brutality," at 150.

108. Robert Polner and Patricia Hurtado, "Rudy Says No: Vows Opposition to Federal Monitoring of NYPD," *Newsday* 24 March 1999: A7.

109. Benjamin Weiser, "Federal Inquiry Criticizes Police in New York City," *New York Times* 10 July 1999: A1, B3; Kevin Flynn. "U.S. Report Expected to Criticize Response by Police to Brutality," *New York Times* 14 June 1999: B1, B6.

110. See, e.g., Kevin Flynn, "Police Consider Plan to Bolster Review Board," *New York Times* 10 August 1999: A1, B7.

111. Polner and Hurtado A7; Weiser, "Federal Inquiry Criticizes Police," A1.

112. See Miller, "Police Brutality," at 169–172 (concluding that attorney general would be able to demonstrate a "pattern or practice" with evidence of a few civil rights violations and an institutional policy sanctioning the violations or from a larger number of related violations and statistical evidence showing disparate impact).

113. "Excerpts from Remarks by the District Attorney," *New York Times* 1 April 1999: B5.

114. See Freeman 704. Opinion polls have suggested that an increasing number of New Yorkers applaud these efforts, especially respondents who are white men or identify themselves as members of the upper middle class. See, e.g., Adam Nagourney, "Poll Finds Optimism in New York, but Race and Class Affect Views," *New York Times* 12 March 1997: A1, B4; Alan Finder and David Kocienewski, "A Safer City Raises Spirits and Questions," *New York Times* 13 April 1997: 1, 34. Of course, these are the groups to which the city's administration has pitched its crime-control rhetoric. More recently, in a poll taken after the Diallo shooting, the *New York Times* found that only 22 percent of the respondents believed that the NYPD treat white and black persons evenhandedly, 51 percent found that most police use excessive force, and 47 percent believed that the crime policy of the Giuliani administration had increased the incidence of police brutality. At the same time, 62 percent of respondents approved of the way Mayor Giuliani has handled crime, and 49 percent agreed that, compared to four years ago, the city is safer today. Dan Barry with Marjorie Connelly, "Poll in New York Finds Many Think Police Are Biased," *New York Times* 16 March 1999: A1, B8.

115. Paul Chevigny, *Police Power: Police Abuses in New York City* (New York: Pantheon Books, 1969), 280.

PART III

ACTIVISM

7

Mothers of Invention

The Families of Police-Brutality Victims and the Movement They've Built

Andrew Hsiao

ONE CHILLY EVENING last year, some twenty people crowded into the cramped, downtown Manhattan office of the National Congress for Puerto Rican Rights to share a mutual heartbreak. Each member of the group—mostly Latinas, though two young Asian women and a middle-aged African American couple were among them—had lost a son or brother to police violence, but the discussion was at once gruesome and remarkably practical. One mother spoke matter-of-factly about the "three kinds of strangulation." Another laid out time limits and deadlines for civil suits. Still another recounted a meeting she had just had with a private pathologist: "The doctor said my son did have a slow death. I don't know what he meant by that, but it's been bothering me ever since."[1]

Like a New York version of the Argentinian mothers of the disappeared, mothers and sisters of police brutality victims have become a ubiquitous and heart-wrenching presence at protests, rallies, and teach-ins across the city. Their extraordinary public role has seemingly been welcomed by both the movement and the media—a *New York Times* profile of Kadiadou Diallo, the mother of the Guinean immigrant who was killed by a hail of police bullets in the spring of 1999, described her as a "telegenic celebrity," and meditated on her "potential" as a "national icon," "figurehead," and "symbol."[2]

But even as the iconography of the police-brutality controversy has increasingly accommodated images of grieving mothers—humanizing brutality for many and helping to contest police narratives of black and Latino male criminality—the more fundamental roles of these women have been largely ignored. Behind the scenes, mothers and family members of police-brutality victims have become leaders of a citywide movement, quietly building and sustaining organizations in the Bronx and Brooklyn, organizing multiracial demonstrations in Manhattan and Queens, producing publications that track police victims and bad cops. Years of meetings and marches have propelled several into exceptional political engagements, yet their movement has remained rooted in street-level community organizing, producing at least temporary alliances with an unlikely array of social forces—youth groups, gay and lesbian organizations, even street gangs. Indeed, just as the police brutality controversy reached its apogee in public consciousness following the shooting of Amadou Diallo and the weeks of mass protests that followed it, the mothers and their grassroots allies found themselves and their activist agenda pushed to the side by politicians, celebrities, and leading liberal establishment figures suddenly eager to bask in the media spotlight.

Meanwhile, these mostly poor women have battled resistance in their own communities—and within their families—as well as political inexperience and the ever-present enemy of debilitating grief. They have been lucky to find allies among some of the city's ablest radical community organizers. That collaboration has built arguably the city's most enduring grassroots protest movement of the last decade, a movement that has helped keep direct-action politics alive while helping to make police brutality one of the defining political issues of our time.

Iris Baez considers herself the unlikeliest of activists. Looking back on the decades during which she raised eleven children—five of them adopted—in a small brick house while her Bronx neighborhood slowly declined, she says, "We never went to meetings, other than church meetings." She and her husband, Ramon, who were born in Puerto Rico, are widely known in their University Heights neighborhood as leaders of the nearby Second Christian Church. For years, police cruisers used to park on the Baez's tiny block, where their only neighbors are a vacant lot and a gas station. Drug dealers and prostitutes occasionally ply their trades beneath the Jerome Avenue subway, across the street from the Baez house. "We always had wonderful relations with the cops," says Baez. "They used to use the bathroom when they were on coffee break."

All of which makes her odyssey since December 22, 1994, she adds, "so ironic." That night, her twenty-nine-year-old son, Anthony, and three of his brothers were playing a game of touch football outside their home when a stray ball hit a parked police car. At the wheel was officer Francis Livoti. The officer ordered the Baez brothers home, and when the youngest, seventeen-year-old David, refused, Livoti arrested him. Then Anthony Baez protested the arrest, so Livoti arrested him too, by grabbing him from behind and choking him. Anthony was declared dead at Union Hospital about an hour later. He died with the edges of his eyeballs bleeding, his tongue swollen, and his windpipe splattered with hemorrhages.[3]

Five years later, one can write that simple scenario without qualification, but only after three indictments, two criminal trials and a departmental hearing, an inexplicable judicial acquittal, a bevy of civil suits, and countless demonstrations. For after Anthony Baez was killed, the police—there were several other officers on the scene with Livoti—said Baez had caused his own death by violently struggling with cops and then apparently suffering a fatal asthma attack. Iris Baez remembers that the police story left her "in shock": "It didn't make any sense. He was violent? He was a Sunday school teacher. All of a sudden he had an asthma attack?"[4]

Amid her grief, Baez "started asking questions. I didn't know anything about coroners or police procedures. I just wanted to ask questions." The queries accumulated after the city's chief medical examiner ruled the death a homicide—an autopsy found the cause of death to be asphyxiation from compression of the neck and chest. Baez's questions got louder and more insistent. "I was always the one with the biggest mouth. And I had to be vocal because of my son." Besides, she found herself buoyed by the community. "The day they laid out Tony," she recalls, "the family all got together, and we went to the precinct and we started chanting. By the time the family got from here to the precinct, there were about 250 people. And then from the precinct, by the time we got to the funeral parlor, the streets were filled."

The outpouring of community outrage over the Baez killing had something to do with the Baez family's stature in the community, but it also drew on the mounting frustration with brutal and bullying police officers. (Francis Livoti, Baez soon found out, had accumulated twelve other complaints of brutality in eleven years on the force.) Then, less than a week later on January 12, eighteen-year-old Anthony Rosario and his twenty-one-year-old cousin, Hilton Vega, were killed by cops in a nearby Morris Heights apartment. The following Monday, Martin Luther King Day, Baez and hundreds of others marched to the Bronx courthouse on 161st Street for a raucous, angry rally.

Margarita Rosario, Anthony Rosario's mother, went to that protest, or rather, she was "taken there, sedated." She had spent the previous weekend "submitted to my bedroom. My pain kept bringing me down, and I didn't want to leave my room." Her son had been shot by two detectives on a stakeout who had fired at him, at Vega, and at another man because, the police department said, the cops were in "imminent danger." But "from the very beginning," says Rosario, she "knew that something was wrong" with the police version. It turned out that though three guns were recovered from the three men, none had been discharged. Still, the police had fired a fusillade of twenty-eight bullets, striking Anthony Rosario fourteen times, each time in the back or sides. Hilton Vega was shot eight times in the back and in the back of his head. None of the bullets that missed were lodged in the walls; all were in the floor. Says Rosario now, "They slaughtered those boys like dogs."[5]

Grief overwhelmed Rosario in the days following the shooting. Then a niece "came into my room and said, 'Look at you. While you're laying there, they're putting out lies about your son.' And I guess with her help, I was able to get out of bed, and decided, okay, I will get up and fight." On the steps of the Bronx courthouse, she says, "I heard people speaking about King, and I knew from that day forward what I had to do. I knew that if I was going to get any justice it was going to have to be by doing it his way, by marching and organizing." The thirty-nine-year-old had, after all, "grown up seeing Martin Luther King fighting for justice." Though she and her siblings had weathered terribly rough times as children when the family immigrated to New York from Puerto Rico, she had always been outspoken. "We used to cut class and have walkouts in the early '70s to protest the Vietnam War."

Early on, says Rosario, a truant officer, she realized "I had to become my own investigator." In the controversial aftermath of the shooting—when Mayor Rudolph Giuliani had immediately injected himself into the case by calling the two detectives to console them—Rosario's family became intimidated. "They probably felt that there was no way of finding out anything else," she says, "because we're dealing with the police department, an organization that has a lot of power, and there's really nothing we can do." The medical examiner's initial public statements were equivocal (they turned out to be wrong). Rosario remembers coming home from the ME's office and saying, "This is all bullshit. And I got angry with them. Because I had decided to fight with all my life." Eventually, the family hired a pathologist, who concluded that Vega and Rosario had been "prone on the floor at the time of the shootings" by the two cops—who, it turned out, had both been volunteer bodyguards for Giuliani during his election campaign.

Iris Baez met Margarita Rosario at the Martin Luther King Day rally, along with a number of other mothers and families of police-brutality victims, some of whom came to the rally with activists from the National Congress for Puerto Rican Rights and the Center for Constitutional Rights. The meeting would turn out to be immensely fruitful, signaling a new stage in the anti-brutality movement, though the political groundwork for that meeting had been developing for years. In the late 1980s, says Richie Perez, a cofounder of the congress, the organization had begun working closely with families of victims of racial violence; the work almost immediately slid into anti-police-brutality advocacy. Founded in 1981, the congress had long organized protests around racist violence and police killings of Latinos, and along with the Black United Front, led by Brooklyn minister Herbert Daughtry, had helped spur two congressional hearings on police misconduct in New York. But the sustained engagement with families of victims—Perez says that early on, the group told families that if it took on their case, it would stay with them till they "won justice"—involved the congress in "a new kind of work," an amalgam of social work and political organizing involving a subdued sense of ideology.[6]

"When we began working with Altagracia Mayi (the mother of a nineteen-year-old Dominican student, Manuel, who was killed by a racist gang in 1991 in Corona, Queens)," says Perez, "we realized that the best organizing was empathetic. We were entering her life, and the lives of other families, at a time of great loss, and trying to help them convert their pain into political anger. It called for us to get really close to them and free of rhetoric. We had to learn to walk through the process with them."[7]

Meanwhile, activists in other communities were adopting similar strategies. Charles Barron, who was Daughtry's chief of staff and has worked alongside the Reverend Al Sharpton for years, was concerned about the way "families are neglected when the cameras are gone." Indeed, says Barron, what often happens after a killing "is a race to the family. Because they're in pain, they're at the mercy of whoever gets to them first, though they later get left behind. We've learned over the years that we've got to protect the families. Because in the end, if you don't have the family, you don't have the story." Staying with the families, however, is intense and time consuming; Perez concedes that the congress has had to drop many of its other activities as its advocacy on behalf of the families has grown. "Sometimes the pain is so great," adds Barron, "that it's hard to get political." But the approach has fostered leadership from the ground up. Moses Stewart, for example, the father of Yusuf Hawkins, a sixteen-year-old who was beaten to death by a racist mob in Bensonhurst in 1989, is a key member of Sharpton's National Action Network today.

But no grassroots group has been more persistent than the mothers initially brought together by the congress. Throughout 1995, the roster at the weekly meetings at the congress grew—a testament both to the proliferation of police violence and the outreach of the activists. Both Baez and Rosario began to draw in other families, one by one. "When I heard of a loss," says Rosario, "I would get the address of the family, then get some mothers together and knock on the front door." The house call would be for consolation, but inevitably "we would talk about the fight."

The struggle prompted other realizations. Says Baez, "I didn't know I was poor until my son was murdered. The shock of it: I didn't have the money to bury my son. It never dawned on me that there's a million people out there just like me, that work every day just to live every day. And I began to see that it's poor communities that they're attacking." Baez responded both practically and ideologically: she started scouting funeral parlors, "looking for the cheapest coffins," so she could advise others. But she also started talking about broader injustices.

The women's practical knowledge and expertise were grounded in the byzantine details of their fight for justice for their own sons, while each fight exposed the interlocking levels of the criminal justice system that maintain systemic abuse. The Baez case illustrated the conspiracy of silence within the department: Livoti received favorable treatment as a Patrolmen's Benevolent Association official, a judge would later complain about "a nest of perjury" among the cops, and one officer who bucked the blue wall to tell the truth was drummed out of the department. The Rosario case revealed the ineffectuality of the Civilian Complaint Review Board—whose investigators were nonetheless spied on by the police—not to mention the corrupting intransigence of high officialdom. In the midst of multiple investigations, Giuliani loudly continued to defend the detectives. Meanwhile, Police Commissioner William Bratton refused even to read the CCRB report that found excessive force had been used, while Bronx district attorney Robert Johnson not only failed to get the grand jury to indict the cops, but participated in the surveillance of the CCRB.[8]

In both cases, as in so many others, the system responded, if at all, only after intense pressure: both Baez and Rosario launched multimillion dollar civil suits. In July 1995, Rosario and Baez were among five hundred people who confronted Bratton at a town hall meeting in the South Bronx. The commissioner dissolved in anger, snapping at the crowd, "You're acting like a bunch of fools. You're the same group that shows up at every one of these meetings." In October 1995, Baez, Rosario, and a dozen others occupied the office of Bronx D.A. Johnson, who had also botched Livoti's indictment. Livoti was reindicted.[9]

By this time, Rosario had given their movement a moniker, Parents Against Police Brutality, though, she says, "We gave ourselves a name just to have a name. Then calls started. Press, families: It turned out to be something the community needed." And something that other communities needed as well. In April 1995, the growing roster of families joined with black, Asian, and white activists to block access to the Manhattan Bridge. The action was part of a coordinated demonstration with homeless groups, students, and AIDS activists that stopped rush-hour traffic at four major arteries to the city, forcing the arrest of 185 people. The shutdown was brief, but it threw activists from all over the city together at a time when multiracial, multi-issue protests had become virtually nonexistent. The alliances that were formed in the months of organizing—and arguing—about the demonstration have been productive.[10]

One group that spearheaded that coalition effort, the Committee Against Anti-Asian Violence (CAAAV): Organizing Asian Communities, developed particularly close ties with the National Congress for

Puerto Rican Rights. Founded in 1986 to combat racial violence against Asians, CAAAV had quickly found that police brutality made up a quarter of the bias attacks to which they were responding. One of the most outrageous was the death of Yong Xin Huang. On March 24, 1995, the sixteen-year-old Chinese boy was playing with a BB gun in a Sheepshead Bay backyard when a police officer was called. The cop would later claim his gun went off when Huang struggled with him, but an autopsy revealed the teen had been shot in the back of the head. That the 115-pound honors student would have fought a cop was unfathomable to the boy's family. "He was so quiet, such a good kid," says his sister Joyce. "Before, we all had the same opinion of the police. They protect us. We didn't know anything about police brutality."[11]

The death of their brother upended Joyce and sister Qing Lan's world. Because their parents speak mainly the Toishanese Chinese dialect, the two became spokespersons for the family. But despite the fact, says Qing Lan, that "I really don't like to speak in front of hundreds of people," the sisters became a constant presence at rallies, and along with CAAAV organizers, began to work closely with the congress and Parents Against Police Brutality. In March 1996, the two invaded Brooklyn D.A. Charles Hynes's office, and were arrested—along with ten others, including Milta Calderon, whose son Anibal had been shot in the back by a cop blocks from his Flatbush home on January 25, 1995. The mothers and sisters had gone to Hynes's office to demand action in both cases.[12]

Possibly the most remarkable coalition sparked by the new anti-brutality movement involved street culture. In 1996, after months of talks, Richie Perez had helped to broker a truce among some of New York's most notorious street gangs. So in the spring of 1996, when some 2000 people turned out for a Racial Justice Rally at City Hall (held on the fifth anniversary of Manuel Mayi's death), Parents Against Police Brutality was joined not only by the Huangs, the father of Leonard Lawton, a twenty-five-year-old African American killed by a cop in Washington Heights that year, and other families, but by members of the Universal Zulu Nation, the Association Pro-Inmates Rights/Netas, and the Almighty Latin King and Queen Nation. Minutes after the mothers finished speaking, Antonio Fernandez, King Tone of the Latin Kings, went up to the rally platform. A swarm of teenage boys and girls raised their hands in a tricky looping motion and saluted their leader. "Gangstas shed tears, too," said Fernandez.[13]

At weekly meetings presided over by ex-Young Lord Perez, Fernandez had shared the floor with the mothers—and with erstwhile enemies from the Netas and Zulus—in planning the rally. And he had vowed to make his "independent street organization" political, eschewing criminal activity for activism. The mothers had fully accepted the young people. "The dynamic there," enthuses Perez, "was powerful. The mothers, the political activists, the gangs, and all these other youth groups. It was multiracial and powerful." In October, Francis Livoti was acquitted, and following angry demonstrations led by the Latin Kings, a police captain was shot outside the Bronx's 46th Precinct house. The mothers came under pressure to denounce the Kings. Their response was to hold a press conference in which they declared, "These are our children." Still, the alliance has not lasted. In 1998, the police arrested ninety-five Latin Kings in a sweep the department said would "crush" the group forever. Perez acknowledges now that "we had no illusions that these groups would turn around completely, but there was and is a core that was trying to transform themselves." Given that the Latin Kings were heavily infiltrated, Perez says that, in a tactic recalling COINTELPRO strategy, the leadership most committed to the political turn was targeted.

Which is not to say that the mothers' movement has not had self-generated problems. Many of the women have had to wrestle with their own families while they fought a seemingly impossible battle. "When I first started," says Rosario, "my husband thought I was losing it. I remember when we came home from the medical examiner's office, and I said that I wasn't going to bury Anthony, a lot of my family said, 'You can't. It's not the proper thing to do.' And after the first year most of them dropped out. They often wished that I would stop. Because they feel that what's best for you is to let go."

Resentments have flared as some families' stories have captured the fickle media's fancy while others languish. Pain saps energy, especially around anniversaries and holidays, and political inexperience has led to missteps. Parents Against Police Brutality has guided almost one hundred victims, but, laments Rosario, "Parents lose faith, communities move on. Sometimes the family gets angry, sometimes they give up." Then there is the matter of sexism. Many in the macho universe of the police-brutality controversy have been uneasy accepting leadership from these women. Skirmishes developed over accepting women as strategic planners. Some men did not want women—or gay and lesbian activists—as security officers. When Jane Bai, the executive director of CAAAV, was put in charge of security for a march of five hundred last winter, it was a gender milestone. As if to underscore the centrality of women in the movement, a newly minted women's group, Women for Justice, drew some five hundred—mainly women—to City Hall for a protest last year.

But perhaps the movement's greatest challenge has involved its relationship with New York's liberal political establishment. The mothers' movement has remained remarkably radical, even as it has won some partial victories. Five months after Francis Livoti was acquitted of homicide, a police tribunal found him guilty of using an illegal choke hold and he was fired. A year and a half later he was convicted in federal court of violating Anthony Baez's civil rights and was sentenced to ten years in prison (meanwhile, he had also been found guilty of assaulting a teenager in a separate Bronx confrontation). In the fall of 1998 the Baez family settled its civil suits against the city for $3 million. Throughout, however, Iris Baez has continued to demand changes in the system that forged Livoti. She started a foundation that tracks cops with brutality records—"I want communities to know their cops, the good and the bad"—and has relentlessly inveighed against politicians to fight for an independent agency to investigate the police. When Bronx borough president Fernando Ferrer announced a run for mayor in 1997, Baez announced her own run for Ferrer's seat. To the Bronx Democratic machine, her Green Party candidacy—backed by Al Sharpton—was a terrifically unwelcome blast from below. The insurgency became moot when Ferrer decided to forgo his mayoral run.

Meanwhile, Margarita Rosario has been unwavering in holding top politicians responsible for police brutality. In July 1999 she dramatically confronted Giuliani on the mayor's radio show, just a month after blaming him for her son's death at a congressional hearing. Giuliani responded in typically gelid fashion, cutting her off to declare, "Maybe you should ask yourself some questions about the way he was brought up," and adding that "I also have an obligation to deal with the hurt and the harm done to these police officers who were put in a position where they had to kill your son."[14]

But as police brutality has moved toward the center of New York's political consciousness, the radical edge of the anti-brutality movement has discomfited many. When a march across the Brooklyn Bridge was hastily assembled to protest the brutal sodomization of Haitian immigrant Abner Louima in a Brooklyn station house in August 1997, jockeying among activists led to some disarray. Some march organizers wanted no explicit criticism of Giuliani, though the large march ultimately contained a spectrum of views. Still, the Louima case turned up the spotlight on the movement, until even that glare was eclipsed by the explosion caused by the killing of Amadou Diallo.

Soon after Diallo was gunned down amid a hail of forty-one bullets on February 4, 1999, Charles Barron met with Herbert Daughtry and Al Sharpton. Sharpton had been debating the merits of calling for civil disobedience with the board chair of his National Action Network, the Reverend Wyatt T. Walker. A month after the Diallo shooting, Sharpton and Walker were arrested on Wall Street, along with nine others. Nineteen others were arrested for staging a sit-in outside the World Financial Center. But Barron and Daughtry had something more ambitious in mind. Recalling the two months of daily arrests in front of Washington's South African consulate in the 1980s, Barron and Daughtry argued for a similar extended effort. Walker was opposed, but in the end, the tactic prevailed. None of them, however, predicted it would be as spectacularly successful as it was.

When a dozen people—most from Sharpton's group—were arrested for blocking the entrance to police headquarters on March 9, Sharpton announced that twelve people would come to Police Plaza and repeat the action until the four cops who had shot Diallo were arrested. The mothers and other longtime activists were there, of course. Evadine Bailey, whose twenty-two-year-old unarmed son Patrick was killed by Kenneth Boss—one of the four cops who shot Diallo—came to the plaza with her husband, who was arrested. Milta Calderon remembers her own arrest as a high point: "In jail, the women were shouting and chanting. A police officer asked me, 'Are you going to commit suicide?' I said, 'No. We have a long way to go to get justice.'"[15]

Years of constructing alliances paid off, helping to convince Sharpton that the stream of protesters could be counted on for two weeks at least.

But after former mayor David Dinkins was arrested six days later, the protest quickly exploded. Within two weeks, hundreds—including many political novices—were being arrested at Police Plaza every day, along with Susan Sarandon, Ossie Davis, Ruby Dee, Jesse Jackson, and virtually every Democratic politician in the city—even a former NYPD chief of patrol. In the end, more than 1,200 people were arrested, occasioning the biggest crisis of Rudy Giuliani's mayoralty (his approval rating plunged almost 20 points). On April 3, 25,000 people marched on Washington to demand an end to police brutality.

But even as the movement was reaching its zenith, the mothers and their allies were being marginalized, or as Charles Barron puts it, "the movement was hijacked." Though Sharpton had orchestrated the protests in behind-the-scenes strategy sessions, leaders of the city's liberal establishment, like Democratic National Committee vice-chair Bill Lynch and powerful union leader Dennis Rivera of Local 1199, were setting an agenda alongside Democratic politicians and black business leaders. At a March 27 summit they approved a set of ten demands and plans for a march across the Brooklyn Bridge. The demands included some of the longtime demands of the grassroots movement, as well as a pay raise for cops, but more disturbing, says Perez, was "the process. They presented it as a fait accompli." Baez and Rosario, among others, had been invited to the summit, but, adds Perez, "it was an insult to invite us in after everything had been done."

Most damaging, says Barron, is that following the summit, "even the language of the movement changed." When the procession across the bridge, dubbed the March for Justice and Conciliation, was finally held on April 15, 1999, "every speaker emphasized, 'We're not talking about all cops.' Elected officials dominated the roster, and they kept saying the problem is a few bad apples." There was no talk of public grand juries, little talk of systemic racism. Ten thousand people participated in the march, but only a few near the front saw an extended scuffle at the side of the stage as Harry Belafonte and a phalanx of Democratic politicians spoke: a dozen mothers and family members had pushed up to the stage and were fighting for an opportunity to speak. After almost an hour of argument, most went home. That denouement left many in the grassroots movement bitter about the opportunism of the politicians who had taken up their cause.

The mainstreaming of the movement raised the profile of police brutality in New York, but, says CAAAV's Jane Bai, it also "turned out

Ten-Point Plan. March to Brooklyn Bridge, April 15, 1999. (Photo by Richard McKewen.)

to be a pacification for the anger that was generated. It got a lot of people out there, but didn't lead us anywhere." And in the months following the Police Plaza protests, the high-profile figureheads faded from the scene. The mothers and grassroots activists regrouped and pressed on. By the spring of 2000, when trials began of three police officers for covering up the torture of Abner Louima and of four cops for shooting Amadou Diallo, longtime activists had organized a coalition of coalitions, People's Justice 2000, that brought a broad band of grassroots groups together, allowing coordinated action.

Indeed, following the dramatic acquittals of the four officers who shot Diallo, a wave of actions was unleashed throughout the city. People's Justice 2000 called for forty-one days of protests following the verdict. Ninety-five protesters were arrested the day after the acquittals, one thousand marched to the United Nations the next day. The next week, two thousand demonstrators rallied in Washington, D.C., and several hundred high school students skipped classes to march across the Brooklyn Bridge. When Mayor Giuliani responded to the March police shooting of another unarmed black man, Haitian American Patrick Dorismond, by attacking the dead man and releasing his juvenile arrest record, more than a thousand Haitians took to the streets of Flatbush, filling five city blocks in a political funeral procession that culminated in a clash with cops and twenty-seven arrests.[16]

The mothers and family members have been pivotal to this galvanization, says Bai, because "for people who first got involved because of Diallo or Dorismond, hearing the mothers speak at these rallies makes clear how it isn't isolated acts of injustice." Their movement now includes groups that had little connection to the issue before: in February, a contingent of Irish gays and lesbians got arrested outside the city's police academy; in April, South Asians held a solidarity rally in Jackson Heights; People's Justice 2000 includes immigrant advocates, youth groups, and feminist organizations. And their years of collaboration—along with increasing strategic smarts born from experiences like the April 15, 1999, March for Conciliation conflict—have sharpened the politics of the movement. In marked contrast to the disarray leading up to the 1997 Haitian community march across the Brooklyn Bridge, a new group affiliated with People's Justice 2000, the Haitian Coalition for Justice, responded to the Dorismond killing by swiftly calling for Giuliani's resignation.

Just as ACT UP revived street activism in the late eighties, the antibrutality movement has helped keep direct action protest alive in the late nineties. New York in the last decade saw large demonstrations over the Gulf War, a massive student protest over tuition hikes at CUNY, and disruptive marches following Matthew Shepard's murder. But no other community movement has endured as long, produced equally explosive political protests, kept its grassroots nature, and remained as radical—connecting racism, the war on the poor, and government manipulation of state violence.

Still, after years of increasingly impressive protests, there have been no fundamental reforms of the police department. The media seem increasingly inattentive to the issue: in the two months following the Diallo acquittals—a period that included the Dorismond shooting and the Louima coverup trial—New York's four major daily newspapers devoted only two-thirds the number of stories to police brutality than during the equivalent period following Diallo's death.[17] The movement has clearly helped wound Giuliani: in the spring of 2000 the mayor's approval ratings fell to their lowest point in seven years—and this before his widely publicized marital woes. But, of course, the question remains: what can the movement win?

Will the movement merely help one Democratic buffer supplant a Republican? Or can it spark a change in what Iris Baez calls "the overall system"? Baez says she will not be remotely satisfied unless the system is completely remade. Because, she says, "The system—not just a police officer—took my son."

NOTES

1. Unless otherwise noted, all quotations are from interviews I conducted in the spring, fall, and winter of 1999, and descriptions of events are based on my reporting. An abbreviated version of this article, cowritten with Deirdre Hussey, appeared in the *Village Voice*, 6 April 1999: 48. For additional material and help, thanks to Esther Kaplan of Jews for Racial and Economic Justice and Jane Bai of CAAAV: Organizing Asian Communities.

2. Susan Sachs, "From Grieving Mother to Forceful Celebrity," *New York Times*, 12 April 1999: A1.

3. For another account of the Baez shooting, see a report by Amnesty International, *United States of America: Police Brutality and Excessive Force in the New York City Police Department* (June 1996), 29 (hereafter "Amnesty report"). Other portraits of the Baez family include David Gonzalez, "Family Paints Tender Portrait of Man Who Died in Custody," *New York Times*, 7 January 1995: A25; Jim Dwyer, "Asphyxia, Say Experts: Quiet Nabe, Irate Cop & Ugly Death for Baez," *Daily News*, 17 September 1996: 8.

4. Coverage of the various trials includes Juan Gonzalez, "Verdict a License to Kill: Tells Police They Can Get Away with Murder," *Daily News*, 8 October 1996; David Kocieniewski, "Dismissal Is Urged for Police Officer in a Bronx Death," *New York Times*, 8 February 1997: A1; Benjamin Weiser, "Ex-Officer Guilty in Choking Death," *New York Times*, 27 June 1998: A1; David Rohde, "Despite Deal, Family of Man Who Died in Arrest Assails Mayor, *New York Times*, 3 October 1998: B1; Benjamin Weiser, "Former Officer Gets 7 1/2 Years in Man's Death," *New York Times*, 9 October 1998: B1.

5. Additional details are available in Amnesty report, 53. See also Matthew Purdy, "Pathologist Says 2 Men Killed by Police Were Shot While Lying on the Floor," *New York Times*, 3 August 1995: B5.

6. For contemporary coverage of those Congressional hearings, see, e.g., Sam Roberts, "A House Panel Will Hear Charges of Police Brutality to City's Blacks," *New York Times*, 17 July 1983: A1; Margot Hornblower, "About 1000 Blacks Disrupt Hearing in Harlem on Alleged Police Brutality," *Washington Post*, 19 July 1983: A3; Sam Roberts, "Police Brutality Charged at Forum," *New York Times*, 20 September 1983: A1.

7. The gang chased Mayi for sixteen blocks and beat him to death after he

drew his graffiti tag on a wall in a largely Italian section of Corona. A high school senior was acquitted after the principal witness fled to Sicily and refused to return to testify. See Curt Simmons, "Mom: Justice Denied," *Newsday*, 11 April 1993: 20. In 1997, the New York City Council named the corner where Mayi was killed Manuel Mayi, Jr., Corner. See Donald Bertrand, "Streets Named for 3 Who Mattered," *Daily News*, 26 June 1997: 2.

8. For more on the surveillance of the CCRB by the police, see Matthew Purdy and Garry Pierre-Pierre, "Police Barrage Still Resounds; Investigators Feud over Bronx Killings," *New York Times*, 20 August 1995, A35.

9. On Bratton and the town hall meeting, see David L. Lewis and Corky Siemaszko, "Bratton Blows Top," *Daily News*, 12 July 1995.

10. For more on the rush-hour protests, see Andrew Hsiao with Karen Houppert, "Birth of a Movement? Behind the Rush Hour Revolt," *Village Voice*, 9 May 1995, 12.

11. On Yong Xin Huang and police brutality against Asian Americans, see CAAAV's essay in this collection. Also, a report by CAAAV, "Police Violence in New York City's Asian American Communities, 1986–1995," (1996). On the Huang case, coverage includes Ying Chan, "Deadly BB Drama," *Daily News*, 25 March 1995: 5; Dennis Hevesi, "No Indictment for Officer Who Shot Brooklyn Youth," *New York Times*, 17 May 1995: B3; Tomio Geron, "New York Story: Anti-Asian Violence Group Wants New Investigation into the Killing of Yong Xin Huang," *AsianWeek*, 13 October 1995; Maureen Fan, "400G For Slain Teen Kin," *Daily News*, 13 March 1996: 16.

12. For more on the Anibal Carrasquillo, Jr., case, see Sheila Maldonado, "Maternal Instincts: Anibal Carrasquillo Was One of Brooklyn's 'Disappeared,'" *Village Voice*, 9 April 1996: 12. See also, Amnesty report, 44.

13. Coverage of the Lawton case includes Chuck Sudetic, "Man Is Slain by Police Officer at Pool Hall," *New York Times*, 23 January 1996: B3; Yusef Salaam, "Leonard Lawton: Promising Young Songwriter Laid to Rest," *New York Amsterdam News*, 3 February 1996: 3; Barbara Ross, "No Charges vs. Cop in Project Shooting," *Daily News*, 20 April 1996: 8. More on the Rally for Racial Justice in Ed Morales, "Kings of New York: As Top Cops Shuffle, Antibrutality Ranks Grow," *Village Voice*, 9 April 1996: 12.

14. Giuliani's comments drawn from David M. Herszenhorn, "Radio Caller and Giuliani Clash on Son's Death at Hands of Police," *New York Times*, 17 July 1999: B1; and Michael Finnegan, "Rudy Radio Lecture Criticizes Mother of Suspect Killed by Cops," *Daily News*, 17 July 1999: 7.

15. For more on the Patrick Bailey case, see Peter Noel, "Raising Patrick Bailey," *Village Voice*, 9 March 1999: 41. Also Herb Boyd, "Kenneth Boss Cleared in 1997 Shooting Death amid Controversy," *New York Amsterdam News*, 14 April 1999: 5.

16. For the Dorismond funeral procession, see Ron Howell and Ray

Sanchez, "Mourning and Melee: Clash with Police Follows Dorismond Funeral in Flatbush," *Newsday*, 26 March 2000: A06.

17. Between 4 February 1997 and 4 April 1997, the *New York Times, Daily News, New York Post*, and *Newsday* ran 497 stories on police brutality. Between 25 February 2000 and 25 April 2000, the same newspapers ran 319 stories on the subject.

8

International Human Rights Law and Police Reform

Paul Hoffman

I. INTRODUCTION

Recent reports by Amnesty International (AI) and Human Rights Watch (HRW)[1] have defined the problem of police abuse in the United States as an international human rights issue. This may come as a surprise to many Americans accustomed to believing that international human rights problems arise only in far-off lands.

International human rights norms do apply to law enforcement officials within our borders and the international community will subject U.S. police practices to increasing scrutiny in the future. Amnesty International has already done so in New York City with the publication of its 1996 report on excessive use of force by New York police officers.[2]

In this chapter I discuss the relevance of international human rights law to police misconduct issues in the United States. What is the reach of international human rights law? Can U.S. tribunals—civil or criminal—enforce these international norms against police misconduct? Could the police officers in the Abner Louima case have been prosecuted in New York for the crime of torture under international standards? Can Amadou Diallo's survivors bring a claim against the City of New York and NYPD under the Alien Tort Claims Act?

To address these and other questions, we first examine the international human rights norms most relevant to policy debates and police misconduct issues. Second, we consider the enforceability of these norms in the domestic legal system. Although the chapter is written from a litigator's perspective, international human rights norms will be useful for a wide range of advocacy, including the lobbying of legislatures and administrative bodies.[3] These issues are addressed in section 8.4 below.

There are two primary sources of international law relevant to police abuse issues in the United States: treaties and customary law.[4] The United States has ratified only a handful of the dozens of international human rights treaties that have been negotiated since the end of World War Two.[5] Indeed, it has been only in the last decade that the United States has ratified the multilateral human rights treaties most relevant to police misconduct issues.

These treaties include the International Covenant on Civil and Political Rights (ICCPR),[6] the Convention on the Elimination of All Forms of Racial Discrimination (CERD),[7] and the Convention Against Torture and Other Forms of Cruel, Inhuman and Degrading Treatment (CAT or Torture Convention).[8] Under Article VI of the United States Constitution, these treaties are the "Law of the Land" and supreme over inconsistent state and local laws. As explained in section 8.3.2 below, it has been difficult to enforce this principle in practice.

In addition to treaty norms, the United States is bound by international customary law, a form of international common law.[9] A customary norm may be found when there is universal, or near universal, agreement among nations that a norm (e.g., the prohibition against torture) exists and is binding on all states as a matter of international obligation.

Theoretically, customary law is also part of United States law and is supreme under Article VI.[10] As the Supreme Court stated in *The Paquete Habana*, 175 U.S. 677, 700 (1900), customary law is "part of our law, and must be ascertained and administered by the Courts of Justice of appropriate jurisdiction, as often as questions of right depending upon it are duly presented for their determination." In practice, United States courts have been reluctant to employ customary norms to displace the decisions of domestic political institutions.[11]

Since 1980, litigators have relied upon the Alien Tort Claims Act (ATCA), 28 U.S.C. §1350, to bring claims for "torts committed in violation of the laws of nations and treaties of the United States." Most of these cases have been brought against foreign human rights violators who have washed up on our shores;[12] however, increasingly ATCA cases are being brought against domestic defendants in police abuse and INS detention conditions cases.[13] The possibilities and limitations of such actions will be discussed below.

The limitations on using international human rights norms in addressing police misconduct issues in the United States is primarily the result of a larger political resistance to international law generally within our domestic legal and political culture. This attitude toward international human rights law is changing and as international law becomes more accepted, this evolving body of law will be another important tool in the arsenal of those involved in advocacy to control police misconduct.

For this reason, civil rights advocates should become familiar with international human rights norms and identify ways in which international law can be used to advance their advocacy on behalf of the victims of police misconduct.

2. INTERNATIONAL HUMAN RIGHTS NORMS PERTAINING TO POLICE ABUSE

2.1. Treaties

In the last decade the United States has ratified three important multilateral international human rights treaties. Each of these treaties contains provisions that are relevant to police misconduct issues. The following is a brief summary of the most relevant provisions.

The Convention against Torture

The CAT contains prohibitions against torture and other cruel, inhuman, and degrading treatment (CID). CAT also contains provisions for the practical enforcement of these anti-torture norms.[14]

Though systematic torture of criminal suspects may be a thing of the past in the United States,[15] the Abner Louima case in New York demonstrates that there continue to be acts of police brutality that fit within the international definition of torture and many more acts that would be considered cruel, inhuman, or degrading treatment or punishment.[16]

Under CAT, the United States must provide civil remedies for the victims of torture. In addition, in Article 14 of CAT, the United States must "ensure" that its legal system allows a victim of torture to obtain redress and "fair and adequate compensation, including the means for as full rehabilitation as possible." If a victim dies, his relatives should obtain compensation.

Though the United States has an elaborate body of civil rights laws for the redress of police misconduct,[17] aspects of these laws may be open to challenge under international law. For example, immunities from liability or proof-of-intent requirements may prevent compensation in a particular case.[18] Similarly, the limitations on liability of municipalities in *Monell v. Department of Social Services*, 438 U.S. 902 (1978) and its progeny, are likely to preclude municipal liability for acts of torture unless the plaintiff can identify a municipal "policy" or "custom" that contributed to the torture.[19] Similar jurisprudence under the Eleventh Amendment to the United States Constitution[20] precludes federal courts from awarding liability judgments against state governments.[21]

The United States also has an obligation under Article 4 of CAT to make torture a violation of our criminal law and to investigate and punish acts of torture occurring within the United States. Congress passed implementing legislation in 1996 but paradoxically created criminal penalties only for torture committed outside the United States.[22] Thus, the police officer who admitted to torturing Abner Louima could not have been tried for this international crime whereas a police officer from Mexico who tortures a Mexican citizen in Mexico City in exactly the same manner may be tried in the United States under this new legislation. Human rights groups have criticized this double standard.[23]

Under Article 10 of CAT, the United States must "ensure" that education and information about the prohibition against torture is fully included in the training of all law enforcement personnel who may be involved in arrest, detention, or imprisonment. In Article 11, the United States must keep its instructions, methods, and practices regarding arrest, detention, or imprisonment under "systematic review" with "a view to preventing any cases of torture." This obligation includes issues such as the "code of silence," internal investigations into complaints, and the discipline of officers.

Article 12 requires "prompt and impartial investigation, whenever there is reasonable ground to believe that an act of torture has been committed" within the United States. Article 13 provides that individuals subjected to torture have a right to complain to and have their cases "promptly and impartially examined" by competent authorities. Coming under growing scrutiny, many internal investigation procedures in police departments across the United States may fall short of this international standard of "promptness" and "impartiality."

The Torture Convention also requires the United States to "undertake to prevent . . . other acts of cruel, inhuman or degrading treatment or punishment which do not amount to torture." The obligations described above in Articles 11, 12, and 13 apply equally to acts of cruel, inhuman, or degrading treatment or punishment. However, the effectiveness of CAT is undermined because the United States is not required to criminalize such conduct and need not provide civil penalties and rehabilitation for the victims of CID.

The prohibition against CID is of great long-term importance to U.S. police reform advocates. There is a growing body of case law at the international level that gives a core of meaning to CID, and this concept may well be broader than U.S. constitutional standards in at least some circumstances.[24]

The Convention on the Elimination of All Forms of Racial Discrimination

The CERD is a comprehensive treaty dealing with all aspects of racial discrimination, including discrimination by law enforcement agencies. One of the most significant features of CERD is its definition of "discrimination" in Article (1)(1) as "any distinction, exclusion, restriction or preference based on race, colour, descent, or national or ethnic origin which has the purpose or effect of nullifying or impairing the recognition, enjoyment or exercise, on an equal footing, of human rights and fundamental freedoms in the political, economic, social, cultural or any other field of public life."

Further, under Article 2(1)(c), the United States must "take effective measures to review governmental, national, and local policies, and to amend, rescind, or nullify any laws and regulations which have the effect of creating or perpetuating racial discrimination wherever it exists."

Thus, laws and practices that have a disproportionate adverse impact based on race, and policies such as those that sanction "driving while black" highway stops, must be reviewed and corrective measures must be taken under CERD.

The International Covenant on Civil and Political Rights

The ICCPR contains a long list of civil and political rights that will be familiar to Americans. Of these, Article 7 embodying the prohibition against torture and other cruel, inhuman, and degrading treatment is the most pertinent to the police abuse issues for the reasons discussed earlier in relation to CAT.[25]

In addition, Article 10 of the ICCPR provides that "[A] ll persons deprived of their liberty shall be treated with humanity and with respect for the inherent dignity of the human person." The pervasive overcrowding and conditions in U.S. detention facilities and prisons were in clear conflict with these requirements.[26] The use of practices like chain gangs and other punishment by shaming that have recently been in vogue may also violate Article 10 and prohibitions against cruel, inhuman, and degrading treatment.

The ICCPR also safeguards the "right to life" in Article 6. This right is relevant to police shooting cases and other situations where police action or inaction is alleged to result in loss of life.[27] There is a substantial body of jurisprudence relating to constitutional protections for the right to life. Cases like *Tennessee v. Garner*, 471 U.S. 1 (1985), limit the use of deadly force beyond the ordinary Fourth Amendment restrictions relating to bodily searches and seizures.[28]

International restrictions on the use of deadly force appear to be more stringent than U.S. constitutional standards. Article 3 of the Code of Conduct for Law Enforcement Officials provides that law enforcement officials may use force only when strictly necessary and to the extent required for the performance of their duty.

The Basic Principles on the Use of Force and Firearms by Law Enforcement Officials elaborates on these standards.[29] For example, Article 9 provides that "law enforcement officials shall not use firearms against persons except in self-defense or defense of others against imminent threat of death or serious crime involving great threats to life, to arrest a person presenting such a danger and resisting their authority, or to prevent his or her escape, and only when less extreme means are insufficient to achieve these objectives. In any event, international lethal use of firearms may only be made when strictly unavoidable in order to protect life."

A good example of the careful analysis that international tribunals have given to lethal police operations is *McCann and Others v. United Kingdom*,[30] in which the European Court of Human Rights found that a British special forces team violated the right to life of three members of a suspected IRA bomb detail in Gibraltar. What is significant about the judgment is that while it absolved the officers who actually fired the shots, the court found a violation on the basis of inadequacies in the ways in which the operation was controlled and organized.

The court's rigorous and broad analysis would be useful to United States police misconduct advocates in certain categories of cases. For example, in Los Angeles, numerous lawsuits have challenged the operations of the LAPD's Special Investigation Section (SIS), a unit that has been alleged to follow suspected criminals, to allow them to commit crimes, and then to confront them in a manner that frequently has led to the deaths of the suspects.[31] An operation planned to maximize the possibility of killing suspects contradicts international "right to life" standards, as articulated in cases like *McCann*.

2.2. Customary Norms

Many of the key treaty provisions described above reflect international customary law. For example, there is little doubt that the prohibition against torture is a customary norm. This was one of the primary holdings in the landmark case of *Filartiga v. Pena-Irala*,[32] in which the United States Court of Appeals for the Second Circuit upheld the jurisdiction of the federal courts over claims of torture committed in Paraguay during the Stroessner dictatorship when the torturer, the former Inspector General of Asuncion, Paraguay, was found in Brooklyn. Indeed, U.S. courts have held that the prohibition against torture is a *jus cogens* or peremptory norm of international law.[33]

Systematic racial discrimination has also been recognized as a violation of international customary law.[34] It is likely that the restrictions on the use of deadly force discussed above in connection with the "right to life" are customary norms, or are becoming so. On the other hand, the courts have been more reluctant to accept the standing of the prohibition against cruel, inhuman, and degrading treatment or punishment as a customary international norm despite international law experts' widespread acceptance of this norm.[35]

Although the United States has now ratified several important international human rights treaties, as discussed below, the issue of whether a norm has become part of customary law is still extremely important for litigators trying to restrain police abuse using international standards in U.S. courts. In addition, because torture is a *jus cogens* norm, reference to international human rights law will assist advocacy against practices that fall within the definition of torture.[36]

2.3. "Soft" International Human Rights Law

There are international standards relevant to police misconduct that are not embodied in treaties and may not yet have ripened into customary norms.[37] Such standards often emerge as sets of guidelines or principles, a kind of international set of "best practices." Sometimes these principles may be said to reflect customary norms, and sometimes the creation and use of such standards may be relevant markers in the determination that a customary norm has emerged.

The most important of these standards for police reform advocates are the U.N. Code of Conduct for Law Enforcement Officials and the Basic Principles on the Use of Force and Firearms. As noted above, the Code and Basic Principles contain important limitations on the use of force, especially deadly force, which may be helpful in domestic police abuse cases. These principles may also be helpful in the cases arising out of the use of intermediate force by police officers, including the use of police dogs, stun technology, taser guns, and other potentially lethal intermediate force.

3. THE ENFORCEABILITY OF INTERNATIONAL HUMAN RIGHTS NORMS IN THE U.S. DOMESTIC LEGAL SYSTEM

3.1. Introduction

The brief description of international human rights norms in section 2 above suggests the promise of more extensive protections from police abuse in the United States based upon international law. Of course, these theoretical advantages will remain theoretical without effective enforcement mechanisms.

This section starts with an overview of methods for enforcing international human rights law in U.S. courts. I will illustrate the issues facing litigators seeking to use international human rights law by discussing several cases in which these arguments challenging police misconduct in United States courts have been advanced.

3.2. Litigating International Human Rights in U.S. Courts

The Enforceability of Treaties

As noted at the beginning of this chapter, under Article VI of the U.S. Constitution treaties are the "Law of the Land." Indeed, the language of Article VI speaks directly to the judiciary.[38] Notwithstanding the apparently clear constitutional directive to courts to enforce international treaties, the Supreme Court for two centuries has given effect to the doctrine that some treaty provisions are "non-self-executing."[39]

Initial attempts to enforce the antidiscrimination norms of the United Nations Charter and the Universal Declaration of Human Rights, despite early success, foundered on the shoals of the non-self-executing treaty doctrine.[40] Indeed, concerns that international human rights treaties might alter domestic law were one reason why the United States did not ratify such treaties for decades.

The immediate post–World War Two battles over international human rights treaties have had a lasting effect on the ratification process. Each of the major human rights treaties ratified by the United States in the last decade has been saddled with a long list of reservations, declarations, and understandings (RDUs) that limit United States acceptance of these treaty obligations in various respects.[41]

An analysis of each of the RDUs is beyond the scope of this chapter;[42] however, three RDUs are most pertinent to police reform efforts.

First, each of the treaties is subject to a declaration that the treaty's provisions are non-self-executing. In essence, this is a declaration to the judiciary from the executive and legislative branches of government that these treaties should not be viewed as creating enforceable rights in U.S. courts. Although litigators will argue that these declarations are not binding on the courts,[43] this argument will be a hard sell before judges who are already inclined to defer to the political branches in the foreign affairs arena.[44]

Second, the ratifications of CAT and the ICCPR were accompanied by reservations limiting the scope of cruel, inhuman, and degrading treatment or punishment to the content of the relevant provisions of the United States Constitution. These limitations are especially harmful in the area of police abuse and prisoners' rights because CID is a broader concept under international law than it is within the United States Constitution, or within United States law, especially after the Prison Reform Litigation Act limited the right to sue with respect to prison conditions.[45]

Finally, CERD and the ICCPR were restricted by a reservation limiting the scope of discrimination to what American lawyers understand as the "rational basis" test, the lowest level of judicial scrutiny given to allegedly discriminatory laws or practices.

In a recent case, a death row inmate in Nevada challenged a reservation to Article 6 of the ICCPR concerning juvenile execution. Article 6 prohibits execution of a capital offender who was under the age of eighteen at the time of the offense. The Senate conditioned the United States's ratification of the ICCPR with a reservation on this provision. The Nevada inmate argued that this reservation was not binding on the judiciary and that Article VI of the Constitution mandated that the courts treat Article 6 of the ICCPR as the "Law of the Land."

In 1998, the Nevada Supreme Court rejected that argument by a 3-2 vote, finding that the political branches could limit the terms of U.S. acceptance of a human rights treaty.[46] It is likely that litigators will continue to challenge the RDUs attached to these treaties. In the current judicial climate, however, these challenges face considerable obstacles.

The Enforceability of Customary Law

As noted above, customary law is the "Law of the Land" enforceable in U.S. courts. There are many examples of such enforcement in United States jurisprudence.[47] However, U.S. courts have been reluctant to enforce customary norms when they appear to be in conflict with federal statutes or executive action. The recent District Court decision in *Hawkins v. Comparet-Cassani*, 33 F. Supp. 2d 1244 (C.D. Cal 1999), illustrates the problems facing litigators who assert customary norms in police abuse cases.

The *Hawkins* case arose out of a well-publicized incident in July 1998: a criminal defendant facing life imprisonment under California's "Three Strikes" law was subjected, at the Court's direction, to a 50,000-volt electric charge from a stun belt when he continued to speak in court after he had been told to stop. Mr. Hawkins brought a civil rights damages action, and his attorneys raised claims under a variety of treaties and customary international law, in addition to §1983 claims to recover for violation of federal rights committed by persons acting under color of state law.

Relying heavily on the "non-self-executing" declaration in reaching this conclusion, the District Court found that the treaties Hawkins relied on were "non-self-executing" (*Hawkins*, 33 F. Supp. 2d at 1257, citing *In re Extradition of Cheung*, 968 F. Supp. 791, 803 n. 17 [D. Conn. 1997]). The District Court also rejected Hawkins's claims that the court should imply a cause of action for damages from the *jus cogens* prohibition against torture (*id.* at 1254–1256). In denying the claim for damages, the court went through a familiar analysis under the *Bivens* line of cases that have implied a right of action to enforce certain federally protected rights.[48] Concluding that remedies were available, and that Congress had acted in the field of torture, the court expressed its hesitance "to interfere in an area that is traditionally entrusted to the legislative and executive branches" (*id.* at 1256).

The District Court did not, however, address the plaintiff's claims for injunctive relief based upon customary law. This issue is analytically distinct from the issue of whether a court should imply a cause of action for damages from a customary norm. Indeed, the basic principle in *The Paquete Habana* is that courts must enforce customary norms, at least in exercising their equitable powers.

It is not easy to explain the District Court's failure to confront this issue.[49] The court went on to grant a preliminary injunction against the future use of stun guns in courtrooms (*id.* at 1260–1263). In light of the court's factual findings, there was ample basis for issuing an injunction to prevent future acts of torture or cruel, inhuman, or degrading treatment or punishment under traditional principles.[50] The *Hawkins* decision is another example of the practical difficulties of enforcing international law in U.S. courts, even in cases of alleged torture.

The Alien Tort Claim Statute

The obstacles to enforcement of international human rights norms illustrated by the *Hawkins* decision do not exist for aliens seeking redress from at least certain forms of police misconduct. Under the ATCA, "aliens" may sue for "torts committed in violation of the law of nations and treaties of the United States." Since most police misconduct claims are torts, the central question in ATCA cases is whether the conduct alleged violates the "law of nations."[51]

Since the landmark *Filartiga* decision, most ATCA cases have involved claims against foreign human rights violators and obvious international human rights claims.[52] In 1998, two decisions applied the ATCA in the context of claims against domestic law enforcement officials.

In *Martinez v. City of Los Angeles*, 141 F.3d 1373, 1383 (9th Cir. 1998), the Court of Appeals for the Ninth Circuit considered a claim of arbitrary arrest and detention against LAPD officers who allegedly had caused the arrest and two-month detention of an elderly Mexican man in Mexico by supplying false information against him to Mexican law enforcement officials. The court agreed that there was a "clear international prohibition against arbitrary arrest and detention" (*id.* at 1384). However, the court found that the fact that the plaintiff's arrest was pursuant to an arrest warrant, and that the plaintiff had access to a judge and a prompt hearing and was released fifty-nine days after his arrest, undermined the plaintiff's claims that his arrest and detention were "arbitrary." Though the court applied the criteria for *prolonged* arbitrary detention claims under the Restatement of Foreign Relations Law to arbitrary arrest and detention claims based on the provision of false information, the court had little difficulty applying the ATCA to the conduct of local police officers.

Because the *Martinez* court found that the plaintiff's claims did not rise to a violation of international customary law as a matter of law, it did not reach a host of other issues, which will be the subject of future ATCA litigation. For example, are police officers entitled to claim any immunities in response to ATCA claims? May an ATCA claimant sue a municipality under the ATCA without satisfying the §1983 requirement of stating a municipal "policy" or "custom" under *Monell*? If ATCA suits are unencumbered by the same limitations, non–U.S. citizens may find the ATCA a more attractive option than civil rights statutes, at least in some cases.

In *Jama v. INS*, 22 F. Supp. 2d 353, 361 (D.N.J. 1998), a district judge in New Jersey found subject matter jurisdiction under the ATCA over claims by INS detainees who claimed that they had been subjected to cruel, inhuman, and degrading treatment, including filthy conditions of detention, sleep deprivation, torture by guards, invasion of privacy, and other forms of physical and sexual abuse. The *Jama* court rejected the argument, accepted by the court in *Hawkins* in the context of torture claims by a United States citizen, that the existence of constitutional and statutory claims precluded the plaintiff's ATCA claims (*id.* at 364).[53] The court allowed these claims to proceed against both INS officials and officials of the private company that ran the facility (*id.* at 365–366).

The use of the ATCA against domestic law enforcement officials is still novel. With millions of immigrants living in the United States and with tens of thousands in some form of detention, there will be many opportunities to bring ATCA cases to challenge police misconduct. For example, the Amadou Diallo case in New York is a candidate for an ATCA claim. Diallo had emigrated from Guinea;[54] and his family has a claim that his right to life under international law was violated in light of the allegations of police misconduct surrounding his shooting by NYPD officers. The ATCA may offer broader protection than federal or state civil rights laws in these circumstances.

The use of the ATCA in cases involving U.S. law enforcement officials is in keeping with the known original purposes of the ATCA—to provide a federal remedy for assaults on foreign diplomats in the United States.[55] If a body of jurisprudence emerges in these cases, Congress may be moved to provide an explicit claim for relief under customary or treaty law for United States citizens in similar circumstances.[56]

The "Charming Betsy" Principle

Another approach used by litigators seeking to implement international law in U.S. courts has been to rely on the venerable principle of statutory interpretation originally derived from *Murray v. The Schooner Charming Betsy* that "[w]here fairly possible, a United States statute is to be construed so as not to conflict with international law or with an international agreement of the United States."[57]

In the context of police misconduct claims, the argument that the U.S. Constitution should be interpreted in harmony with evolving customary norms and treaty norms[58] has met with resistance in the U.S. Supreme Court's Eighth Amendment jurisprudence for juvenile execution cases. In *Stanford v. Kentucky*, 492 U.S. 361, 770 (1989), the majority sharply rejected the relevance of international customary law for determining the "evolving standards of decency" in traditional constitutional analysis.[59] Justice Antonin Scalia, writing for the five-Justice majority, emphasized "that it is *American* conceptions of decency that are dispositive, rejecting the contention of petitioners and their various amici . . . that the sentencing practices of other countries are relevant." In rejecting the relevance of international standards to the constitutionality of juvenile execution, the Court disregarded not just "sentencing practices" but a customary law prohibition of this practice. The majority did not similarly address the significance of this norm in light of the history of reviewing international practice in Eighth Amendment analysis.[60]

4. NONLITIGATION ALTERNATIVES TO IMPLEMENTATION

In this section I will discuss nonlitigation alternatives to enforcement of international human rights norms. In fact, nonlitigation uses of international human rights norms are perhaps the most important area for U.S. civil rights advocates to pursue. If these international norms are to become effective tools, they must be accepted and utilized more widely in the U.S. political and legal culture generally.

4.1. The Treaty Bodies

Introduction

Each of the treaties described in section 2.1 above has similar international enforcement mechanisms.[61] Under each treaty, an independent body of internationally recognized experts is elected by the states parties. These experts serve in their individual capacities and perform similar tasks under each of the treaties. These include providing general comments on implementation reports submitted by states parties, and general comments concerning the interpretation of the provisions of each of the treaties.

States parties must file reports within one year of ratification and on a regular basis after that about the steps they have taken to implement their treaty obligations. By commenting on state reports and providing interpretive evidence to states in the form of general comments, committees constituted by states parties are developing a body of jurisprudence that American advocates may use in arguing that the United States is not in compliance with its international obligations under these treaties. Thus, police reform advocates should follow the interpretations provided by these committees and use them to fashion arguments based on the treaties.[62]

The Reporting Process

The reporting process may provide important opportunities for police reform advocacy. First, the United States must prepare a public report on the implementation of its treaty obligations. Second, the United States must defend its record in a public session before the treaty body under such treaty.

To inspire needed reforms, human rights advocates in many countries produce counterreports and use the public sessions to focus attention and publicity on the shortcomings of the government's human rights record. So far, the United States has issued only one of its required reports. In July 1994 the United States issued its initial report on the implementation of the ICCPR.[63] The report, submitted more than a year late, was mainly a summary of basic constitutional and statutory provisions and case law, not the analysis of actual implementation that is required under the treaty.

Several human rights groups published reports challenging the United States' human rights record, including its record on police issues.[64] These reports were used by committee members to ask United States officials, including Assistant Secretary of State for Human Rights John Shattuck, Attorney General for Civil Rights Deval Patrick, and State Department legal advisor Conrad Harper, about specific human rights issues. The Human Rights Committee issued general comments concerning the protection of human rights in the United States.[65]

In theory, the committee will inquire further of U.S. representatives at the public session on the next U.S. report. This report should have been issued by 1998 under the ordinary schedule; as this is being written, the United States has not issued its second report.

The United States has yet to issue its initial reports under CAT or CERD. Each of these reports is years overdue by now. So far, there has been little public pressure on the United States to comply with these obligations, limiting the effectiveness of these procedures. Police reform advocates have an important stake in pushing for the timely publication of reports under CAT and CERD, given the relevance of these treaties to police issues.

International Complaint Procedures

Each of the three major human rights treaties that the United States has ratified has a complaint procedure. Although each makes provision for state-against-state complaints, no state has ever filed such a complaint. Moreover, the United States has declined to accept the competence of these treaty-based committees to hear such complaints.

The ICCPR has an individual complaint mechanism in its Optional

Protocol,[66] which the United States has neither signed nor ratified. The complaint mechanism in CERD has seldom been used by anyone.

The United States *is* subject to individual complaints before the Inter-American Commission on Human Rights (though the United States contests the commission's jurisdiction). In fact, many complaints have been filed against the United States, leading to some significant decisions, especially on the death penalty.[67] Indeed, police misconduct appears to be a natural arena for increased litigation before the commission, especially concerning racially motivated, or racially disproportionate, police abuse. The problem in this area is that the United States does not take the commission very seriously, and the United States still has not ratified the American Convention on Human Rights or become party to the Inter-American Court of Human Rights.

4.2. Executive Order 13107

In December 1998, on the fiftieth anniversary of the Universal Declaration of Human Rights, President Bill Clinton promulgated Executive Order 13107, intended to remedy some of the problems described here. In particular, the executive order states that "it shall be the policy and practice of the Government of the United States, being committed to the protection and promotion of human rights and fundamental freedoms, fully to respect and implement its obligations under the international human rights treaties to which it is a party, including the ICCPR, the CAT and the CERD."

The executive order creates an assortment of bureaucratic initiatives designed to ensure that the relevant agencies of government assign people to implement this directive. Section 4 creates an intra-agency working group on human rights treaties to monitor the progress of these efforts. The working group is assigned a variety of tasks, including coordinating the preparation of the reports under each treaty, preparing responses to complaints to the UN, the OAS, and other international organizations, reviewing legislation for conformity with international human rights obligations, and developing plans for public outreach and education. Section 3 requires all agencies to respond to "inquiries, requests for information, and complaints about violations of human rights obligations that fall within its areas of responsibility."

The executive order in Section 6 pointedly states that it does not create any enforceable rights against the United States, its agencies or instrumentalities, its officers or employees, or any other person. Further, "this order does not supersede federal statutes and does not impose any justiciable obligations on the executive branch."

Despite its limitations, the executive order provides a strong policy directive to the federal bureaucracy to implement the ICCPR, CERD, and CAT. The working group, and indeed all agencies, may be reminded of these obligations by human rights advocates whenever the federal government acts inconsistently with its international human rights obligations or fails to act to implement those obligations.

One example of a possible pressure point is the Justice Department's exercise of its new statutory authority to bring civil "pattern and practice" lawsuits against law enforcement agencies.[68] The Justice Department should consider patterns and practices that violate U.S. treaty obligations in deciding when to investigate and sue under the statute.

5. CONCLUSION

U.S. civil rights and civil liberties advocates have a long-term stake in advancing the cause of practical enforcement of international human rights norms within the United States and around the world. This chapter gives only a brief overview of the international human rights tools available to advocates in the United States. Utilizing international human rights norms may offer broader protections, now and in the future, for victims of police misconduct. It will not be easy to use these tools effectively in police abuse litigation or advocacy when international norms collide with U.S. legal doctrine. More importantly, an ambivalent attitude toward international law and initiatives in U.S. society continues to hamper enforcement efforts.

Yet advocates can overcome these obstacles by a combination of effective organizing, education, and outreach efforts. The growing strength of the international human rights movement will make it difficult for U.S. decision makers, whether politicians or judges, to ignore our international human rights obligations in the long run.

NOTES

1. See Amnesty International, "USA: Race, Rights and Police Brutality," AMR 51/147/99 (September 1999); Human Rights Watch, *Shielded from Justice:*

Police Brutality and Accountability in the United States (1998). See also Chevigny, *The Edge of the Knife* (1995) at 271–73. In 1998–1999, Amnesty International launched an international campaign about human rights violations in the United States. *Rights for All,* 17–54 (1998). Police abuse issues were a central focus of Amnesty International's concerns. In 1998, the UN Special Rapporteur on Extrajudicial, Summary or Arbitrary Executions, Bacre Waly Ndiaye, issued a report on the United States which also addressed issues of police brutality. See E/CN.4/1998/68/Add.3 ("Ndiaye Report").

2. Amnesty International, "United States of America: Police Brutality and Excessive Force in the New York City Police Department," AMR 51/36/96 (June 1996).

3. There is a vast body of literature on international human rights issues. One useful practical introduction to international human rights issues is Hannum, *Guide to International Human Rights Practice* (3d ed. 1999). For a discussion of the relevance of international human rights law to civil rights litigation, see De La Vega, "Civil Rights during the 1990s: New Treaty Law Could Help Immensely," 65 Univ. of Cincinnati L. Rev. 423 (1997).

4. Article 38, Statute of the International Court of Justice.

5. The most comprehensive collection of human rights treaties is published by the United Nations in a two-volume paperback set called *Human Rights: A Compilation of International Instruments.* In 1996, the United Nations also published a compendium of human rights standards specifically for law enforcement officials, *International Human Rights Standards for Law Enforcement,* HR/P/PT/5/Add.1 (1996). A great deal of international human rights information is also available on the Internet. See Hoffman, "Guide to Human Rights Research on the Web," in the 1999 edition of the ACLU International Civil Liberties Report (available from the ACLU Foundation of Southern California, 1616 Beverly Blvd., Los Angeles, CA 90026).

6. International Covenant on Civil and Political Rights, *opened for signature* December 19, 1966, 999 U.N.T.S. 171, *entered into force* March 23, 1976, *ratified by United States* September 8, 1992.

7. Convention on the Elimination of All Forms of Racial Discrimination, *opened for signature* March 7, 1966, *entered into force* January 4, 1969, *ratified by the United States* November 20, 1994.

8. Convention Against Torture and Other Cruel, Inhuman and Degrading Treatment or Punishment, G.A. Res. 39/46, annex, 39 UN GAOR Surp (No. 51), at 197, UN Doc. A/39/51 (1984), *opened for signature,* Dec. 10, 1984, 1465 U.N.T.S. 85, *entered into force* June 26, 1987, *ratified by the United States,* Oct. 21, 1994.

9. See generally Symposium, "Customary International Human Rights Law: Evolution, Status and Future," 25 Ga. J. Int'l and Comp. Law 1 (1995–1996). One of the difficulties in enforcing customary law is that it is not easy to find customary law because it is not codified or readily accessible in a format

familiar to United States lawyers or judges. This unfamiliarity has created practical litigation and advocacy difficulties in a political and legal culture that is ambivalent about international law to begin with.

10. Henkin, *Foreign Affairs and the Constitution* (2d ed. 1996) at 198–203.

11. In particular, the courts have given effect to federal statutes and executive action, even in conflict with customary norms that arguably crystallized after their adoption. See Henkin, *supra*, note 10 at 198–203. See also, e.g., *Garcia-Mir v. Meese*, 788 F.2d 1446 (11th Cir.), *cert. denied sub nom, Ferrer-Mazorra v. Meese*, 479 U.S. 889 (1986). See also Kirgis, "Agora: May the President Violate Customary International Law?" 81 Am877. J. Int'l L. 371 (1987).

12. See, e.g., *In re Marcos Human Rights Litigation*, 94 F.3d 539 (9th Cir. 1996). Stephens and Ratner, *International Human Rights Litigation in U.S. Courts* (1996). This book is a comprehensive practical guide to bringing lawsuits under the ATCA.

13. See *Jama v. Immigration and Naturalization Service*, 22 F. Supp. 2d 353 (D.N.J. 1998) (§1350 available to detainees in an INS detention facility to challenge cruel, inhuman, and degrading conditions).

14. A good analysis of CAT can be found in Rodley, *The Treatment of Prisoners under International Law* (2d ed. 1999). Professor Sir Nigel Rodley is the UN Special Rapporteur on Torture.

15. There have been such allegations from time to time recently. Amnesty International, "United States of America: Allegations of Police Torture in Chicago, Illinois," AMR 51/42/90 (December 1990). See also the discussion of police abuse in fourteen U.S. cities in *Shield from Justice, supra*, note 2.

16. Under Article 1 of CAT, "torture" is defined as

any act by which severe pain or suffering, whether physical or mental, is intentionally inflicted on a person for such purposes as obtaining from him or a third person information or a confession, punishing him for an act he or a third person has committed or is suspected of having committed or intimidating or coercing him or a third person, or for any reason based on discrimination of any kind, when such pain and suffering is inflicted by or at the instigation of or with the consent or acquiescence of a public official or any other acting in an official capacity. It does not include pain or suffering arising only from, inherent in, or incidental to, lawful sanctions.

17. See Nahmod, *Civil Rights and Civil Liberties Litigation*, (4th ed. 1997); Avery, Rudovsky, and Blum, *Police Misconduct* (3d ed. 1998).

18. The most common form of immunity in police misconduct cases is the qualified immunity given to officers unless they are shown to have violated clearly established constitutional norms. *Harlow v. Fitzgerald*, 457 U.S. 800

(1982). In the context of torture, it seems unlikely that surmounting qualified immunity will be difficult in all but the most unusual case.

19. This obstacle is mitigated in most states because the municipal entity will indemnify officers found liable under 42 U.S.C. §1983. See, e.g., California Government Code §825. Such indemnification is not required by federal law, though, and it is possible that a municipality would refuse to indemnify an officer for an act of torture, leaving the victim without a practical manner of collecting a civil rights judgment for torture.

20. The Eleventh Amendment provides: "The judicial power of the United States shall not be construed to extend to any suit in law or equity, commenced or prosecuted against one of the United States by citizens of another state, or by citizens or subjects of any foreign state."

21. See *Quern v. Jordan*, 440 U.S. 332 (1979); *Will v. Michigan Department of State Police*, 491 U.S. 58 (1989) (State is not a "person" for 42 U.S.C. §1983 purposes).

22. The Congress passed such legislation in 1996 providing criminal penalties for torture. This legislation is codified at 18 U.S.C. §2340. To date, there have been no prosecutions of torturers in the United States under this legislation. The Justice Department has recently set up an inter-agency task force to pursue torturers and other human rights violators who are found within the United States. Hopefully, the work of this task force will result in prosecutions under §2340.

23. Human rights groups have called upon the Congress to enact legislation making torture committed in the United States a criminal offense. Massimino, "Torture in the U.S. Is Still Torture," *L.A. Times*, October 14, 1998, at B7.

24. See Rodley, *supra*, note 14, at 101–106. In *Tomasi v. France*, Eur. Ct. of H. Rts, Ser. A, No. 241-A (1990), *Ribitsch v. Austria*, Judgment, December 4, 1995, the European Court of Human Rights found beatings not amounting to torture to qualify as CID. See also *Selmouni v. France*, Judgment of July 28, 1999, 20 H. Rts. L. J. 228 (1999), where the Court found sustained police beatings to be torture.

25. Articles 2, 3, and 26 provide for equal protection safeguards. The Human Rights Committee has stated that "not all differentiation of treatment constitutes discrimination if the criteria for such differentiation are reasonable and objective and if the aim is to achieve a purpose which is legitimate under the Covenant." U.N. GAOR, Hum. Rts. Comm., 37th Sess., 984th mtg., at 4, U.N. Doc CCPR/C/21/rev. 1/Add. 1 (1989).

26. This chapter has focused on police misconduct issues. International human rights norms are extremely relevant to prisoners rights issues in the United States and conditions in U.S. prisons and detention facilities have drawn international scrutiny and criticism. See note 1. In particular, human rights groups have given much greater attention to abuses against women prisoners starting with a seminal report by the Women's Rights Project of Human Rights

Watch in 1996. Human Rights Watch, "All Too Familiar: Sexual Abuse of Women in U.S. State Prisons."

27. See *Ndiaye Report, supra*, note 1, at 26–30 (recounting evidence of death as a result of excessive force by law enforcement officials). Mr. Ndiaye did note that the written policies of U.S. police departments appear to comply with international standards. *Id.* at 29.

28. See *Graham v. Conner*, 490 U.S. 386 (1989).

29. The Code and Basic Principles may be said to reflect a common understanding of the "right to life" in international human rights treaties, or evidence of the customary prohibition on arbitrary killing. At a minimum, they are "soft" law. See sec. 2.3 *infra*.

30. Judgment of Sept. 27, 1995, no. 17/1994/464/545.

31. See, e.g., *Trevino v. Gates*, 99 F.3d 911 (9th Cir. 1996).

32. 630 F. 2d 876 (2d Cir. 1980).

33. See *Siderman v. Republic of Argentina*, 965 F 2d 699, 717 (9th Cir. 1992).

34. Restatement (Third) of the Foreign Relations Law of the United States, §702 (1987).

35. The high-water mark for such skepticism in the face of expert opinion came in *Forti v Suarez-Mason*, 672 F. Supp. 1531, 1543 (N.D. Cal. 1987) ("*Forti I*"). Judge Jenson found that cruel, inhuman, and degrading treatment or punishment ("CID") was not enforceable under §1350 and declined to reconsider this position in the face of expert affidavits filed by renowned international law scholars Richard Falk, Thomas Franck, Louis Henkin, Richard Lillich, and others. *Forti v. Suarez-Mason*, 694 F. Supp. 707, 709 n.2, 711-12(N.D. Cal. 1988) ("*Forti II*"). Other courts have found this norm to be enforceable. See, e.g., *Abebe-Jira v. Negewo*, 72 F. 3d 844 (11th Cir. 1996), and *Xuncax v. Gramajo*, 886 F. Supp. 162 (D. Mass. 1995).

36. For the same reason, in cases where the police conduct does constitute torture, like the Louima case, litigators should consider the advantages (and possible disadvantages) of placing a torture claim before the jury.

37. Toman, "Quasi-Legal Standards and Guidelines for Protecting Human Rights," in Hannum, *supra*, note 3, at 203.

38. Article VI provides that "Treaties . . . shall be the supreme Law of the Land; and the Judges in every State shall be bound thereby." Treaties may not supersede the United States Constitution. *Reid v. Court*, 354 U.S. 1, 17 (1957) (plurality opinion). If a treaty and a federal statute conflict, the last in time prevails, though courts should attempt to give effect to both. *Asakura v. City of Seattle*, 265 U.S. 322, 342 (1924).

39. *Foster v. Neilson*, 27 U.S. 253, 314 (1829). See Vazquez, "The Four Doctrines of Self-Executing Treaties," 89 Am. J. Int'l L. 695 (1995).

40. See *Fujii v. State of California*, 242 P.2d 617 (1952). For an argument that the human rights clauses of the U.N. Charter should be found self-executing,

see Burke et al., "Application of International Human Rights Law in State and Federal Courts," 18 Texas Int'l Law J. 291, 302 (1983). The late California Supreme Court Justice and human rights activist Frank Newman urged advocates to use treaties in administrative proceedings where the non-self-executing doctrine would not apply. Newman, "United Nations Human Rights Covenant and the United States Government: Diluted Promises, Foreseeable Futures," 42 De Paul L. Rev. 1241 (1993). For an argument that the use of international human rights law in the antidiscrimination challenges of the 1940s and 1950s was successful, see Lockwood, "The U.N. Charter and United States Civil Rights Litigation: 1946–1955," 69 Iowa L. Rev. 901 (1984).

   41. For a comprehensive analysis of the enforceability of human rights treaties and the politics and significance of the non-self-executing declarations attached to human rights treaties, see Sloss, "The Domestication of International Human Rights: Non-Self-Executing Declarations and Human Rights Treaties," 24 Yale J. Int'l L. 129 (1999). S. Res. 4783-84, 102nd Cong. (1992) (ICCPR); 140 Cong. Rec S 7634-02 (1994) (CERD); and U.S. Senate Treaty Doc. 100-20, 100th Cong., 2d Sess. (Torture Convention).

   42. See De La Vega, *supra*, note 3, at 452–462; Daniel P. Stewart, "United States Ratification of the Covenant on Civil and Political Rights: The Significance of the Reservations, Understandings and Declarations," 42 De Paul L. Rev. 1183 (1993).

   43. See Quigley, "The International Covenant on Civil and Political Rights and the Supremacy Clause," 42 De Paul L. Rev. 1287 (1993).

   44. See *Hawkins v. Compurel-Cassani*, 33 F. Supp, 2d 1244 (C.D. Cal, 1999).

   45. The PRLA, Pub. L. No. 104–134, 110 Stat. 1321, limited the Supreme Court's holding in *Hudson v. McMillan*, 503 U.S. 1 (1992).

   46. *Dominguez v. Nevada*, 961 P.2d 1279 (Nev. 1998). See Fiore and De La Vega, "The Supreme Court Has Been Called Upon to Determine the Legality of the Juvenile Death Penalty in *Michael Dominguez v. State of Nevada*," 1999 ACLU International Civil Liberties Report 81. Dominguez had argued that the United States reservation to Article 6 violated the "object" and "purpose" of the ICCPR and thus was invalid under international law and unenforceable. In October 1999, the United States Supreme Court denied Dominguez's Petition for a Writ of Certiorari.

   47. Paust, *International Law as Law of the United States* (1996) at 81–142.

   48. *Bivens v. Six Unknown Named Agents of the Fed. Bureau of Narcotics*, 403 U.S. 388 (1971). The court relied on *Handel v. Artukovic*, 601 F. Supp. 1421, 1428 (C.D. Cal. 1985) ("To imply a cause of action from the law of nations would completely defeat the critical right of the sovereign to determine whether and how international rights should be enforced in that municipality"). It should be remembered by advocates that a decision that an international norm is "non-self-executing" does not mean that the United States is not bound to enforce the

norm. Thus, in cases where enforcement is denied by courts, it will be important to put pressure on the political branches of government to enforce these norms. See sec. 4, *infra*.

49. The author presented this argument at the hearing on the motion to dismiss in *Hawkins* on behalf of Amnesty International, appearing as *amicus curiae*. The court's extensive written tentative decision did not address the issue, and the court did not materially change his tentative order when his final ruling was issued. This may be an example of the "blank stare phenomenon." Hoffman, "The 'Blank Stare Phenomenon': Proving Customary International Law in U.S. Courts," 25 Ga. J. of Int'l and Comp. L. 181 (1995/1996).

50. The issue of stun technology is a growing problem. See *Amnesty International*, "Cruelty in Control? The Stun Belt and Other Electro-Shock Equipment in Law Enforcement," AMR 51/54/99 (June 8, 1999).

51. The "treaty" prong of the ATCA has not used much in ATCA litigation. The issue is whether the ATCA serves to make otherwise non-self-executing treaty provisions enforceable in U.S. courts. A similar, though not identical, issue may arise under the "and laws" language in 42 U.S.C. §1983. See *Maine v. Thiboutot*, 448 U.S. 1 (1980). See De La Vega, *supra*, note 3, at 450–451. The issue here is whether treaties or customary norms are included in the term "laws." To date, there are no reported cases on this issue.

52. See, e.g., *Abebe-Jira v. Negewo*, 72 F.3d 844 (11th Cir. 1996) (torture). It is now well established that the ATCA provides both subject matter jurisdiction and a claim for relief. Id, at 848. See also *In re Estate of Marcos Human Rights Litigation*, 25 F.3d 1467, 1474–75 (9th Cir. 1994).

53. The court did raise the possibility that if international law were inconsistent with domestic law, a different result might obtain. *Id.* at 364.

54. Kolbert, "The Perils of Safety: Did Crime-Fighting Tactics Put Amadou Diallo at Risk?" *New Yorker*, March 22, 1999, at 50.

55. Randall, *Federal Courts and the Human Rights Paradigm* (1990) at 59–90.

56. This was one of the reasons for the passage of the Torture Victim Protection Act (TVPA) in 1992. The TVPA applies only to torture or extrajudicial executions committed under the color of foreign official authority. 28 U.S.C. §1350.

57. Restatement (Third), §114. This principle derives from *Murray v. The Schooner Charming Betsy*, 6 U.S. (2 Cranch) 64, 118 (1804). See Steinhardt, "The Role of International Law as a Canon of Domestic Statutory Construction," 43 Vanderbilt L. Rev. 1103 (1990). For a good example of the principle in operation, see *Rodriguez-Fernandez v. Wilkinson*, 654 F.2d 1382, 1388–90 (10th Cir. 1981) (construing Immigration Act to avoid conflict with international norms prohibiting prolonged arbitrary detention).

58. See Christenson, "Using Human Rights Law to Inform Due Process and Equal Protection Analysis," 52 U.Cin. L. Rev. 3 (1983).

59. The relevance of international standards in Eighth Amendment analy-

sis had been affirmed as far back as the Supreme Court's decision in *Trop v. Dulles*, 356 U.S. 86 (1958).

60. In *Thompson v. Oklahoma*, 487 U.S. 815 (1988), and *Stanford*, four members of the Court dissented and affirmed the relevance of this customary norm.

61. For a basic partial introduction to treaty implementation bodies, see Lewis-Anthony, "Treaty-Based Procedures for Making Human Rights Complaints within the UN System," and Coliver and Miller, "International Reporting Processes," in Hannum, *supra*, note 3.

62. There are many other sources of interpretive guidance available to human rights advocates and courts. For example, the European Court of Human Rights, created to enforce the European Convention of Human Rights, has developed an extensive body of jurisprudence in litigated cases that may be relevant to the interpretation of CERD, the ICCPR, and the Torture Convention. See Martin, "How the European Convention on Human Rights and the Case Law of the European Court of Human Rights Are Important to U.S. Law Governing Civil Liberties," 1999 ACLU International Civil Liberties Report, at 29. Several European Court cases discuss the affirmative obligation of states to investigate police brutality. *Id.* 32, *Assenov v. Bulgaria*, Eur. Ct. H. R. (Ser. A) (1998).

63. *Civil and Political Rights in the United States: Initial Report of the United States of America to the U.N. Human Rights Committee under the International Covenant on Civil and Political Rights* (July 1994).

64. See ACLU and Human Rights Watch, Human Rights Violations in the United States (December 1994); the working group is assigned a variety of tasks, including coordinating the preparation of the reports under each treaty, preparing responses to complaints to the UN, the OAS, and other international organizations, reviewing legislation for conformity with international human rights obligations, and developing plans for public outreach and education.

65. General comment reports by the Human Rights Committee under Article 40, paragraph 4, of the International Covenant on Civil and Political Rights, CCPR /c/21/ rev. 1/App. 6, November 2, 1994.

66. Optional Protocol to the International Covenant on Civil and Political Rights, March 23, 1976, 99 U.N.T.S. 171.

67. See, e.g., Case 9647 (James Roach), Inter-Am. C.H.R. 147, OEA/Ser.L/ V/II. 71, Doc. 9 rev. 1 (1987) (system of juvenile execution in United States violates American Declaration on the Rights and Duties of Man).

68. This authority was part of the Police Accountability Act of 1993, codified at 42 U.S.C. §14141. 42 U.S.C. §14142 requires the attorney general to collect data on the excessive use of force. Such data-collection efforts may also be relevant to the implementation of U.S. treaty obligations.

Yong Xin Huang, Cadman Plaza, Brooklyn, New York, April 15, 1999.
(Photo by Richard McKewen.)

9

Police Brutality in the New Chinatown

Committee Against Anti-Asian Violence: Organizing Asian Communities

ON MARCH 24, 1995, sixteen-year-old Yong Xin Huang, a Chinese American youth from Brooklyn, was killed by Police Officer Steven Mizrahi. Using a Glock 9-mm pistol, Mizrahi fired one shot—at point-blank range—into the back of Huang's head. According to Mizrahi and the New York Police Department (NYPD), the shooting was an accident. The police story claims that Huang and three friends were in possession of what appeared to be a real pistol while playing in the driveway of the Brooklyn home of one of the friends. Responding to a call from a neighbor, Mizrahi arrived on the scene with his gun drawn. In the driveway, he saw Huang holding an air gun. Taking no chances, Mizrahi ordered the teenager to put down the toy gun. According to the police, Huang—induced by either intense panic or intense fearlessness (take your pick)—did not respond to this order and continued to hold on. From this point forward, the police account turns fuzzy: somehow a struggle ensued between Mizrahi (who stands six feet tall, and over two hundred pounds) and Huang (who stood at five feet, three inches, and barely one hundred pounds). So fierce was this struggle that it sent both Huang and Mizrahi crashing through a glass door. As the two fell to the ground, Mizrahi's Glock 9-mm fired the fatal round—by accident.

But eyewitness accounts from the scene and an independent autopsy report tell a drastically different story: Huang put down the toy gun when ordered; Mizrahi then approached the "unarmed" Huang, who was facing a glass door with his back to the officer, trying to go inside his friend's house; Mizrahi grabbed Huang with his gun still drawn. Now Mizrahi's pistol was aimed at the back of Huang's head. Mizrahi then slammed Huang's face into a glass door, shattering the glass. At this point, Mizrahi's gun was fired—point-blank into the back of Huang's head.

The shooting of Huang instantly became headline news in both the mainstream and ethnic press. Yet, rather than begin with an investigation at the scene of the shooting, news reporters, encouraged by the police, initially searched for evidence that would point to justified police force: Why was he not in school on the day of the incident? Was the incident gang related? Does the toy gun resemble a real one? Whose is it, and what was he doing with it?[1] The media's attempt to criminalize Huang should come as little surprise. To be sure, in similar police shootings of unarmed Black and Latino youth during the early 1990s, the immediate impulse is to invoke popular media tropes concerning urban criminality to justify the police action.[2] An investigation into the youth's personal past, however, yielded a portrait of a sixteen-year-old boy— the son of a working-class immigrant family, with a mother who is a garment worker, the father a restaurant worker, three older sisters who went straight to work after high school to support the family, and all of whom had invested their hopes and dreams of upward mobility in their youngest and only son, now deceased. The daily struggles of Huang's family as immigrant laborers in a sweatshop economy is a story that was never told by the press. Having failed to uncover evidence to criminalize Huang and render a hasty and easy verdict in the case, the media then quickly turned to "model minoritism"—the characterization of Asian immigrants in the U.S. as hard-working, law-abiding endorsers of majoritarian values. Headlines highlighted Huang's above-average school records as the press characterized the incident as an aberration— "good kids" who follow the rules are not supposed to be killed by the police. Such is the bipolar racial profile of the working-class Asian immigrant: the hopelessly unassimilable criminal who dodges government authorities, on the one hand, and the quiet and obedient "model minority" who achieves the American dream through hard work and assimilation, on the other.

The community reaction to the Huang shooting commanded a moral authority rare for a police shooting case.[3] The shooting functioned as a "clarion call" for New York's Chinese immigrant community—a community undergoing intense polarization along class, generational, and geographical lines. From the Chinatown working-class laborer to the middle-income Chinese professional, there were very few who could not find reason to support the Huang family in its struggle for justice, and who did not seriously question the overly aggressive policing practices that led to Huang's death.

In the days following the shooting, the Committee Against Anti-Asian Violence (CAAAV)[4] worked with the Huang family to pull together the broad base of support that would be needed to pressure the Brooklyn District Attorney's Office to seek an indictment against Mizrahi. Yet, within this united front, CAAAV was particularly interested in generating support among the working-poor residents of Chinatown. Anti-police-brutality activity in Chinatown has invariably focused on the plight of working-class residents, especially the violence experienced by young people whom police consider to be members of notorious Chinatown gangs or "tongs." But in the early 1990s, CAAAV also noticed an increase in the number of brutality incidents against the working-poor adults of Chinatown—street vendors, sweatshop laborers, dollar-van drivers,[5] as well as small entrepreneurs. In 1994 alone, CAAAV documented over thirty cases of police raids and claims of harassment and physical violence against Chinatown street vendors, and a dozen accusations of harassment and false arrests of Chinatown workers traveling to and from work.[6] As these cases flooded CAAAV's office, allied groups such as the Chinese Staff and Workers Association documented the harassment of workers who, at the renowned Silver Palace restaurant, staged one of the largest restaurant workers' strikes in Chinatown's history. During the strike, the NYPD was a daily presence at the restaurant, disrupting and at times preventing the workers' protests.[7]

As these daily forms of police harassment and violence against the Chinese working poor continued, they went largely unnoticed by those outside of Chinatown. Even the most seasoned veterans of the anti-police-brutality movement in New York City knew very little about Chinatown's new policing campaign. The killing of Huang in March 1995, however, began to shed some light on the issue. The justice campaign for Huang gained momentum, due in large part to the tireless efforts of Huang's older sisters, Qing Lan and Joyce Huang. This campaign opened the possibilities for a popular discussion of the more subtle and routine forms of police brutality in new immigrant communities, particularly in Chinatown and its satellite community in Brooklyn. This is not to suggest, however, that Huang's death was merely an opportune vehicle through which to discuss less sensationalized forms of police brutality that did not appear on the radar screen of the dominant media or the mainstream of the anti-police-brutality movement. To the contrary, CAAAV sought to make the connections between the killing of Huang—a killing that seemed the result of identifying Asian youth generally with the category of the "exceptionally intelligent and exceptionally violent" Asian gangster[8]—and a broader, albeit more mundane, campaign aimed at confining, both territorially and socioeconomically, Chinatown workers and small entrepreneurs. For CAAAV, the task was to uncover the ways in which these two seemingly discrete police responses to Chinese immigrant communities were a product of the same economic and political processes that have rendered Chinatown a veritable "internal colony."

In this essay we explore the connections among various episodes of police brutality directed against Chinese immigrants in New York City. We begin by looking at the recent history of policing in Chinatown, which crystallized in the NYPD's anti-gang campaign during the 1970s and 1980s—and the anti-brutality organizing it provoked. For nearly thirty years, representations of the ruthless and cold-blooded Chinese gangster or tong enforcer have permeated American popular culture, adding to Chinatown's aura of exoticized danger. To be sure, gangsterism in Chinatown is a very real problem, one that not only affects the Chinatown economy and its social order, but also the daily lives of working-class immigrant youth. These youth are commonly assumed to be dangerous gang members and thus become subject to criminalization, racial profiling, and harassment by the police. But the roots of contemporary gangsterism and anti-gang policing in Chinatown have been largely obscured and oversimplified by explanations that lay blame on disaffected and alienated immigrant youths, an inscrutable Chinese culture, or the mysterious Chinese "underground economy." In this essay we offer an alternative analysis. We argue that Chinatown gangs are a product of seemingly legitimate Chinese business interests and their links with mainstream institutions, not the least of which has been the NYPD. These gangs expanded as a result of Chinatown's capital boom of the 1970s, and reportedly provided "enforcement" services for Chinatown's property owners—extorting money, intimidating business competitors, or profiting from the drug trade.[9] With this rise in gang activity came a rise in police violence in Chinatown, linked to the NYPD's deployment of anti-gang task forces.[10]

Following our discussion of the roots of contemporary Chinatown gang activity and the attendant police crackdown against Chinese youth, we turn our attention to the new policing campaigns that target the working poor of the Chinese immigrant community. Using examples from CAAAV's advocacy cases from 1994 through 1996, we discuss the ways in which policing in Chinatown has recently shifted its focus from anti-gang enforcement to the disciplining of Chinatown sweatshop workers (particularly in the garment and restaurant industries), and those who participate in the so-called informal economy: street vendors, dollar-van drivers, and other small, unregulated service providers. Similar to our analysis of contemporary gangsterism, we note how these working-poor sectors have emerged as a direct consequence of the economic and political solidarity of Chinatown's business elites during the 1970s. Although the informal economy provides much-needed food and transportation services to the newly proletarianized Chinatown, we note how it is nonetheless viewed as a threat to these elites; indeed, it is a lingering reminder of Chinatown's inability to break from its legacy of "primitive" capitalism. Coupled with Mayor Rudolph Giuliani's campaign to "resurrect" the dirty streets of New York City—by removing vendors, artists, and homeless people—we are confronted with an all-out policing campaign against those in the Chinatown informal economy.

By exposing the shared roots of police brutality experienced by Chinatown youth and the adult working poor, we hope not only to provide an incisive analysis of state violence in Chinese communities, but also to identify the potential for unifying the poorest sectors of present-day Chinatown. Much has been written about the ever-growing disparity between the wealthiest and poorest sectors of the Chinese American community. At the same time, there is a growing division within the poor sector itself. At the level of rhetoric, that division is captured in a set of oppositional constructions: the poor are either hard working and self-sacrificing, or criminal minded. Of course, neither conveys the complex experience of poor people in Chinatown. Yet both "groups" are equally punished under the economic and political rules of the new Chinatown. Our goal, then, is to explore the possibilities for a liberation politics benefiting the entire poor sector. We begin that process by exposing the ways in which Chinatown's ethnic elites stand to benefit from certain forms of crime, the criminalization of youth, and the police crackdown against the disenfranchised residents and workers of Chinatown.

TARGETING YOUNG RADICALS

To be sure, in general terms, the police shooting of Yong Xin Huang stems from policing practices that target young men of color from poor communities as dangerous criminal subjects. Yet the process of criminalization is also quite specific. In other words, racialized police violence does not uniformly occur in relation or response to the homogeneous category "young men of color," but rather attends to a set of diverse cultural factors and stereotypes such as the "pathologizing of African-American violence." This point is neither new nor profound. Indeed, activists in the anti-police-brutality movement in New York City, particularly those who can trace their roots to the revolutionary nationalist left of the late 1960s and early1970s, long emphasized the need to pay careful attention to the particular practice of police brutality within a specific racial community. During this period, groups such as the Black Panther Party and the Puerto Rican–based Young Lords Party recruited local gang members, out-of-work persons, and ex-prison inmates—young men who were excluded from the formal labor market and were most often targets of the police. The goal of this organizing was to liberate poor, intensively policed sectors by promoting solidarity across non-white, working-class communities. These groups provided leadership for Black and Latino community struggles for racial justice and won the support of many Black and Puerto Rican youth by taking an unwavering stand against police violence in their respective communities.[11]

For both the Panthers and the Lords, police brutality was not simply a matter of racist police officers who attacked black and brown youth carte blanche. Rather, these activists understood policing to consist of highly localized campaigns aimed at segregating and disempowering the Black and Puerto Rican communities in distinct ways. For this reason, both groups suggested that the struggle for empowerment among poor, disenfranchised people of color should begin with the struggle for local autonomy—in effect, from the bottom up. The Panthers and Lords viewed their respective activisms as a domestic example of the struggles for self-determination being fought throughout the anticolonial "Third World."[12] In this spirit, they regarded the African American community and the Puerto Rican *barrio* within the U.S. nation-state as "internal colonies."

In 1969, young Asian Americans, strongly influenced by the Black liberation movements, began to organize similar revolutionary collectives in the Asian communities of New York City, San Francisco, and Los Angeles. Among the most well known groups were the Red Guard Party and I Wor Kuen ("the righteous fist"). Drawing upon the theory of an internal colony, these groups sought to uncover the particular forms of state repression directed against the Asian working class, particularly against the people of Chinatown.[13] Much like the Panthers and Lords, these Asian American radicals also understood that the local police force—or the "occupying army" of the internal colony—did not operate in isolation but in a loose conjunction with a broad range of interests, not the least of which was the consolidated business interests of Chinatown.

Although ethnic business elites have dominated Chinatowns since the mid-nineteenth century, the McCarthy era of the early 1950s solidified their influence. That period was marked by the particularly reactionary leadership of the Koumintang (KMT)—those who opposed the Maoist revolution in China and who maintained deep ideological ties to nationalist exiles in Taiwan and Hong Kong. Throughout the 1950s, the KMT had developed an anti-Communist league that worked closely with the Federal Bureau of Investigation (FBI) to expose, arrest, and in some cases deport Chinatown labor activists, many of whom had ties to the Communist Party.[14] But since the early 1960s, following the KMT and the FBI's effective campaign to drive Chinatown's left underground, Chinatown youths—the baby boomer generation—became the primary targets of the KMT's stranglehold and local police repression. Angered by the growing poverty in their community, and inspired by the escalating antiwar and Black liberation movements, these young people sought to build a Chinatown that was liberated from right-wing elites. In many instances, this intergenerational struggle against the power structure manifested itself in confrontations with the police, as many young radicals—well aware of the police's role in driving out the old Chinatown left—viewed the agenda of the local police to be inseparably intertwined with that of the local KMT leadership, as both guarded the interests of capital and acted as disciplinarians of the working poor.[15]

Attacks against young radicals such as the left-oriented members of the youth gang known as Leway[16] were perhaps the most obvious form of police repression against Chinatown youth during the late 1960s and early 1970s, mirroring the police crackdown on numerous political organizations, including the Panthers and Lords. But police targeting of the youthful new left tells only a fraction of the story. Indeed, the outspoken left was merely a part of a larger youth movement that threatened KMT control; this movement included a heterogeneous grouping of youth, many of whom were new immigrants wishing to seize power—and not necessarily for the broader liberation of the Chinatown masses. In this group were youth who participated in the informal economy of the street, acting as extorters, strong-arm men, and drug dealers. Although many of these youths were carrying out business for the elites—to all appearances their services were in high demand as Chinatown business expanded during the 1970s—they were also viewed as an impending, and unpredictable, threat to Chinatown's unofficial power structure and to law enforcement.[17] For this reason, they became the targets of high-intensity policing campaigns throughout the 1970s and well into the 1980s.

ECONOMIC GROWTH AND THE GANG HYSTERIA

Since the mid-1960s, Chinatowns in many U.S. cities, particularly in New York, have undergone an economic boom characterized by large capitalist investment and development. Before the 1960s, Chinatowns were made up of small service businesses that could not reproduce themselves or invest in development projects. But according to Peter Kwong, this process of community decline began to change its course with the influx of cheap labor in Chinatown following the passage of the Immigration Act of 1965.[18] By the early 1970s, Chinese laborers, particularly Chinese immigrant women, became available to the New York–based garment industry that was looking for ways to stay competitive with an expanding global workforce.[19] Many Chinese business owners opened small-to-medium-sized garment firms that often paid far below the minimum wage, and offered little or no benefits.[20] With the profits made from the garment industry, Chinatown business leaders began to develop banks, luxury office buildings, and condominiums in Chinatown, and large restaurants sprouted there throughout the 1970s.

There are those who claim that this economic boom, coupled with the normalization of international relations between China and the United States, led to the increasing irrelevance of the KMT elites who had long dominated Chinatown. But critics such as Kwong dispute this conclusion. To the contrary, the KMT elites only expanded their consolidated business ventures under the new economic boom. With a new generation of young immigrant gang members, there were reports of extortion, not only from small shopkeepers, but from new garment and restaurant owners. When workers in these garment shops and restaurants struck for higher wages, it was reported that gang members—similar to the enforcers who had worked with the anti-Communist league during the 1950s—threatened violence against labor organizers.[21] Finally, there were claims that some business elites, who now had ties to international capital, financed the trafficking of heroin into the United States.[22]

But the youths who provide enforcement for this new Chinatown economy are not the venerated tong soldiers who once held power and prestige within the tong itself. In keeping with their new image as legitimate businessmen and real-estate owners, the tongs have rid themselves of soldiers, relying instead on disconnected youth gangs who function as subcontracted "guns for hire." This is especially true for New York's Chinatown. In his discussion of New York's two most powerful tongs, the Hip Sing and An Leung, Kwong notes that "today, tongs sponsor youth gangs who are not members of tongs; they subcontract the dirty work to these gangs. A tong pays a coordinator to recruit and organize a gang. . . . Gang members follow orders from this dai low [elder brother] and have no relations to the tongs."[23]

As such, these youth are in many ways expendable to the tongs and their businesses. It comes as no surprise, then, that numerous teenage gangs have proliferated in Chinatown from the 1970s through the 1990s. These gangs experience a quick rise and an even quicker fall, with little cost to the tongs. Most importantly, these youth absorb the brunt of police criminalization, arrests, and brutality for the tongs.

Police crackdowns against the new set of Chinatown youth gangs are contradictory, to say the least. To all appearances, the police permit Chinatown businesses with gang connections to carry on with business as usual. But when gang violence escalates in Chinatown, creating a precarious situation for the city's tough-on-crime political pundits, and threatening the downtown tourist industry, the police are often called in to clean up the streets. The NYPD and the Manhattan District Attorney's office initiated numerous anti-gang campaigns during the 1970s and 1980s. Meanwhile, federal prosecutors, particularly former U.S.

attorney Rudolph Giuliani, ended a ten-year investigation of the Ghost Shadows gang, securing the first-ever federal conviction of Chinatown gang leaders.[24]

For the most part, however, these anti-gang campaigns were cosmetic initiatives: by cracking down on young Chinese "toughs," the police could reassure the public that they were on top of organized crime in Chinatown. But rarely, if ever, did the police connect these relatively disorganized youth gangs to the highly organized tongs—and it is uncertain whether or not they ever desired to do so. Before long, working-class Chinese youth became the embodiment of crime and punishment in Chinatown. As youth gangs continued to spread throughout the 1980s and into the 1990s, their chaotic proliferation and permeability have allowed the NYPD easily to accuse any Chinatown youth, particularly the unemployed and working poor, of being "gang related."[25]

Young people in Chinatown and in the satellite Chinatowns of Queens and Brooklyn have accused the NYPD of photographing them while they play in public parks, on street corners, and even in front of their apartment buildings. The youths' allegations are consistent with those of other youth in Philadelphia and southern California, where the police have been found to compile "Oriental mugbooks" in a further effort to police Chinatown youth during the 1980s. The photos are inserted in unofficial mug books and are used whenever a crime involving an Asian suspect is reported. As a more routine practice, the police will round up a group of Chinese youth for "questioning," take Polaroid snapshots of the youth while they are being detained, and then add these photos to similar mug books.[26] Thus, even though the youth in the mug book has not committed a crime, and has no criminal record, he or she is automatically a potential suspect in crimes involving Asian perpetrators.

The story of Chinatown's economic boom, its proliferating sector of youth gangs and violence, and the resulting police crackdown against Chinatown youth, illuminate the way in which the emerging Asian American movement, applying a revolutionary nationalist critique, could characterize Chinatown as an internal colony. At the same time, Chinatown's conditions were idiosyncratic. During the early 1970s, as liberal policymakers, sociologists, and even community activists insisted that an increase in jobs and an expansion of businesses in the Black inner city would lead to a decrease in class polarization and gang violence, just the opposite held true for Chinatown under KMT control.

Moreover, police abuse in Black communities was viewed as a systemic program to control the growing sector of unemployed and angry Black youth who were seen as a threat—particularly in the post-riot (post-1968) period. There was wide support for the view that providing these youths with greater opportunities to participate in an economy in which Blacks held a modicum of control might bring an end to brutal policing. But in Chinatown, conversely, capital consolidation of an ethnic elite, the expansion of business, and the exponential growth of low-wage labor *exacerbated* gang violence and the militarized response of the police.

Understanding the ways in which crime and policing in Chinatown thus are deeply connected to capitalist growth allows us to analyze more accurately other sectors of Chinatown that recently have become prime targets of police brutality. CAAAV has documented the effects of an emerging police campaign, particularly active under the Giuliani administration, to control the informal trade in Chinatown. This campaign has focused its efforts against street vendors, small-shop owners, and dollar-van drivers.

STREET VENDORS IN CHINATOWN

The same economic boom that gave rise to Chinatown gangs during the 1970s has also spurred the growth of the informal economic trades, the most popular of which has been street vending. As mentioned earlier, the influx of cheap immigrant labor into Chinatown led to mass proletarianization in the garment and restaurant industries over the past thirty years. Paralleling this growing workforce was an expanding street-vending industry that had become a vital commercial resource to the new Chinatown worker. Workers rely on food vendors for a quick lunch, or for something to take home to their children after a long day of work. Much like the sweatshop workers to whom they sell their goods, food vendors work a difficult twelve-hour shift. Yet, unlike the sweatshop worker, the vendor is located in public or semipublic spaces, and must therefore frequently interact with the general public as well as the police.

For over twenty years, food vendors have been permitted to sell vegetables, hot plates, and fish along the thoroughfares of New York City's Chinatown. But during the mid-1990s, the 5th Precinct in

Chinatown began an initiative that would mark the beginning of the end for the Chinatown industry. In 1996, Mayor Giuliani, at the urging of downtown Business Improvement Districts (BIDS), formed the Street Vendor Review Panel, a committee of mostly Giuliani appointees. As New York City remakes its image to present itself as the financial capital of the world, the Vendor Review Panel's task is to draft legislation that would significantly delimit, if not eliminate, street vendors who had become a thorn in the side of property owners and real-estate developers in gentrifying neighborhoods. Under the pretense of preserving the city's "quality of life"—decongesting sidewalks, beautifying parks, and keeping streets clean of debris—the Review Panel introduced several proposals that would drastically curtail vending on virtually all major city streets.[27] Those facing the most serious removals, however, were vendors from Harlem, Midtown, and Chinatown—neighborhoods marked for gentrification.[28]

Anticipating the proposed vending bill, Mayor Giuliani and the NYPD began clearing the streets. Before introducing any proposed legislation, the NYPD initiated a campaign to remove vendors from the key vending sites in Chinatown that, in effect, reduced the strength of organized protest to emerge when the Review Panel issued its proposal. Fifth Precinct officers began issuing tickets to vendors for the slightest infractions. A food vendor's every action, from the size of her display to where she set it up, from where she kept her cardboard boxes, to how she kept her fingernails, became subject to police regulations and fines. Before long, her very presence on the street was criminalized, as she became the scapegoat for street congestion. Meanwhile, only a few blocks away in Little Italy, cafes were routinely allowed to block sidewalks with their tables and chairs in summertime.[29]

By the late 1990s, paying heavy fines for the smallest violation had become so routine to Chinatown vendors that many had figured these fines into their monthly operating cost.[30] Some vendors still claim to be fined up to four times per week, which amounts to an annual total of about $6,000 in fines. Even if a vendor stood a chance of fighting these tickets in court, most immigrant vendors cannot afford to take a day off from work. Paying the fine turns out to be less expensive than closing shop for a day. Such vigilant policing resulted in a dramatic decline in the number of street vendors in Chinatown, from three hundred in 1993 to sixty in 1997.[31]

The most glaring act of police harassment of vendors came in the fall of 1998, as the "Triangle Vendors"—those who vend on a triangular-shaped pedestrian mall located at the intersection of Baxter and Canal Streets—were being forced from their spots. The enforcers of the removal claimed that the vendors were to be blamed for street congestion, which gives rise to traffic accidents and incidents of pickpocketing, and hence posed a threat to public safety. Outraged over the absurdity of the charge, the vendors, many of whom had worked on the triangle for over ten years, refused to leave the site. The NYPD ticketed and confiscated their carts, citing them with "sidewalk obstruction" and "refusal to move." Vendors interviewed by CAAAV reported that those who spoke up in protest were punished with additional tickets.[32]

In addition to the food vendors, the NYPD has also targeted the vendors who sell watches, bags, perfumes, and miscellaneous items along Chinatown's busiest strip, Canal Street. On any given day, one can witness a Midtown South Task Force van parked in plain view outside a watch- or perfume-vending stall, which, vendors say, the police indiscriminately raid, confiscating merchandise and cash. The NYPD justified these raids under the pretext that Canal Street vendors violate trademark laws by selling counterfeit items under such brand names as Guess, Gucci, and Ralph Lauren. While there are few, if any, New Yorkers or Chinatown tourists who actually believe they are buying a genuine brand-name item, the police routinely raid the vending stalls. According to the Canal Street vendors, the police simply come into the stalls with garbage bags and confiscate merchandise and cash. No vouchers are made out for goods that are seized; and after the raid is complete, the vendors are never told what happens to the merchandise.[33]

DOLLAR-VAN DRIVERS

Paralleling the growth of satellite Chinatowns was the expansion of the "dollar van" industry. These vans shuttle Chinatown workers, most of whom live in Sunset Park, Brooklyn, and Flushing, Queens, to and from the Chinatown factories and restaurants. They provide a vital service to the workers, as public transportation to Brooklyn (along the N and R

train lines) is considered slow and unreliable, especially for Chinatown's workers who work long hours and whose travel times, therefore, do not coincide with rush hour when public transportation is more
frequent and convenient. In the early to mid-1990s, dollar-van driving,
on the whole, was an unregulated trade. But this lack of regulation was
not the choice of van owners and drivers; rather, it was the consequence
of city politicians who refused to legalize dollar-van driving fully because the Metropolitan Transit Authority cried foul at the potential loss
of Chinatown subway riders.[34] Here, too, in an effort to crack down on
the dollar-van driving industry, the NYPD targeted the van drivers.

Although the regulation of dollar-van driving traditionally rested
under the jurisdiction of the Taxi and Limousine Commission (TLC),
Mayor Giuliani transferred TLC street regulation to the control of the
NYPD in 1994. This transfer allows the NYPD to be virtually the sole
regulators of the entire taxi and livery economy of New York City. The
result, many dollar-van drivers claim, has been a pattern of uneven enforcement and the targeting of these drivers. At the time of CAAAV's
investigation of police practices in the dollar-van industry, drivers were
given tickets on a daily basis for violations ranging from parking in "no
parking" zones, seat belt violations, and "improperly displayed licenses," to operating a vehicle without a first-aid kit. Under some circumstances, vans were towed away by police inspectors, costing the
van driver close to one thousand dollars in tickets and tow fees. In several instances, drivers and their passengers had been stopped by police
on the Brooklyn-Queens Expressway where, following an inspection,
the police evacuated the passengers (leaving them on the side of the
highway) and towed the van away.[35]

In many ways, the selective enforcement that has limited the
growth of Chinatown's new informal economy starkly resembles similar policing tactics that were once deployed in Chinatowns during the
late nineteenth century. The San Francisco ordinances that closed down
nearly three hundred Chinese laundries in 1870, and New York City
building restrictions that targeted overcrowded Chinatown tenements
during the 1890s, are but two examples. That these racist and anti-immigrant ordinances have experienced a revival in the late twentieth
century—a period marked by heightened xenophobia and anti-immigrant legislation—should not come as a complete surprise. Yet what is
perhaps most surprising is the apparent complicity of contemporary
Chinatown business elites in the assault on the informal economy.

CHINESE BENEVOLENCE

At the height of their struggle to remain on the Triangle, the Triangle vendors appealed to Chinese Consolidated Benevolent Association (CCBA), a community organization operated by pro-KMT business elites. For the greater part of the twentieth century, the CCBA has insisted on positioning itself as a veritable welfare state for Chinatown community members. Yet the vendors' appeal for help fell on deaf ears, as leaders of the CCBA refused to use their influence in negotiations with the 5th Precinct. The police, meanwhile, suggested that the vendors move into the Dragon Gate market, a vacant lot on Grand Street that the Parks Department had designated for vending. In order to vend in Dragon Gate, however, vendors had to pay several hundred dollars a month to the Parks Department. In addition, they were required to build vending stalls that adhered to city regulations—another huge cost. In the meantime, Dragon Gate, the only open-air market in Chinatown, had been secretly marked for demolition by the Parks Department. The plan, many vendors claim, was to push the vendors into Dragon Gate by the winter of 1998/1999 and then shut the entire market down by the spring of 1999.[36]

When news of the impending demolition of Dragon Gate reached the vendors and the broader Chinatown community, CAAAV worked with vendors to organize a community takeover of the market. The objective was to have community members squat the market and prevent the demolition. This action, coupled with a temporary stay of eviction secured in court by the vendors, was successful in delaying the city's plans. Both Mayor Giuliani and Parks Department commissioner Henry Stern were furious with what had occurred, but their anger was far outmatched by the fury of Chinatown's business leaders. The squatting of Dragon Gate and the concomitant anti-Giuliani protests among Chinatown community members no doubt were inconvenient to Chinatown business leaders, whose interests are consolidated in the CCBA. For years these business leaders had courted the Giuliani administration, hoping to become one of the administration's favored downtown business interests. If the Dragon Gate protests were successful, it would be a serious embarrassment for the efforts of the Chinatown business elites, sending a clear message that they could not keep their house in order.[37] Several days into the takeover, representatives of Chinatown's business interests intervened in the guise of brokering a truce but seemed more intent on disrupting the protests. Some co-opted absentee vendors who advocated vacating the market and negotiating with the city on a more formal basis. Others claimed to have a direct line to the mayor's office, assuring protesters that the mayor would meet with representatives to work out a reasonable compromise.[38]

The actions of Chinatown business leaders during the Dragon Gate struggle are perhaps the clearest example of the crucial role the elites play in the regulation and disciplining of Chinatown's working poor. Although the informal economy supplements the economic boom of Chinatown by providing basic services to the Chinatown worker, it is paradoxically viewed as a threat to the restructured economy. Much like the youth gangs who reportedly perform enforcement services, the informal trades are both necessary and despised by Chinatown's unofficial power structure. The informal trades remind Chinatown investors that the capital-heavy "new" Chinatown fundamentally rests on the old: unregulated, ephemeral, and impoverished small trades. The role of the police is to mediate this contradiction.

But it is also worth mentioning here that the function of the police is not limited to protecting the interests of Chinatown elites. Indeed, their regulation of Chinatown has much to do with maintaining of racial segregation of urban space. It is no news that racial tensions have always existed on the borders of Chinatown and Little Italy/SoHo. Chinatown—a community founded in response to historical racist exclusion of Chinese people in the United States labor markets and residential neighborhoods—finds itself having to accommodate the growing number of Asian immigrants while being geographically hemmed in. Bound by the courts and the financial district on one side, and the East River on the other, the only direction in which it can expand is northward. Chinese merchants who pioneered the northern expansion by setting up shops in abandoned streets in the 1980s now find themselves the targets of harassment and apparent anti-immigrant sentiment in the form of lawsuits filed by local merchants and residents who want to eliminate certain loading and forklifting operations of Chinatown wholesale produce businesses. In addition to alleging sidewalk congestion and safety issues, these lawsuits cite the adverse effect of these operations on the "historic" character and "aesthetic" value of the Little Italy and Soho neighborhoods that these businesses border.[39] (Apparently, the presence of café tables and chairs on the sidewalks of tourist-drawing Little Italy does not qualify as a "nuisance" or improper use of public space.) Ostensibly to improve the "quality of life" of the neighborhood, the police, acting as a border patrol, reinforce the targeting of these wholesale businesses by subjecting Chinese merchants to excessive fines and other forms of harassment.[40]

Due to such systemic efforts to delimit Chinatown geographically, Chinese immigrants have formed Chinatowns in other boroughs. In Sunset Park, Brooklyn, historically a white neighborhood, the increase in the number of Chinese residents and stores in the past decade has led to racial tensions between Chinese and white neighbors. Some NYPD officers, apparently acting as self-appointed agents to police white turf, have refused to protect Chinese crime victims and used physical force to discipline Chinese residents. In 1993, when a Chinese woman went to the local police and sought the arrest of her white neighbor who vandalized her home and threatened her children with a gun, she reported that the police response was, "Arrest them yourself," and "If you don't like it here, you can go back to China."[41] In 1996, the Committee Against Anti-Asian Violence saw an increase in police-brutality claims against Chinese people arising out of landlord-tenant disputes in Sunset Park. In one claim, a Chinese woman reported the following exchange: after physically attacking the woman, an officer said to her, "I'm teaching you a lesson, because you Chinese people are taking over this neighborhood."[42]

CONCLUSION

Following the killing of Yong Xin Huang, activists organized a series of demonstrations to pressure the Brooklyn district attorney to present a strong case before the grand jury called to consider possible criminal charges against Officer Mizrahi. When the grand jury failed to return an indictment, scores of protesters from around the city descended on the steps of the Brooklyn District Attorney's Office to condemn the decision. Among these protesters was a strong showing of Chinatown workers: sweatshop workers, restaurant workers, and vendors. Their presence represented both a demonstration of solidarity with the Huang family (Huang's mother was a member of the International Ladies Garment Workers Union) and an expression of frustration over the intense and brutal policing that the working poor of the Chinese community experience on a day-to-day basis. The killing of Huang and the failure of the criminal justice system to prosecute Mizrahi awakened these workers from any ambivalence they may have felt toward the criminalization of Chinatown youth by the police.

While justice marches for Huang were being organized in China-town, workers at Jing Fong, Chinatown's largest restaurant, were in the middle of an intense labor struggle with owners. The combination of anti-police-brutality and labor protests turned Chinatown into a poten-tially volatile arena of protest during the summer of 1995. Both sets of protests seemed to be feeding off each other. Apparently fearing a po-tential tidal wave of protest, some business leaders in Chinatown sought to decouple the two protest struggles by holding a private meet-ing with the Huang family. During this meeting, they promised the Huang family that they would do everything in their power to secure justice for Yong Xin, so long as the family signed a letter stating that the Justice for Yong Xin campaign was in no way tied to the labor struggle at Jing Fong.[43] The letter later appeared in the Chinese language news-paper, *Sing Tao Daily*.[44]

This move anticipated something that the protesters had yet to see: the most dangerous threat to the Chinatown power structure was a united front among the different sectors of the Chinatown poor. The ex-tent to which Chinatown's poor population works toward a solidarity of this kind will determine the shape of local politics in Chinatown in the new century—and offers the best case for empowering Chinatown's most disenfranchised members.

NOTES

1. These questions were posed to the family of Yong Xin Huang as well as to CAAAV by reporters covering the incident.

2. The most notorious instance was that of Anthony Rosario and Hilton Vega, who were found face down, spread-eagled, shot twenty-one times. See David Stout, "Failed Robbery Tactic Led To Fatal Shootout in Bronx," *New York Times*, January 14, 1995:28; Matthew Purdy, "Pathologist Says 2 Men Killed by Police Were Shot While Lying on the Floor," *New York Times*, August 3, 1995:B(5); Matthew Purdy and Garry Pierre-Pierre, "Police Barrage Still Re-sounds; Investigators Feud over Bronx Killings," *New York Times*, August 20, 1995:35. Another is Anibal Carasquillo, who had been shot in the back. See "Man Is Fatally Shot by Officer in Brooklyn," *New York Times*, January 23,

1995:B(2); Bob Herbert, "In America; Sickness in the N.Y.P.D.," *New York Times*, October 11, 1996:39.

3. Other cases having a claim to "moral authority" included the shooting of Eleanor Bumpers, an African American grandmother shot and killed by police after they mistakenly targeted her apartment for a raid; Anthony Baez, who died after Officer Francis Livoti administered a chokehold; and Amadou Diallo, fired upon forty-one times by four Street Crime Unit officers who claimed they thought Diallo was involved in several rapes in the area. Linking these incidents is the fact that innocent blood had been shed; most of these victims were unarmed and none had criminal records. See Bob Herbert, "In America; Sickness in the N.Y.P.D.," *New York Times*, October 11, 1996:39; Michael Cooper, "Officers in Bronx Fire 41 Shots, and an Unarmed Man Is Killed," *New York Times*, February 5, 1999:1; Clifford Krauss, "Clash over a Football Ends with a Death in Police Custody," *New York Times*, December 30, 1994:B(1); Benjamin Weiser, "Ex-Officer Guilty in Choking Death," *New York Times*, June 27, 1998:1.

4. In 1997, the Committee Against Anti-Asian Violence was renamed CAAAV: Organizing Asian Communities. Although the acronym has been kept for reasons of familiarity, we have added the subtitle in an effort to emphasize our focus on community organizing as opposed to anti-hate-crime advocacy.

5. A dollar van is an informal car service for Chinatown workers. The vans take workers to and from their homes in Brooklyn and Queens. These vans cost less than public transportation; more importantly, they cut travel time in half for women workers who must return home to care for young children.

6. CAAAV, *Police Brutality in New York City's Asian Communities: A Ten-Year Report (1986–1996)* (on file in the offices of CAAAV, 191 East Third Street, New York, NY).

7. "News Briefs: Settlement in NY Chinatown Labor Dispute," *Asian Week*, October 1997, 10.

8. See K. Connie Kang, "Asian Gang Rise Strikes a Paradox," *Los Angeles Times*, January 25, 1996:3.

9. See Michael Daly, "The War for Chinatown," *New York Times*, February 14, 1983:33.

10. See Paul Tagaki and Tony Platt, "Behind the Gilded Ghetto: An Analysis of Race, Class, and Crime in Chinatown," *Crime and Social Justice*, Spring–Summer 1978:17.

11. They organized street patrols, engaged in direct actions against precincts with police officers who were identified as racist, and were involved in countless shootouts. See, e.g., Elaine Brown, *A Taste of Power: A Black Woman's Story* (New York: Pantheon Books, 1992); Huey Newton, *Revolutionary Suicide* (New York: Harcourt Brace Jovanovich, 1973); Bobby Seale, *Seize the Time: The Story of the Black Panther Party and Huey P. Newton* (New York: Random House, 1970); David Hilliard and Lewis Cole, *This Side of*

Glory: The Autobiography of David Hilliard and the Story of the Black Panther Party (New York: Little, Brown, 1993).

12. See, e.g., The Black Panther Editorial Collective, "To the Brave People of North Vietnam," *The Black Panther: Black Community News Service*, May 2, 1969.

13. Thirteen Point Platform of I Wor Kuen, *Roots: An Asian American Reader* (Los Angeles: UCLA Press, 1971); John Lui, "Towards an Understanding of the Internal Colonial Model," *Counterpoint: Perspectives on Asian America*, 160–168 (Los Angeles: UCLA Press, 1976).

14. See Him Mark Lai, "An Historical Survey of the Chinese Left In America," *Counterpoint: Perspectives on Asian America* (Los Angeles: UCLA Press, 1976).

15. Alex Hing, formerly minister of information for the Red Guard Party and founding member of I Wor Kuen, interviewed by Fred Ho and Steve Yip, in *Legacy to Liberation*, ed. Fred Ho (San Francisco: AK Press, 2000), 288; Getting Together Collective, "Chinatown Youth as Chinese American Workers," *Past and Present: An Anthology of Getting Together* (San Francisco: Getting Together Collective, 1978).

16. See, e.g., Stanford Lyman, *The Asian in North America* (Santa Barbara : ABC-Clio Books, 1977); Jennifer L. Thompson, "Are Chinatown Gang Wars a Cover-up?" *San Francisco Magazine*, February 1976.

17. See Tagaki and Platt, "Behind the Gilded Ghetto."

18. See Peter Kwong, *The New Chinatown*, 26 (New York: Hill and Wang, 1987; 2d ed., 1996).

19. See Kwong, *The New Chinatown*, 29.

20. See, e.g., Victor Nee and Brett de Barry Nee, *Longtime Californ': A Documentary Study of an American Chinatown*, 253 (Palo Alto: Stanford University Press, 1972).

21. See Kwong, *The New Chinatown*, 123.

22. See Seth Faison, "U.S. Indicts Two Businessmen as Chinatown Gang Lords," *New York Times*, September 10, 1994:A4; Arnold H. Lubasch, "Ex-Head of Chinatown Gang Is Guilty of Leading Drug Ring," *New York Times*, December 15, 1992:B1.

23. See Kwong, *The New Chinatown*, 111.

24. See Joseph P. Fried, "New City Unit Combats Chinese Gangs," *New York Times*, June 10, 1981:B(7); Albert Scardino and Alan Finder, "Chinatown Indictments" *New York Times*, February 24, 1985:4(6). See also *U.S. v. Lee*, U.S. Dist. LEXIS 6621, *2–3 (S.D.N.Y. 1990).

25. Recent studies show that nearly half of the youth in Chinatown are not enrolled in school. They are either laboring in sweatshops or looking for work. City of New York, *The Newest New Yorkers: Annual Report 1997*.

26. See Daniel C. Tsang, "Moral Panic Over Asian Gangs," *the ricepaper* 4, no. 1 (Autumn 1993):18.

27. See Hyun Lee, *History of Vending Bill # 511*, official CAAAV document, June 1999 (on file with CAAAV).

28. See proposed Vending Bills #100 and #511.

29. See *CAAAV Internal Bulletin*, August 1997, 6 (on file with CAAAV).

30. See CAAAV, *Chinatown Research Synopsis*, Summer 1997:3.

31. See id. at 8.

32. Interview with Chinatown street vendor, CAAAV, *Chinatown Research Synopsis*, Summer 1997:8–9.

33. See id. at 8–9.

34. See Jonathan Hicks, "Vans of the People Shifting into Legality," *New York Times*, August 17, 1995:B(3); Anthony Ramirez, "Judge Rejects Most of Law on Commuter Van Licenses," *New York Times*, March 24, 1999:B(4).

35. See Affidavit dated June 15, 1996, of L. M., a dollar-van driver (on file with CAAAV).

36. See "Struggle at Dragon Gate," *CAAAV Voice*, Fall 1999:10 (on file with CAAAV).

37. See Andrew Hsiao, "Chinatown Take Out," *Village Voice*, February 23, 1999:29; Julian Barnes, "Street Vendors Protest Ouster from a Busy Site in Chinatown," *New York Times*, December 6, 1998:64.

38. See id.

39. See, e.g., *Buckmiller Automatic Sprinkler, Inc. v. Cheong Mei, Inc.*, Order to Show Cause, and supporting papers, Index No. 97/121892, New York State Supreme Court. See also *Soho Alliance v. World Farm Inc.*, Index No. 96/115769, New York State Supreme Court. Reply Affidavit of Carl Rosenstein, para. 10; Sur-reply Affidavit of Benjamin Zelermyer, paras. 14–16.

40. Reports by wholesale vendors to CAAAV organizers during summer and fall 1997.

41. *See* CAAAV, *Police Brutality in New York City's Asian Communities: A Ten-Year Report (1986–1996)*, 13–15.

42. See id.

43. Statement of Joyce Huang and Qing Lan Huang to Hyun Lee, 1995.

44. See letter, *Sing Tao*, 1995.

Polite police state, Cadman Plaza, Brooklyn, New York, April 15, 1999. (Photo by Richard McKewen.)

10

An Interview with Derrick Bell

Reflections on Race, Crime, and Legal Activism

Andrea McArdle

ON AUGUST 3, 1999, lawyer-scholar-author-activist Derrick Bell joined me for a long, wide-ranging conversation about race, crime, law, direct action, and a pedagogy for a new generation of lawyer-activists. Reflecting on his forty years of advocacy and activism, he encourages us to think about police brutality in a broader economic and political context, keeping the focus on how police violence is connected to, and a symptom of, the racism that persists in our political and social structures. He does not romanticize his years of protest and challenge; neither has he become a defeatist. In the end, it is a question of doing "what you think you can do." We have included here highlights from that conversation.

AM: Derrick, one of the points we want to bring to light in this anthology is that the police are part of a larger picture, serving larger economic and political forces.

DB: Absolutely. And whatever problems there are in having authority, and having to deal with that authority in a measured way, a political and economic climate that encourages excessive responses exacerbates the problem that already exists. So you know, in that sense the economic and political problems that you identified are directly linked up with the way the police are being encouraged to behave. It seems clear to me that the police respond not only to direct instructions as to how to do the job, but also to silently conveyed instructions, which blend with what many of them have known and believed most of their lives about the dangerous character of black people, particularly black men. If the public has this deep sense that blacks are basically dangerous, and if elected officials see it's politically advantageous to focus on black street crime, they will do it. If the whole prison industry sees an advantage in filling prisons with blacks and Hispanics to bring in employment to local communities, and if the police are a part of that complex, they are contributing to the perpetuation of racism even when they are not actively abusing people. Even when they are doing the job according to the book. When they are not pulling out guns and shooting folk, when they are not beating them up and torturing them. It's not only those brutality incidents, but the whole function of the system has been twisted.

AM: Yet, when people do step back and acknowledge racism and become critical, what seems to exercise them, or at least the media, the most, are instances of abuse by the police. Why the focus on abusive policing as opposed to other ways in which racism manifests itself in the administration of criminal law?

DB: I think there is an unconscious willingness to let abuse go on unless it is beyond the pale. Look what it took before Governor Whitman finally conceded that there was a problem with racial profiling by the New Jersey state police. The evidence indicated that profiling was not only happening but was being encouraged, that it was ongoing for several years, that if you wanted to be promoted, you had to bring in any number of blacks. I notice now some officers in New York's Street Crime Unit are going back to plainclothes operations after six months in uniform, because they haven't picked up as many guns. Now we have to take it for granted that the police are telling us the truth about the reduced number of guns that have been taken. But it's clear, if they did that in the white community, if they stopped everybody coming down the street, they would pick up a whole lot of white folks for guns and drugs.

I guess I'm saying that I don't know that it is a cause for either praise or potential for improvement that the major incidents of brutality get a lot of media attention for awhile. As far as the media goes, you know the word is that "if it bleeds it leads." Now usually that's blacks committing crime and particularly blacks committing crimes against whites. That gets plenty of attention, but serious incidents of police brutality do also, people turn on the television and they talk about it and debate it one way or the other. Mayor Giuliani responds one way and Al Sharpton responds the other way, and this is theater.

AM: It's theater. These are egregious incidents.

DB: And even with the egregious cases, like Louima, the only people who were convicted in the [first federal] criminal case were those officers against whom other white officers testified, corroborating Louima. The cops charged with assaulting him in the car, when Louima was the only source of testimony, were acquitted.

AM: I'd like to raise with you a more specific question about the impact of race upon police culture. Many critics have suggested that one way to improve the situation in communities like New York City is to require officers to live in the communities where they work. Would that result in less pernicious stereotyping?

DB: Certainly less fear. For the NYPD really to go forward with the community policing plan that Lee Brown, former police commissioner and a black man, really got started (and didn't get much credit for)—having police there live in the community, it would be a great thing. But, as a political reality, to require officers to live within the city limits, it would be easier to repeal the lottery than to get the state legislature to change the rules and then get the city officials to actually implement residence rules for police.

AM: Some critics call for altering the demographics of police forces so that they are more reflective of the city's population. Certain patterns of employment are entrenched. Often, white police officers come from families and past generations of police, but there has not been a comparable long tradition of black police officers.

DB: That's right, and it makes recruitment of minority officers difficult. But I think one of the things that kind of pattern encourages is solidarity among those in the minority. Groups of black police organize and speak out against abusive treatment of people in the community. It takes great courage to do that.

AM: Others suggest that there's an autonomous police culture out there. No matter what one's race or sexuality or gender, police officers become socialized and a part of this larger culture, which obscures all of those differences that some people think could make a difference. And I wondered what you thought about that?

DB: I think there is a little truth in that. If all police officers were minorities born in poor neighborhoods, that wouldn't guarantee that there wouldn't be abuses.

AM: There's been some evidence of greater community activism in New York City (and around the country as well). The very heavily covered campaign of civil disobedience back in March 1999 at One Police Plaza, where people were coming in daily and being arrested, made a very powerful statement, and got a lot of coverage. There were fairly heavy turnouts at a series of rallies this past year, protesting police brutality. Does this suggest to you a revival of the kind of direct action associated with the civil rights movement during the late '50s and '60s, or do you see this response from the community as something different, coming from a different source?

DB: I think that there are a number of blacks and other people of color, and many whites, who are really outraged by this. Now, what it took to organize the outrage is someone like Reverend Al Sharpton who does not get anywhere near the credit he should. Very few people could do what he has done. He has a very sharp mind. He might not be able to get elected to office, but that's not his role. But I think that there has got to be somebody to organize, to bring together what it is that folks are willing to do. So if he said, "Are we just going to lie down on the street and get run over?" it might not work, but he was able to carefully orchestrate that whole movement so that people kept coming out. A lot of work was done. I think it was worthwhile. It doesn't mean that if we had a referendum on an issue about policing that Giuliani wouldn't get a clear majority. It does show that where there is the right kind of organizing and leadership around a particularly egregious event, folks will respond. That's good news. Sometimes it leads to a little change and sometimes not. I guess the sad part is the reluctance of much of society to recognize brilliance when it comes in black skin. I think about Sharpton and of course I think about Jesse Jackson.

AM: What will it take to sustain the kind of mass response that occurred in the spring? Do you think Al Sharpton can?

DB: No. Nobody can. [Martin Luther] King couldn't. But that doesn't mean you don't try. It's not a reason for defeatism or despair.

AM: That's something you suggested in *Confronting Authority*[1]—that there is something self-affirming about individual action.

DB: Sometimes you can't easily predict when one person who does something will bring about something else. Not total reform but improvement over what was. Rosa Parks created a spark, a feeling that carried people along for quite a while. I guess the goal for some of us, particularly the seniors in the group, is at least to utilize our experience to look beyond or behind the surface issues and to what creates the turmoil to the system. You don't have to win in the usual measure to do it. What's key is the willingness to do it.

AM: What about the possibility of coalitions? In New York City, for example, there are members of many communities who have had violent encounters with the police, and these communities have reason to bring police misconduct to light. Yet there hasn't been much of a history of communities working together. You've written, in *Afroatlantica Legacies*,[2] for example, that coalitions have possibilities and limitations. Many of us believe that collaborative strategies are more likely to have an impact. Would you address this issue?

DB: The potential of coalition work is always great. The reality is not as great. Each of those interest groups has interests, and they don't necessarily conform except at some very base level. Trying to harmonize various groups' interests is very tough. You'd think that there would have been a great coalition among the civil right groups in the '60s, and for a little while there was. But you didn't want to go too far beyond the surface because there were tensions and rivalries even then. People are people. For example, the NAACP was always a little leery of Dr. King. He was a celebrity, and he didn't necessarily see the big picture that NAACP had mapped out. I think that other minority groups are very leery about joining black groups, because the groups have their own interests. I think they have the sense that blacks are already getting more than their share. But some people are better at working across groups. I think Al Sharpton has done a good job. I think Jesse Jackson was starting to do a good job of organizing groups when he was running for president because he was able to speak beyond race. It's a tough situation, to go from the personal, to the national, to the community. Somebody should be doing it because, as with litigation, you don't want to put all your efforts in one strategy. That's what I tell my students. You should do what you think you can do.

AM: To pull people together and get them to work creatively?

DB: I think that Sharpton has been able to pull people together. He does that amazingly. He motivates people to action. We all need to do what we can, even if it is simply writing a letter, because power does not like any challenge to itself. And all we can do, it seems to me, is nibble away, we'd like to take big nibbles if we could, but nibble away in doing what we can.

AM: There's also the strategy of using litigation to implement a law-reform agenda. You've written more recently that there are limitations to over-reliance on litigated solutions. Yet part of the problem with the police is the failure of the legal system to respond to police criminality. There are options—criminal prosecution or affirmative litigation strategies; for example, the class action brought on behalf of the National Congress for Puerto Rican Rights and others to enjoin the current operations of New York's City's Street Crime Unit. What role can litigation have?

DB: I think some. I think that our problem was we [the NAACP Legal Defense Fund] thought we could do it all. Litigation can be some help. I think using litigation as an affirmative tool also gives an opportunity for real innovation. I guess one example is the city suing gun manufacturers—going after the producers instead of consumers of the instrumentalities of crime. And litigation can be supportive of other activities, like a legislative agenda. It's helpful. I think one of the things we did was to try to set general policy, but our problems are too serious and our power too limited to have a universal strategy. We need to be flexible and do little things that look like they have some potential. What we need is litigation that has as a major thrust protecting white people against the threat of police violence.

AM: This brings to mind a quote from Patricia Williams, "Police states are always safe until you step on a crack in the sidewalk."[3] Ultimately, everybody is at risk. In a trivial way there already has been a hint of that in the effort to enforce some of the quality-of-life ordinances. Mayor Giuliani announced that anybody who didn't cross at the corner was subject to prosecution for jaywalking, do you remember? The plan raised such a hue and cry that the city abandoned it. Obviously, this is a very minor example of overpolicing. But the idea that something like that was contemplated suggests what is happening as we move to a police state. As a strategist, how do you articulate that threat so people see it as something that isn't just confined to one part of the population?

DB: One of the great difficulties of reform is coming to grips with the fact that most people are not reformers and accept existing policies. Let me give you an example. I imagine how tough it would be to try to organize people to do away with the state lottery. Changes in law that we think are very important can be difficult to bring about through litigation. Partly it's a problem of how lawyers are trained to think about these strategies. I think that one of the things that we who teach in law school miss is the opportunity to portray more vividly those kinds of challenges. There are a lot of folks who come to law school and get sidetracked. They come with the idea of doing good through the law, and learn that it's tough to do good.

AM: But that raises a point too, that constitutional law and other legal doctrine can be taught in a very abstract way. And students can learn what the principles of the cases stand for, but there are also human stories that generate these cases. You teach a law course that, among other things, asks your students to write Op Ed pieces that draw on constitutional law doctrine but also on policy and the students' personal experience. If you're habituating a generation of lawyers to come up with innovative litigation strategies to fight a systemic problem, maybe it has partly to do with the ability to get beyond the abstraction and think about the impact that certain rules have on people's lives.

DB: It's hard. It's not for every student. Some feel they don't learn the rules that way, but that's part of the matrix. There is evil out there, but some people perceive it differently. The police brutality problem gives us an opportunity, gives us an entry, maybe only a look through a keyhole more than a real entry, into ways of getting advocates to stay focused on the human problem.

AM: Can we follow up on that point? Can we give the generation of lawyers to come a different kind of orientation about the law that is less tied to precedent—to think differently about the law, to create opportunities for change? Could this be a way to combine legal activism and individual direct action?

DB: Audre Lorde said that you can't destroy the master's house with the master's tools.[4] Well, I think there is a message there for even the best-intentioned lawyers. We look at the civil rights movement from a long perspective, and we see that the gains that were made were the gains that benefited overall society. Even though most of that society was resistant. There was tremendous resistance to school desegregation, and most black kids are still not attending good schools; but the school systems no longer are burdened with the need or pretense of maintaining a dual school system. They can discriminate on a whole range of bases and not ever deal with overt segregation. And those blacks who have moved up are seen as proof that there is no discrimination. So it's hard to get across the fact that much of the civil rights progress has been really progress for white people rather than for blacks. And the seeming compulsion to subordinate blacks remains. I think that part of lawyers' training is making them aware of the fact that their work is likely going to do more to support the system that they despise than it does to help the people they are trying to help. When I left Harvard the first time in 1980 to become dean of University of Oregon Law School, my friend Reverend Peter Gomes said to me that "as a law school dean you are an evil."[5] He said as dean you are going to reward expectations that you should disappoint and you're going to disappoint expectations that you should reward. Most of the time you're not going to know the difference, so what you have to do every morning is look in the mirror and say, I am a dean and thus I am an evil, but today I'm going to try to be a necessary evil. Well, that's the message to get across to law students thinking about their role in relation to the system. As lawyers working in the system they are evil, but with real care and even more real humility, they can from time to time be a necessary evil.

NOTES

1. Derrick Bell, *Confronting Authority: Reflections of an Ardent Protestor* (Boston: Beacon Press, 1994).

2. Derrick Bell, *Afroatlantica Legacies* (Chicago: Third World Press, 1998).

3. Patricia Williams, "On Innocence and Ignorance: Police Brutality and the Mayoral Race in New York," *The Nation* 265, no. 10 (October 6, 1997), 10.

4. Audre Lorde. "The Master's Tools Will Never Dismantle the Master's House," in *This Bridge Called My Back: Writings By Radical Women of Color*, 98, 99–100, ed. Cherrie Moraga and Gloria Anzaldua (Watertown, Mass.: Persephone Press, 1981).

5. With permission of the Reverend Peter Gomes.

11

Organizing at the Intersections

A Roundtable Discussion of Police Brutality through the Lens of Race, Class, and Sexual Identities

Dayo Folayan Gore, Tamara Jones, and Joo-Hyun Kang

THE AUDRE LORDE Project (ALP) is the nation's only center for lesbian, gay, bisexual, two-spirit,[1] and transgender[2] (LGBTST) people of color communities. In 1997, ALP added a Working Group on Police Violence to its organizing initiatives in response to increasing reports of police violence directed against LGBTST people of color in New York City. At that time, police brutality had once again emerged to plague America's national consciousness. ALP organizers realized the need to expand the public's understanding of police brutality in order to illuminate better the complexities of the problem. Specifically, we addressed the ways in which interactions of both race and sexual identities shape how LGBTST communities of color experience police violence, and how this deepens our understanding of police brutality. This need was especially urgent given Mayor Rudolph Giuliani's nationally and internationally recognized tough-on-crime policies, and his "defend the police at all costs" attitude.

In the past several years, high-profile cases across the country have highlighted the unique and often lethal role of state violence in the everyday lives of people of color. Some of these cases have provided the dominant media images of police brutality in the contemporary United States: the video replays of Los Angeles Police Department officers violently beating a subdued Rodney King; a battered Abner Louima cloaked in hospital garb after being sexually assaulted with a wooden stick (originally thought to be a toilet plunger) by police officers in the bathroom of a Brooklyn precinct; and the bullet-ridden doorway where officers from the New York City Street Crimes Unit, in a case of mistaken identity, fired forty-one bullets and killed the unarmed Amadou Diallo in front of his Bronx home.

White male police officers unleashing their fury on black men has historically provided the framework of mainstream discussions of police violence and abuse. But while the media and many activists have used these images to demonstrate the ways in which racism and abuses of power inform policing in our society, these images most often are driven by an overly simplistic analysis of race and racism in this country. Such analysis understands police brutality as acts by individual officers who harbor racial prejudice. This limited analysis tends to support narrow definitions of police brutality—where the only valid examples of brutality are cases of murder or extreme physical violence by individual officers—and have therefore produced responses that privilege litigation and oversight committees (that are largely symbolic and often lack meaningful power) over grassroots street and community organizing.

In large part, such "solutions" still remain dependent on, and fail to alter, the flawed structures of the state and institutional police power that are at the root of the problem. By focusing on individual cases of "excessive force" and individual "racist cops," they ignore issues of systemic racism. They have produced a silence around the crucial roles that gender and sexuality have played in shaping police brutality and have limited our understanding of policing as a social function. The public emphasis on cases involving the severe beating and murder of black and Latino men leaves little room to discuss other victims of police abuse. For the majority of poor, working-class, and people-of-color communities (including Asian and Pacific Islander, Arab, and Native American/Indigenous peoples), these popular definitions and analyses do not reflect much of their own experiences with police violence and abuse on a daily basis.

As government officials tout the benefits of a larger and tougher police force, link aggressive policing to urban economic redevelopment, and call for increased policing of moral and social behavior, we must be particularly aware of the ways in which the police operate in our communities. For behind celebrations of decreasing crime rates and increasing economic prosperity there hides a much bleaker picture. Recent studies have pointed to an increase in police harassment and abuse in communities of color, the rapid tracking of youth of color and the unemployed into the criminal justice system, and a continued rise in homophobic violence and hate crimes.[3] These numbers only begin to suggest the everyday experiences of violence and abuse that occur in our communities. It is these experiences, often silenced in the media and mainstream consciousness, which so demand our attention.

Thus, it was within this context that members of ALP's Working Group on Police Violence (Dayo Gore and Tamara Jones) and ALP's executive director (Joo-Hyun Kang) sat down to talk about police brutality and its intersections with issues of race, class, sexuality, and gender. We enter this work and discussion as lesbian and bisexual women of color working in people-of-color and LGBTST communities.

TAMARA JONES: We define police brutality as any form of abuse of power committed by police officers. When we define the problem in this way, then it's not confined only to physical attacks and murder. It includes all of the other ways in which the police fail to fully serve the people that they are charged with protecting—our communities. Therefore, we include under acts of police violence failure to properly investigate crimes when they are reported, verbal harassment and verbal attacks by the police, illegal stops, searches, and seizures in our neighborhoods which often are a reflection of the police's own racist assumptions and stereotyping.

JOO-HYUN KANG: It's also important to note that police violence can result from the normal operating procedures of police departments if those procedures deny community members a thorough or timely response to reported crimes. For example, New York City Police Department's "forty-eight-hour rule" allows officers who have shot and even murdered citizens to avoid providing an immediate accounting of their actions to authorities. Evidence of possible wrongdoing can therefore be covered up more easily as cops "get their stories straight."

DAYO FOLAYAN GORE: A complete definition of police violence also demands that we examine the ways in which specific social communities—not just geographic neighborhoods—are targeted. For example, we've known for years now that queer youth of color get stopped and frisked on the West Side piers in Manhattan [a popular hangout spot for LGBTST youth].[4] In addition, over the past two years we've been hearing more about how people of transgender experience, especially transgender and transsexual women, have been targeted in the West Village, in the borough of Queens, and in other areas of NYC with harassment and arrests by cops who assume that all transgenders are engaging in sex work.

TAMARA: Apart from the outright physical attacks on members of our communities, the law as it is currently constituted and interpreted allows the police to determine who and how we can be—even within our communities. Many of us have gotten accustomed to the police monitoring and questioning our physical movements, our right to assemble and to speak freely, our organizations, and even our right to be on the street—there is just a general surveillance that takes place on an everyday basis. People don't become outraged as much by these acts because they are so pervasive and constant that they've become normalized. That's why broadening the definition of police violence is important in getting us to recognize that that presence and those actions by the police are also intolerable abuses of power and not acceptable crime-fighting tactics.

DAYO: There's the perception that this everyday surveillance is the price some in our society have to pay in order to have a viable safe life for everyone. The belief is that if you want crime down, then you have to accept the police searching people as they enter the subway in certain neighborhoods, or when they are driving in certain areas. Specific communities are subject to more policing because of this. Certain people and communities have come to be seen as more threatening to society than others.

JOO-HYUN: Who are you talking about specifically when you talk about "certain people and communities"?

DAYO: Poor and working-class people of color are commonly devalued and seen by the police as suspect. Often having limited economic opportunities, their very presence is viewed as a threat to a secure and viable society, or what here in New York City our mayor calls a certain "quality of life." People who are openly lesbian, gay, bi, or transgender are also often marked as not contributing to a proper "quality of life." So these communities often become the easiest targets of police abuse, as people who do not have the economic resources or social power that is deemed valuable or worthy of protection.

TAMARA: The police do not function strictly to apprehend people who violate the law. Part of their function as well is to uphold the values of the community. Mayor Giuliani's "Quality of Life" campaign is a really good example of this, as is the social agenda of the Republican-led Congress. I do think that when you have particularly conservative governments that are sending out strong messages about conservative "values," and at the same time are cutting back on funding for programs that build competent public infrastructure to serve marginalized and poor communities, then at those moments acts of police brutality do go up. Because it's not simply about punishing criminal behavior; there is also the process of criminalizing that which is seen as not valuable. In a Giuliani local environment, in a Republican national environment, and increasingly under Democratic administrations as well, the communities that are most desired don't have a lot of people of color, or LGBTST people, and certainly not LGBTST people of color at the center of those communities. Often we're being tolerated at the margins, if at all, and more often than not our very existence is seen as a threat to the "moral fiber" of the community.

JOO-HYUN: This is especially true the more gender variant[5] a person is, or if they are a person of color, or if they find that the only visible spaces they know to meet other LGBTST people are in public spaces. And this goes back to our definition of the problem as well. Because when we talk about abuse of power, what we're talking about is the police as an extension of the state, and so it's not simply an issue of morals and values. There doesn't have to be a match between the values and morals of individual police officers, the business/corporate-class and elected officials. It's more a matter of the police carrying out what those in power (whether corporate interests, economically privileged sectors of society, or elected officials) set up. I think it's important to note that there is actually a shrinking of public space as spaces become more privatized. Public land is increasingly being sold to private business as part of local development plans. It means that fewer people are able to use those spaces. And their use of the space, which used to be an unquestioned right, is now being questioned and in some cases even made illegal. We've seen this with the Giuliani administration's outlawing of street vendors to protect interests of some business owners— thereby depriving some immigrant communities of workplaces that they had developed. And we see it with the redevelopment going on by the Piers, which used to be one of the spaces where queer young people of color and trans communities and other communities often congregated. While folks still go there, they're also harassed by cops for "loitering" in what used to be assumed as public space.

DAYO: Public space is becoming privatized in very specific ways that are raced and classed. That privatization is linked to the general economic changes happening in cities around the country, as gentrification influences not only housing prices but police presence and the treatment of lower income residents and people of color in these communities. Often this notion of "reclaiming" American cities is used, which raises the question of "from whom?"

JOO-HYUN: And "for whom?"

DAYO: People can really grasp the idea of race being used to profile and to police people. But it's harder for most people to talk about policing linked to other social categories like gender and sexuality. I think it's important to talk about the ways that gender and sexuality stereotypes operate in instances of police violence: how all too often people perceived as nonheterosexual are subject to greater police abuse and surveillance.[6] Whether it is transgender women who are harassed because they're assumed to be prostitutes or the ways in which same-sex cruising has been criminalized here in New York City.

TAMARA: Stonewall[7] is a good place to start because people often think of police violence as these very public and dramatic acts, you know, a case of a clear wrong that outrages. But even before the Stonewall uprising happened, there was a history of the police coming into the clubs under the force of law—perfectly legal—to check people's identifications and to see if people were wearing the "right" kind of clothing for their gender. We all know there were times when members of LGBTST communities were arrested and brutalized in these situations, simply because they did not fit society's gender norms.

JOO-HYUN: We also have a history of lesbians, gay men, and transgender folk fighting back against this abuse. That's an example of historically what queer communities have dealt with in terms of being policed and being the target of state repression. Interestingly, while many folks in the U.S. would point to Stonewall as the start of gay liberation in this country, it is rarely referenced in discussions of police brutality or in contemporary queer discourse as an example of police violence.

DAYO: Yes! I think this is a really important silence to acknowledge. Stonewall powerfully highlights some of the ways police violence has historically affected LGBTST communities, yet as you said there is this erasure of Stonewall as an example of police violence—and community rebellion against it, in LGBTST activism and in most LGBTST organizing against police brutality. I think such historical amnesia helps to silence or to mask the ways conceptions of sexuality and gender have shaped police violence.

JOO-HYUN: In New York City we're hearing more and more stories of people who identify as transgender being harassed and beaten by cops on a consistent basis, especially if they are suspected of being sex workers—and almost any visibly gender-variant trans folk, particularly women of transgender experience, are automatically suspected of being sex workers. In August of this year, a woman of transgender experience was falsely arrested for soliciting right across the street from the Lesbian and Gay Services Center in Manhattan. And this was just minutes after she had left a meeting for outreach workers who work with transgender communities. Her "crime" was to chat with a man who beckoned to her from across the street. And for this she was handcuffed and spent several days at Rikers Island prison. All of this under the guise of a "morals sweep" that officers were conducting that night.

Because of the transphobic[8] environment of precincts, people of transgender experience will often not go to report these incidents. Other issues emerge for folks of transgender experience, including which holding pen they get put into when they are arrested—the women's or the men's. Also, there is a lot of ridicule and embarrassment involved in these incidents.

DAYO: Such policing of gender and sexuality is often done under the guise of lowering crime and ensuring public safety. This form of justification isolates so many LGBTST people and people of color by presenting our rights and safety as being in conflict with the "public good." I do think the type of police surveillance that LGBTST people face is connected not only to the enforcement of "moral standards," but also to our increasing visibility and to the assertion of our right to use public spaces. The right to walk around the streets holding hands with my lesbian partner is a way of asserting that this is my community and I can be here as much as anyone else. But policing makes people think about such acts a little more. If being subject to police abuse—in addition to homophobic violence from people on the street—is an everyday occurrence, then you are more likely to change what you do in order to avoid such encounters.

TAMARA: And also knowing that even if the police are not the perpetrators of violence in a particular incident, they might not protect you or take you seriously if you report the incident. In fact, they might use that moment to subject you to additional violence by ridiculing you, making you feel like it was your fault because you're "not normal," charging you with soliciting, or simply not taking your complaint seriously.

DAYO: Who has the economic resources to access and command police power to work on their behalf? I think this question is important in understanding how conceptions of race, class, and sexuality both intersect and overshadow each other in issues of policing. For example, last summer there was an incident of homophobic violence in which several Latino men were reported to have attacked a white lesbian (calling out homophobic slurs and cutting her with a knife) who had just left a lesbian bar in Brooklyn. In response to the attack, the bar owners held a community meeting in which a group of mostly white lesbians demanded increased police presence on the streets outside the bar as the first step in addressing the problem of homophobic violence. While such a response is not surprising, I found it particularly troublesome considering the bar is located in a predominantly people-of-color and immigrant neighborhood, and faces increasing rents and policing as white-owned businesses and residents are gentrifying the area. Yet those putting forth this call for increased policing seemed to have few misgivings about the impact such a strategy might have on neighborhood relations, or how it would feed into a racialized and classed "us versus them" mentality.

JOO-HYUN: In that case, increased police presence was offered as the primary solution to anti-gay attacks in that neighborhood, even though some of us pointed out that this wouldn't stop those of us who are also people of color from being harassed by the police, who are generally white. But that seemed to be of secondary concern to many of the white gays and lesbians in the room that day. It's important to note that some of the women of color reacted in similar ways—which makes me wonder about the ways in which women

are so victimized by violence on a daily basis that the illusion of police protection becomes increasingly appealing.

All of this in spite of the fact that because of the way race, class,
and sexuality operate together, the police usually are more likely to
view LGBTST people of color, especially men of color, as criminals—because of their race—than as possible victims of anti-gay violence. Thus, race masks sexuality, and the complexities of the lives
of gay men of color are sacrificed to the more familiar racial stereotypes. Unfortunately, this is also mirrored among white LGBTST
people. So even though LGBTST people of color fall victim to anti-
gay violence, these incidents rarely promote a public outcry in the
white LGBTST community for action by the police.

DAYO: And we saw that clearly just last year. In 1998, there were a number of reported cases of anti-gay attacks and murders. In NYC, a
significant number of unsolved murders of LGBT people were of
gay men of color and transgender people of color. Yet, many white
LGBTST activists largely ignored this fact. Much of the mobilization of white LGBT people focused on attacks against white victims
or on attacks which took place in the West Village and Chelsea, both
of which are predominantly white gay neighborhoods.

JOO-HYUN: In other words, it's easy for race to trump all other identities in the eyes of the police who would be on the lookout for attackers who are working class and/or of color, and in the eyes of activists who see victims as targeted only by sexual orientation. For
those of us who identify as both people of color *and* LGBTST *and*
working class, the complexities of our lives can be reduced to just
one identity by those incapable of grasping it in its fullness. Our position at the intersection means that we have to consider the impact
of policing on ALL of our communities. There is no "them," only
"us." So even when we are not personally targeted by the police, we
know our heterosexual brothers and sisters of color will be—especially young people who are often scapegoated as the main perpetrators of homophobic and transphobic attacks.

TAMARA: But the reason there is this automatic turn to the police for
protection is that LGBTST communities are under such attack that
our very survival is at stake, so there's a lot of short-term decision
making.

JOO-HYUN: Those of us who are taxpayers feel like we can demand that
our tax dollars get used for police protection. And it gets further

complicated because women—lesbians, bisexual, and women of transgender experience—face daily acts of verbal assault and threats of physical attacks. Many of us don't even see it as unusual. Unfortunately, we've incorporated it into how we approach our daily lives—knowing that it's a rare and precious day when we're not subjected to some form of misogynist abuse.

TAMARA: And marginalized communities—particularly working class, poor, people-of-color communities—often either lack the resources to create alternative policing institutions, or community-based institutions located in poor or people-of-color communities are simply overtaxed because the demand for their services outweigh what they can supply. So, you're caught in a bind if you're in a marginal community coming under attack.

Also, people-of-color communities are not necessarily more immune to homophobia and anti-gay violence. Fighting racism doesn't mean that people of color automatically fight against other systems of oppression, like sexism and heterosexism.[9] In fact, communities of color have internal struggles against gender bias. Black women have been speaking out against this for a long time. The sad truth is that marginalized communities often mimic oppressive forces on one front even as we fight against them on another. So when we are talking about anti-gay attacks and police violence directed against LGBTST people of color, homophobia in communities of color also throws a blanket of silence over our battered bodies.

Dayo, I want to go back to your image of walking hand in hand with your girlfriend on the streets. In talking about our experiences as LGBTST people of color with this problem of police violence, it's clear that our relationships to our home communities are very complex. It's not very easy to imagine myself walking hand in hand with my girlfriend in black communities, in Caribbean neighborhoods, because of homophobia in those communities.

DAYO: And as we pointed out earlier, within the broader LGBTST community there is racism. For example, certain lesbian and gay clubs won't let us in if there are too many people of color already inside. So that compounds the problem, because even within these marginalized communities there is still a valuing going on, so that when LGBTST people of color become the target of police brutality or police violence, there is no sense of public outrage or that it's a real problem. We have to think about the degree of isolation and alienation LGBTST people of color face, even within our own home communities because of our location at the intersection of multiple marginalized groups.

JOO-HYUN: And we certainly don't get much social support around such occurrences because of that.

TAMARA: Exactly. As activists against police violence, we all need to be aware of the ways in which oppression can work both against us and against others who may not be exactly like us. If straight activists never integrate gender and sexual identity into their analyses and action programs, then they are supporting and strengthening police abuse of power against women and LGBTST peoples. The same logic holds for white LGBTST activists on this issue; without a solid anti-racist stance, you're not being effective. It's like fighting a Hydra—you need to chop off all the heads to kill it.

JOO-HYUN: You know, it makes me think of the Abner Louima case here in New York City. After the media sensationalized the incident and made it into a national and international cause, what was really terrifying, horrific, and also interesting all at the same time were the ways in which that whole incident was sexualized. The media always said that Louima was innocent because he was a "legal" immigrant—they always said "legal"—and he was a family man, and that he was not gay. And that the cops were wrong for thinking and suspecting that was gay. The question was never raised, but what if he had been gay? Had he been gay, or transgender, it's hard to imagine that degree of public outrage even if it had been the same exact incident. This reality makes our work a lot harder, I think, in terms of trying to do work around police violence issues, but also maintaining that there has to be an anti-homophobic and anti-transphobic analysis within that.

DAYO: In the Louima situation homophobic language was even taken up in our communities of color. At a number of the marches some protesters would chant "Faggot!" at the police. It was viewed as a way of insulting the police and empowering our communities. But it was very isolating and uncomfortable for LGBTST people of color who also had contingents at the marches. How far can we go with a vision of empowerment that is steeped in homophobic attitudes?

TAMARA: Homophobia weakens social-justice movements in communities of color, broadly speaking. Because if the rumor gets started, or the perception is there that the victim is gay, regardless of whether they are gay or not, then you can expect a lower degree of mobilization . . .

JOO-HYUN: . . . and the victims and incidents of violence against them are delegitimized.

TAMARA: That's something that the police know. They count on homophobia among people of color—and within society as a whole—as another weapon that they can use to get away with the abuse, as a way of delegitimizing their victim. Even though it wasn't believed, the Louima case is a good example of the police trying to use this type of logic.

JOO-HYUN: In fact, we saw Marvyn Kornberg [attorney for one of the defendant cops in the Louima case] insinuate in his opening arguments that Louima's vicious injuries could have been the result of *consensual gay sex!* So not only was Kornberg attempting to delegitimize Louima as a victim and survivor of police brutality, his ridiculous theory also served to sensationalize gay sex, conflating queer sexuality with inhumane levels of violence.

TAMARA: This is why social-justice movements, especially in communities of color, have to take issues of heterosexism and homophobia seriously. These issues have to be part of the central analysis that we're developing, because if you don't do it you become vulnerable to manipulation by the forces that you're fighting.

In our society, women are victimized daily and the society becomes desensitized to that abuse. That desensitization affects media coverage of violence against queer people. For example, because transgender communities are seen as less than masculine, and are feminized in the public's mind, then the violence directed against people of male-to-female transgender experience is not seen as outrageous as when it is directed against a heterosexual man. In my community, where the survival of the entire community is reduced to the survival of the black man, an attack against a young, black, heterosexual male becomes an attack against the entire community. An attack against a young black female is not an attack against the entire community; that pushes a different set of buttons about protecting "our" women. It's about masculinity.

DAYO: It becomes an attack against the black male, again. [Laughter]

JOO-HYUN: Unless it's a butch woman or a woman who people perceive to be contradictory to her societally assigned gender norm.

Women of transgender experience, or gender-variant expression anywhere on the gender continuum, experience a whole other level of violence both by communities and cops, they get attacked for the supposed outrageousness of a "woman trying to be a man" or a "man trying to act womanish."

TAMARA: What we're saying is that when you have police violence directed against transgender or gender-variant communities, then what you have is gender policing, which also reflects the general gender policing in our communities.

JOO-HYUN: Regardless of whether a person of transgender experience identifies as heterosexual or not, it's assumed that they're homosexuals anyway. Activist rhetoric also often tends to play out sexist stereotypes—even among some activists who do really good anti-police-brutality work. The whole idea that "we need to protect our young men of color" or "we need to protect our women" without recognizing the complexities of how such statements get heard in a society where there's a pretty empty vacuum of visible public discussion about what we mean by "man" and "woman." It also ends up sending the message that men of color will do the work and that women are defenseless by nature. And we know that we don't think of ourselves as defenseless.

DAYO: This construction of women of color as a group to be protected by their men against the police reveals some of the ways women of color's experiences of police violence are practically erased. Earlier we hinted at how violence against a heterosexual black woman is often read back as an attack on black manhood. The racist and sexist violence black women experience is often made invisible because those experiences get used simply as background for attacks on black men, who are presumed to be the "defenders" of the black community.

JOO-HYUN: The media and even studies suggest that more men than women are victims of police violence. But I guess having grown up as a woman in this society, we often know that our histories are so hidden that it leads me to question whether we can believe the current statistics and conventional wisdom. While police-brutality statistics don't generally reveal a higher trend of women as victims or survivors of police violence, I think we have to wonder about how much this may have to do with the fact that women generally underreport violence against themselves in the first place—whether physical or verbal. We've been so conditioned as women of color by our daily lived experiences of racist, sexist, and homophobic violence, that we take it for granted. A verbal attack—racist, sexist, and/or homophobic—from a cop on the street just gets catalogued in our minds as one of a string of abuse we've taken that day. It may surprise us because it comes from a cop, but I think many of us would tend to lump it together as "part of what women go through"—the way every woman has at least one story about going past a construction site of male construction workers, and getting harassed but not even thinking to report it to someone. So I would suspect that we end up often not reporting instances where cops have perpetrated violence against us, because if we reported all the acts of violence against us as women, every day, some of us would be reporting twenty-five incidents a week.

DAYO: There's another way in which gender plays out here. What's interesting is that we're three women sitting in this room talking about police work in this city. What does it mean that it's been so hard to get gay men involved in ALP's Working Group on Police Violence? If you look at the other groups working on this issue citywide, there are a lot of women involved, and in some groups women are in leadership positions around this issue more than men. So, what does it mean that many women activists continue to frame the problem of police violence as saving our young men of color?

TAMARA: Part of the reason there are so few gay men fighting police brutality could be sexism among gay men, to the extent that we at ALP talk about victims that are transgendered. I've observed a struggle in the gay male community between men who express their sexuality in ways that don't go too far outside of the traditional gender boundaries, and men who wildly transgress those boundaries. For example, male-to-female transgender populations and drag queens are often not widely respected in the gay community. So when we talk about police violence and brutality directed against transgenders and transsexuals, gay men would have to deal with and talk about why it is that those members of the community are devalued. They would have to talk about sexism and gender biases among gay men themselves. That's a very difficult conversation to have.

DAYO: Historically, particularly in the black communities in the United States, police violence has been framed as an attack on black manhood; and it's the women who do the work because they're the ones left behind. But this also relates to a broader question of the gendering of organizing work in social-justice movements. I do think that a masculine framework dominates America's understanding of police violence, in part, because it provides a clear and less complicated picture. People-of-color communities can more readily grasp a racialized context that is also masculinized; the white male cops out to get men of color.

JOO-HYUN: And not simply men of color . . .

DAYO: Well, specifically in New York City, black and Latino men.

JOO-HYUN: Right. It very rarely takes into account Arab, Asian, or Native men. Race in the U.S. is still most often seen as only black/ white, and sometimes in New York City, folks also include Latino communities. I think it's an important point for understanding the racial divisions that occur within communities of color. For example, those of us from ALP who participated as a contingent in the Abner Louima rally weren't welcome, in part because we were visible as an out LGBTST organization, but it also got played out in racialized ways because some of the folks who joined ALP's banner were also white LGBTST and we were in a Haitian community. Also, some of the people of color in our contingent—like myself, a Korean woman—were very visibly not of African descent. And when media reported on the Louima protests, they most often painted the scenario that it was only black and Caribbean communities that marched, which masked the fact that it was actually a much broader coalition of folks who came out in support.

DAYO: So it becomes part of a very old struggle about where the future of our communities rests and who legitimately belongs in the struggle. The answer, of course, is that we must resist the powerful urge to draw impermeable boundaries around our movements, and we need to seek to build alliance with everyone willing to fight for a more just society.

TAMARA: So now that we've talked for over an hour, where do we go from here? What are the things we want to keep in mind in terms of strategies for action?

JOO-HYUN: Well, I think it's important to first note the contradiction of our fighting against police violence—using a broad, radical definition—while recognizing that most of the demands that many activists see as realistic at this point are simply straight-up reformist.

In fact, what we saw with the organizing after the Diallo murder was several different anti-police-brutality factions working on the issues, often not coordinated, and even sometimes at odds with one another. And that the most conservative, or cautious of these efforts, had the support of many elected officials who were able to buy into the decade-old demands of independent prosecutor, hiring from local communities, civilian complaint review board, etc. In fact, many of these demands, which were somewhat radical back in the day, have now been co-opted by mainstream service and legal organizations as the key pieces that will end police brutality as they know it.

DAYO: But we know that these reformist demands, age-old as they are, are important but really limited. For example, while we support the need for a police force that is reflective of our communities—officers who live in NYC as opposed to outside of NYC, more officers of color—we also know that a diversified police force in itself will not end the epidemic. We know there's a much deeper structural problem that cosmetics will not alter in terms of how, why, and for whom policing is done. And we recognize that it's really institutional issues of racism, sexism, classism, and homophobia that promote the brutality against our communities—not just isolated examples of "bad seed" cops scattered throughout an otherwise great system.

TAMARA: We also know that unless activists build anti-police-brutality movements that reflect the many dimensions that define victims of police violence, then the particular needs of LGBTST people of color will remain largely unaddressed. While some officers may become "sensitized" to LGBTST concerns, what's even more likely is that LGBTST people of color will continue to be targeted and victimized, as we are often the ones with the least access to resources and contacts within the LGBT community.

JOO-HYUN: For ALP, continuing to work with others—many with much longer histories of organizing on this issue—is critical to building our understanding, and our fight-back strategies. The case of Jalea Lamot, a woman of transgender experience, and her family and neighbors[10] is an example of how we benefited from working with a non-LGBT organization—the National Congress for Puerto Rican Rights—because of their many years of experience in the Bronx, their long history of organizing around police brutality, and the fact that non-queer communities were educated and outraged at the incident. And the reality is that they proved in many ways more reliable than one of the gay organizations we had started to work with.

DAYO: So for us, it sounds like rooting our work in communities of color, and other communities most victimized, makes sense for our long-term analysis development, but also to build organizing around. Our work and relationships we've built within the NYC Coalition Against Police Brutality have been invaluable to this initiative's development at ALP. It has allowed us to both go beyond the "gay ghetto" in our understanding of police violence, have homophobic violence taken seriously by mainstream police brutality activists, and also to raise the level of understanding and commitment to police violence issues within LGBTST communities at large in New York City.

Editors' note: Tamara Jones was assisted by a fellowship from the Sexuality Research Fellowship Program of the Social Science Research Council with funds provided by the Ford Foundation.

NOTES

1. "Two-Spirit" is a term that we use at ALP to honor and respect self-naming and self-determination struggles of Native and Indigenous peoples. As stated in the introduction of *Two- Spirit People,* an anthology edited by Sue-Ellen Jacobs, Wesley Thomas, and Sabine Lang (Champaign: University of Illinois Press, 1997), "it has come to refer to a number of Native American roles and identities past and present, including: contemporary Native American/First Nations individuals who are gay or lesbian; contemporary Native American/First Nations gender categories; the traditions wherein multiple gender categories and sexualities are institutionalized in Native American/First Nations tribal cultures; traditions of gender diversity in other, non–Native American cultures; transvestites, transsexuals and transgendered people; and drag queens and butches" (p. 2). Anguksuar [Richard LaFortune]'s "A Postcolonial Colonial Perspective on Western [Mis]Conceptions of the Cosmos and the Restoration of Indigenous Taxonomies" in the same volume further explains that "the term *two-spirit,* which has come into recent popular usage, originated in Northern Algonquin dialect and gained first currency at the third annual spiritual gathering of gay and lesbian Native people that took place near Winnipeg in 1990. What we who chose this designation understood is that *niizh*

manitoag (two-spirits) indicates the presence of both a feminine and a masculine spirit in one person" (p. 221).

2. Leslie Feinberg, in *Transgender Warriors* (Boston: Beacon Press, 1996), explains that "today the word transgender has at least two colloquial meanings. It has been used as an umbrella term to include everyone who challenged the boundaries of sex and gender. It is also used to draw a distinction between those who reassign the sex they were labeled as having at birth, and those of us whose gender expression is considered inappropriate for our sex" (p. x). At ALP, and for purposes of this article, we use the umbrella definition.

3. Amnesty International, *United States of America: Police Brutality and Excessive Force in the New York Police Department* (June 1996). National Coalition of Anti-Violence Programs, *Anti-Lesbian, Gay, Bisexual and Transgender Violence in 1998*, 5th ed. (April 6, 1999).

4. The participants of this discussion use "queer" with respect and as shorthand for LGBTST, recognizing that fundamentally LGBTST liberation is about transforming many of society's values and institutions to value LGBTST peoples—not about LGBTST people becoming assimilated, or the "same as" a mythical norm of heterosexual behavior and lifestyle. In this vein, our use of "queer" seeks to reclaim the term that has been (and in some situations continues to be) used as a derogatory term to describe LGBTST individuals as something other than "normal." "Queer" as a term of empowerment when used by self-affirming LGBTST individuals has also been seen to be more inclusive than "lesbian and gay"; it also draws alliances to others who in mainstream society are not seen as "normal," whether because of race, class/immigrant status, or ability. At the same time, we do acknowledge and honor the fact that not everyone in LGBTST communities is comfortable with the term "queer," and in fact many of those who laid the ground for our liberation fought against the term.

5. By "gender variant," we are referring to appearance and/or behavior that challenges boundaries of mainstream U.S. society's notions of "appropriate" for one's perceived sex and gender.

6. National Coalition of Anti-Violence Programs, 21–24. *Policing Public Sex: Queer Politics and the Future of AIDS Activism*, ed. Dangerous Bedfellows (Boston: South End Press, 1996).

7. The Stonewall Rebellion occurred in the last week of June 1969, when New York City police raided the Stonewall Inn, a gay bar in New York's West Village. The police harassment and demands for identification from those in the bar met with resistance led by black and Puerto Rican drag queens and other LGBT individuals. A crowd soon gathered outside the bar, and a three-day-long protest for "Gay Power" ensued in the streets of the West Village.

8. Similar to how "homophobia" is used in relationship to gays and lesbians, the use of "transphobic" and "transphobia" in this article refers to be-

haviors, actions, and a system that oppresses people based on perceptions of gender variance and/or transgender identity.

9. Heterosexism is used in this article to describe a system of oppression that privileges heterosexual lifestyles and behaviors.

10. Jalea Lamot is a woman of transgender experience who (along with family and others) was subjected to racist, sexist, homophobic, and transphobic violence by the police in the fall of 1998. When officers realized that she was transsexual, they terrorized her and other occupants of her mother's apartment, including her mother, brother, and neighbors. Rather than prosecuting the officers, the Bronx D.A.'s office proceeded to charge family members and a neighbor with various violations. After considerable community pressure, the family was finally offered an ACD. As of this writing, charges against the family and neighbor had been officially dropped. In late November 1999, the family filed a federal civil rights lawsuit against the city of New York and individual police officers who participated in the incident. See Michael Sullivan, "District Attorney Dismisses Charges," *New York Blade*, June 18, 1999, City Desk.

Bearing Witness

Bradley McCallum and Jacqueline Tarry

When does the intensity of an isolated occurrence ripple throughout a community to the point where a collective outcry seems the only resort? Activism is often rooted in empathy. In *Witness: Perspectives on Police Violence,* a multimedia visual art installation, we have created a space to listen to the voices of those who have directly experienced police violence. Central to the artwork are testimonies of victims of police violence, their surviving family members, police officers, and advocates working on the front line of this volatile issue.

Originally installed in the sanctuary of the Cathedral of Saint John the Divine in New York City, *Witness* uses a variety of media, including audio, video, text, and photography. Our advocacy lies in creating an emotional awareness that seemingly isolated incidents of police brutality are in reality pervasive, shared experiences. We strive to counteract the tendency of the press to squeeze the witness accounts into sound bites and focus on only the most extreme cases. The creation of a Media Wall and photographs of emptied streetscapes marked indelibly by police violence are among the ways in which *Witness* memorializes tragic events that so quickly fade from the public eye.

We believe that art can spark civic dialogue. We have chosen to create work outside the sanctioned spaces of museums and galleries to encourage community participation as a means of effecting social change. The installation of *Witness* in the cathedral is only part of a larger project that also involved installing the call boxes during a twenty-day citywide tour at locations where police violence has taken place and at courthouses and civic buildings that determine police accountability (to view interaction, log onto WitnessCallBox.org). The day-long installations of the call boxes provided interaction and exchange among government officials, community activists, and other concerned individuals, proving that artwork can become an impetus for action.

David Baez

Brother of Anthony Baez. Anthony was choked to death on December 22, 1994, at age 29.

"Well, basically, we were getting ready to leave the next morning back to Florida for a little vacation, and we were playing football outside, in front of our home. And, um, one of the footballs accidentally hit the police car. We apologized. Everything was all right. And the cops said, you know, don't worry about it. We continued playing, and the ball bounced and hit the police car again. And that was when Officer Francis Livoti got out of the police car. He told us, cursing, you know, get the f--- out of here, you don't belong here. And we tried to explain to him that we live right where we were playing. So what happened after that was, we tried to play the football game a little bit more up the street. As soon as we started the first play, Livoti jumps out the car and says, didn't I tell you, you know, cursing, to get the f--- out of here. As soon as we tried to explain to him, he just jumped on me…

"He jumped on me, slammed me on top of my brother's car, put the cuffs on me, started pulling the cuffs forward and back, cutting my wrists, slams me inside of the police car, and goes back toward where my brothers were at. And he said, do you want to fight? Who's the leader here? And my, my other brother Raymond was telling Livoti, nobody's a leader here, we're just brothers playing football. Livoti kept, kept trying to make a fight with one of us. So what happened was Livoti went toward my brother Tony and he then told Tony that if he has anything to say, then he's going to get arrested too. So my brother Tony ended up saying that he was a security officer in Florida; he knew his rights. As soon as he said that, Livoti just jumped right on my brother Tony and killed him with a chokehold. And we've been fighting for justice ever since…

David Baez

The mechanism of unconsciousness in Mr. Baez's case in my opinion resulted from two factors. One is the impairment of return of venous blood from his face and brain. The second is the compression of his airway, of his upper air passages, and a backward and upward displacement of the base of his tongue...

WITNESS | PERSPECTIVES ON POLICE VIOLENCE

There is clear and convincing evidence that the police witnesses called by Livoti testified falsely. They each testified that Anthony Baez was conscious, moving and resisting their efforts

Susan Karten
Baez family Attorney.

"I have had a number of police misconduct cases, but nothing ever prepared me for my experience in the Baez case. I can tell you without any reservation that this is a case that points to everything that was wrong with the NYPD–everything that was wrong at the highest level of NYPD.

They allowed someone to stay on the force in the face of having fifteen CCRB complaints against him, in the face of having a recommendation by Francis Livoti's own commanding officer at the 46th Precinct. You don't see that very often, his own commanding officer putting it in writing, saying that this man should be taken out of the precinct. And that recommendation going to the highest levels of the New York Police Department and being ignored. We uncovered, and brought before the public for the first time, the background and the record to show that this is a systemic problem, it's not just about a bad apple...

"It's about how the department allowed someone like Francis Livoti to go on and to murder Anthony Baez. We need lawyers who are willing to go beyond just lawyering but to be zealous in their representation of their clients.

We need that because if we do not have that, then things get swept under the rug, then victims get victimized and demonized by police departments. If anybody thinks that the blue wall of silence has come down because of the Louima case, they can only look at the Diallo case to see how its been resurrected..."

Susan Karten

David Baez

"The cop was showing that he was so brutal and racist and just like an animal. I felt like I couldn't do anything because I was in handcuffs. So many things were crossing my mind, whether I was going to go to jail, what was I being charged for, why was I even being arrested, what was going on with my brothers?

I'm looking from the back of the car, hearing screaming, hearing yelling. I'm hearing my father yelling at Livoti, telling him, stop choking him, he's an asthmatic. As soon as I see all of that, I just get out of the car and went right toward my brother and my father. What I saw was my brother being choked to death....It was like I needed to see what was going on..."

WITNESS | PERSPECTIVES ON POLICE VIOLENCE

DA to Get Testimony On Livoti

Judge calls it 'very, very disturbing'

By Leonard Levitt
STAFF WRITER

A Bronx judge yesterday said he would turn over to prosecutors "very, very disturbing" confidential police testimony related to the case of ex-cop Francis X. Livoti.

Bronx State Supreme Court Judge Douglas McKeon, made his remarks during proceedings in a $48 million civil lawsuit filed against Livoti by the family of Anthony Baez, who died after Livoti used an unauthorized choke hold on him

Francis X. Livoti, kicked off police t trial, now faces a $48 million.use of e

David Baez

"I see my father running across the street. I see police officers pushing my father. I see Officer Livoti choking my brother. So many things were going on at one second, I was aware of everything around me. It's like, it was just hell on earth. Seeing my brother being choked as I was running out the car, I mean, it was like a day in hell. I don't know what a day in hell is, but I've seen the movies that have hell in it. I mean, it was worse than that..."

Iris Baez
Mother of
Anthony Baez.

"After Anthony died, my kids seemed withdrawn. They seem guilty. They seem, you know, not to want to strive for nothing, really. They're destroyed. David never finished school, to this day. They're so withdrawn now that you don't see the happiness. There's anger where there was never anger. There's hate. My grandchildren, they are angry. They're always constantly fighting, arguing..."

Iris Baez "It's totally changed the whole family, where before we always used to be close, we always used to be happy. We haven't had a Christmas dinner since December 24, 1994. We don't have Christmas dinners. Now when I give the gifts, I just give it to them. When I buy them, I don't wrap them up, I don't wait for Christmas. I don't wait for the 25th anymore. I just give it to them when I buy them..."

"Right from there, I was just tackled down, and they beat me up. They stuck a gun to my head. I had handcuffs on, so it wasn't like I was going to do anything. I really didn't accomplish nothing by getting out the car but then again, I had to get out to see what I could do because what I saw that was going on was so brutal. I just couldn't see myself sitting in the car doing nothing, even though I was cuffed..." **David Baez**

```
              CHARGES  AGAINST  OFFICER

    NAME: LIVOTI        FRANCIS     TAX  878015
    RACE: WHITE    APPT: 012682  DOB: 043059   SHIE

   ASE    D-REPT    F A D O              D I S P O SI

  )2592   061584   FORCE               INVEST. CLOS
  \5379   102884     ..  ABU DISCO     CONCILIATED
```

WITNESS | PERSPECTIVES ON POLICE VIOLENCE

Susan Karten "I have to say the most reflective moment for me as an attorney was when I listened to Judge Scheindlin say that there was a nest of perjury in that courtroom and then on Monday acquitted Francis Livoti. Perhaps I was the most downtrodden I had ever been in my career because I very much believe in the system. I believe in the judicial system. When I heard him say that he believed that there was a nest of perjury I remember grabbing a reporter that had covered the trial. I said, he got it, he got it, he got it, he realized that the cops were lying, he's not going to let them get away with it. And Monday we walked into that room and the whole family was with me. And when I started to hear him come down with his decision, I knew we were going down the tubes, and I knew that he was not going to convict Livoti. It was like a balloon that had been popped. Everything that I believed in and thought of and fought for had exploded. The moments after that, when he acquitted him, were very, very difficult because you believe so much in the system, and you believe that things are gonna turn out okay…

"We were in there for like ten hours. It was like ten hours of **David Baez**
really hell on top of hell. We didn't know what we were being
charged for; we didn't know what was going on with our
brother. My father came to get us out. We met up with the
pastor from our church, and from there, he told us what happened to our brother…

Susan Karten "We had received the verdict in the courtroom and there was
an outburst, and everybody was left there just in shock and we
were just sort of left on our own in this bewilderment. And
when we got the presence of mind to leave the courtroom and
go out into the street a crowd of hundreds and hundreds of
people who had heard the verdict over the radio had started
gathering in front of the courthouse. There was actually police
riot gear lined up in front of the courthouse and keeping the
crowds away from us. Coming out into that scene was unbelievable. I had never been through anything like it and I felt
like [I was] just walking through something without feeling
it. But when we got down on the steps of the courthouse, Mrs.
Baez collapsed. She fell to the ground. Everybody ran, and
people had to be kept back, and it was so…incredible to see
how this mobilization of the police was there…

Susan Karten   "When the ambulance was coming Mrs. Baez was on the floor and Maribel was screaming. And as a lawyer I mean you just, you never prepare yourself to go through such a scene...

"I don't blame them all for the murder of my son; I've never blamed them all. I just say that Livoti murdered my son. The ones that were there had a say in it and yet turned their face the other way, so they're just as guilty, they're part of the murder of my son. How could you see somebody hurt another human being and not do nothing about it? That still bothers me. I say maybe my son could have been alive if somebody just would have said, stop. You know, one of the police officers could have said, stop.

Iris Baez

You won't find the justice, but you'll find the relief that you're looking for when something comes to the light. When something is made public, you'll find relief. Like now, police brutality is in the public's eye...

Areas A, B, and C: An Afterword

Andrew Ross

LENNY BRUCE, THE pioneer of avant-garde standup performance, and no stranger to the interior of police precincts, was seldom at a loss when it came to explaining the refractory shape of law enforcement. In one of his rambunctious, routine spritzes, he offers a vignette of the origins of the law. Back "when it started," in what we are invited to imagine as a paleolithic landscape, the need for rules arose:

> "Let's see, I tell you what we'll do. We'll have a vote. We'll sleep in area A, is that cool?"
> "O.K. Good."
> "We'll eat in area B. Good?"
> "Good."
> "We'll throw a crap in area C. Good?"
> Simple rules. So, everything went along pretty cool, you know, everybody's happy. One night everybody was sleeping, one guy woke up. *Pow*! He got a faceful of crap, and he said:
> "Hey, what's the deal here, I thought we had a rule: Eat, Sleep, and Crap, and I was sleeping and I got a faceful of crap."
> So they said, "Well, ah, the rule was substantive . . . "
> See that's what the Fourteenth Amendment is. It regulates the rights, but it doesn't *do* anything about it. It just says, "That's where it's at. . . ."[1]

To give the rules some teeth, an agreement is reached: "If anybody throws any crap on us they get thrown in the craphouse . . . priests, rabbis, they'll all go." But what about enforcement? The person delegated to hire a police officer reveals the predicament of the

hiring class to the prospective employee: "But ya see, I can't do it because I do business with these assholes, and it looks bad for me, you
know, ah . . . so I want somebody to do it for me, you know? So I tell
you what: Here's a stick and a gun and *you* do it–but wait til I'm out
of the room. And whenever it happens, see, I'll wait back here and
I'll watch, you know, and you make sure you kick 'em in the ass and
make sure it's done."

Bruce elaborates further on this division of labor, goes on to explain the
separation of church and state, and winds up describing the dilemma of
the Supreme Court, the Big Daddy who tries to keep all the state and
civil courts in line, but "the minute he turns his back . . . these little guys
keep trying to run the store." Here as always, Bruce is attracted toward
the task of rationalizing the legal system, even though his satire usually
left that rationality in tatters. Despite his long record of persecution by
police at home and abroad, for obscene speech and dope possession
(Phil Spector said he died "from an overdose of police"), he never did
full-frontal attacks on those who sought to silence him. Free speech, in
an age of racial integration and Establishment-shaking, was a fierce as-
piration, not a tried-and-tested weapon.

Toward the end of the routine, Bruce throws out a line about the
current disjuncture between the crime rate and levels of policing:

The crime rate, see, has disappeared, and the task force that we hired
is getting bigger and bigger and bigger—there's never any layoff in the
police department. The welfare is up, and it's getting so there's no
work left. Here's what I figured happened to the crime rate. First—the
basic need to steal is like, for coal, you know, you're hungry. All right.
So now the economy is up, so that went disappear-o. O.K., now the
second need to break the law was for some sort of status, some virility.
O.K., the fact that we now give these people analysis, that went disappear-o. Now there's just nothing left.

Readers might see a plausible resonance between this scenario and
today's socioeconomic climate. Nationally, unemployment has settled
back down to the levels of the early 1960s (when Bruce was performing in the kind of clubs that are increasingly out of place in the newly
sanitized urban order). The crime rate in New York City has substantially declined. In the meantime, the public clamor for beefed-up law

enforcement and zero-tolerance policies continues unabated. Yet many of the authors in this book take pains to show that there is no proven correlation between policing levels, economic indicators, and crime rates (any more than the Giuliani administration's presumed, though equally unproven, correlation between public-order crimes and serious crimes). Rather, they find that the causal glue that binds these together in the public mind is mostly a result of rhetorical manipulation. The absence of *causality* does not mean, however, that there is no narrative in which policing, crime, and the economy are not linked. In fact, the story told in this book attempts precisely to do that.

In many ways, it is a story about the eradication of the kind of world that Lenny Bruce was struggling to bring to life, if not embody, in the years immediately prior to the melting mood of the late 1960s. The puncturing of moral hypocrisy, especially in matters sexual: the erosion of liberal pieties about race, religion, and ethnicity; the expansion of rights regarding public speech, use of public space, and pursuit of public pleasure; the decriminalization of drug use; the skewering of business-as-usual in government; and the desanctifying of corporate power. By the turn of the century, New Yorkers would have seen each of these impulses given partial rein in the years following Bruce's 1966 death, and then come under ruthless siege as business elites accelerated their drive to break down the city's manufacturing base and reconstruct the metropolitan economy along quite different lines. Nor was this transformation confined to New York City limits. The city's fiscal crisis of the mid-1970s provided a model for an emergent neoliberal economics, taken up and emulated around the nation and overseas. So, too, its aggressive redevelopment of downtown neighborhoods pioneered a gentrification pattern that would be imitated far and wide in the 1980s. And in the 1990s, its policing doctrines of zero tolerance, accompanied or not by Mayor Giuliani's "quality of life" morals campaign, were adopted in cities all across the globe.

However widely copied elsewhere, these policies and changes have been most sharply experienced at the core, in a city whose remaking has required authoritarian measures that consistently skirt the limits of constitutionality and offend many residents' sense of what civic freedoms should entail. Outside of Mayor Giuliani's bullying, prosecutorial personality, the "proactive" heavy hand of the NYPD has chiefly carried this despotic stamp. Ironically, this harsh regimen has come at a time when authoritarian management and discipline have fallen out of corporate favor—nowadays the workplace ideal is to be decentralized, so that workers feel "empowered." Most revealing, however, is the disjuncture between the electoral popularity of these policing programs and the plunge in public standing of the police force that implements the street cleaning. Among the populations not targeted by these policies, the sentiment has very much run along the lines of Bruce's characterization: "Here's a stick and a gun and *you* do it, but wait till I'm out of the room." Business elites, who directly benefit from the esthetically purified public spaces of the new urban order, are not the only supporters. The consent of a decisive percentage of nonelite New Yorkers has helped to sustain the NYPD's aggressive enforcement of the mayoral will.

Given the hysteria surrounding racialized crime and the ceaseless capacity of local media to stoke the fires and fan the flames of race hatred ("if it bleeds, it leads"), it is no surprise that the most publicized profile of police repression has been attached to instances of excessive force visited on minority citizens. The evidence presented in this book and elsewhere in the public record points to a racist pattern of abuse, misconduct, and brutality that has attracted the legal scrutiny of the U.S. Justice Department and the international human rights community. The grassroots antibrutality campaign that sprang up in the wake of police violence against Abner Louima and Amadou Diallo, the most well known of the NYPD's recent victims of color, has activated the broad spectrum of the traditional civil rights community and resonated widely and sympathetically with public opinion. While the authors in this book condemn such acts and support the antibrutality campaigns, they also argue that an *exclusive* public focus on instances of excessive force, resulting in severe beatings and violent deaths, diverts attention from the daily normalization of repression, manifest in a thousand nonspectacular and nonheadline-grabbing ways.

To see the big picture, they argue, we must look at the whole spectrum of intrusive operations—systematic surveillance, targeted stop-and-frisk searches and seizures, discriminatory verbal harassment, public-order arrests, and aggressive monitoring of public space—and at the nature of the groups explicitly targeted: youth, homeless and poor people, street vendors, performance artists, protestors, squeegee men, turnstile jumpers, publicly intoxicated citizens, and a host of other "disorderlies," including virtually all black and Latino males, automatically under suspicion on account of their skin color. The challenge of this book is to show that these widespread operations do *not* respond primarily to threatening habits and dangerous vices among the general population. Rather, the book argues, they are a response to the need of elites to secure an effectively controlled, center-city environment for upscale denizens and beneficiaries of the New Economy to inhabit and flourish. In this light, zero tolerance and quality of life are not aimed at restoring order on behalf of a defenseless citizenry cowed in fear of the mean streets, but are directly engaged in establishing new rules for public behavior that answer exclusively to the survivors and winners of the privatizing revolution: "Here's a stick and a gun and *you* do it—but wait till I'm out of the room."

There are other major advances made in these pages. The massive attention devoted to the cases of black heterosexual male victims of police brutality, both by the mass media and by the mainstream civil rights community, overlooks the impact and profile of police aggression among women, gays, lesbians, and the transgendered. The essays collected here provide a more honest portrait of the consequences of heteronormativity and masculinism within the ranks of the NYPD. Nor do the authors present a caricatured portrait of the NYPD as a heavily militarized, and racist, lockstep corps. Extensive interviews with police officers, and historical assessments of the career of women in the NYPD, yield a picture somewhat at odds with the prevailing caricature. Not only do we find a body of public employees who are underpaid and therefore fiercely at odds with City Hall over their labor contract; we also find a covert lack of consensus, and indeed, much evidence of widespread skepticism from within the ranks about the aims and the efficacy of zero-tolerance policies.

Historically, in moments of mounting public resistance, local police forces have not always sided with the draconian policies of their paymasters. While those who break the "thin blue line" of protective silence must be commended, support should also be given to those who would welcome partial democratization of the command structure that implements repressive policies. An independent police commission could very well oversee that process, in addition to monitoring police brutality and corruption. NYPD rank and file might well feel less defensive as a result, and more hospitably animated by the prospect of internal reforms. In an age when the private and public have opened up to each other, perilously eroding the boundaries that separate their domains, a public police force must be given the chance to distinguish itself from the hired guns that patrol the privatized space of the city's numerous Business Improvement Districts.

Ultimately, however, there's no escaping the reality that policing—throwing the crap throwers in the crap house, to use Bruce's formulation—is a dirty job. In a social system that sanctions vast inequalities, it is a fundamentally immoral job. Speaking of law students in his interview in this book, Derrick Bell advises them to acknowledge that "as lawyers working in the system they are evil, but with real care and even more humility, they can from time to time be a necessary evil." Because of the privilege it assumes, it is no easy feat to translate this consciousness from legal professionals to uniformed officers, but the spirit of this kind of mentality is sorely needed within the NYPD and other urban police divisions. But let's not hold our breath. Changes in the education or culture of policing do not lie around the next corner. The lesson we learn from this book is the need to understand some of the broader forces for which policing serves as an evil necessity. We need to see whose specific interests and agendas are being served by public policing before, or in the same breath, as we demand a reform of policing itself.

NOTES

1. Lenny Bruce, "The Law," in *The Essential Lenny Bruce*, ed. John Cohen (New York: Ballantine, 1967), 274–80.

Contributors

HEATHER BARR, a lawyer and advocate for the rights of mentally ill criminal defendants and prisoners, is a Soros Justice Fellow at the Urban Justice Center in New York City. She is counsel to the plaintiffs in *Brad H. v. The City of New York*, a lawsuit regarding New York City's failure to provide discharge planning for people with mental illness being released from New York City jails. She also works as a consultant at the Center for Alternative Sentencing and Employment Services, where she helped create the Nathaniel Project, the first alternative-to-incarceration program for seriously mentally ill felony offenders in the United States.

DERRICK BELL is currently a Visiting Professor of Law at New York University School of Law. He has written extensively on race and racism in American law, including *And We Are Not Saved: The Elusive Quest for Racial Justice, Confronting Authority, Afroatlantica Legacies,* and *Faces at the Bottom of the Well.*

PAUL G. CHEVIGNY is a Professor of Law at New York University School of Law. He has published numerous books on First Amendment issues and on police abuse, including *Police Power: Police Abuses in New York City* (Pantheon, 1969) and *Edge of the Knife: Police Violence in the Americas* (New Press, 1995.)

COMMITTEE AGAINST ANTI-ASIAN VIOLENCE: ORGANIZING ASIAN COMMUNITIES, formerly known as CAAAV, was founded in 1986. It is a pan-Asian grassroots organization that organizes Asian immigrant communities in New York City to combat racist violence in its multiple forms, such as economic exploitation, police brutality, and poverty.

TANYA ERZEN is a Ph.D. candidate in the American Studies Program at New York University. Her essay on the Religious Right appears in *The*

Promise Keepers: Essays on Masculinity and Christianity, and she has written for *The Nation* and *Fairness and Accuracy in Reporting*.

DAYO FOLAYAN GORE is a Ph.D. candidate in History at New York University Graduate School of Arts and Science, writing her dissertation on U.S. political culture and the organizing efforts of black women activists during the 1940s and 1950s. She is also a member of the Working Group on Police Violence at the Audre Lorde Project, a Lesbian, Gay, Bisexual, Two Spirit and Transgender People of Color organizing center based in Brooklyn, and she is active in the New York City–based Coalition Against Police Brutality.

AMY S. GREEN is Assistant Professor of Speech and Theater at John Jay College of Criminal Justice of the City University of New York. She holds a doctorate in theater from the CUNY Graduate School and University Center and is the author of *The Revisionist Stage: American Directors Reinvent the Classics* (Cambridge University Press, 1994).

PAUL HOFFMAN practices civil rights law in Los Angeles. He is the outgoing chair of Amnesty International—USA chapter and former Legal Director of the ACLU Foundation of Southern California. He has written extensively on police brutality.

ANDREW HSIAO is a senior editor at *The Village Voice* and an editor at The New Press, both in New York City.

TAMARA JONES is a Ph.D. candidate in Political Science at Yale University. Her activist background includes work as a member of the Working Group on Police Violence at the Audre Lorde Project; as a union organizer for the Graduate Employees and Student Organization at Yale; as a member of the Black Radical Congress; and as a member of Caribbean Pride—an organization of LGBTs of Caribbean descent. Her other recent publications include "'Top-Down' or 'Bottom-Up'?: Sexual Identities and Workers' Rights in a Municipal Union," in *OutFront: Lesbians, Gays and the Struggle for Workplace Rights*, ed. Kitty Krupat and Patrick McCreery (University of Minnesota Press, January 2001); "Fighting Homophobia versus Challenging Heterosexism: 'The Failure to Transform' Revisited," co-authored with Cathy J. Cohen, in *Dangerous Liaisons: Blacks, Gays in the Struggle for Equality*, ed. Eric Brandt (New

Press, 1999); and "Women of Color in the Eighties: A Profile Based on Census Data," co-authored with Alethia Jones in *Women Transforming Politics: An Alternative Reader*, ed. Cathy J. Cohen, Kathleen B. Jones, and Joan C. Tronto (New York University Press, 1997).

JOO-HYUN KANG is the founding Executive Director of The Audre Lorde Project, a Lesbian, Gay, Bisexual, Two Spirit and Transgender People of Color organizing center based in Brooklyn, New York.

ANDREA McARDLE teaches in the Lawyering Program and is the Co-ordinator of the Lawyering Theory Workshop at New York University School of Law. She is a Ph.D. candidate in the American Studies Program at New York University Graduate School of Arts and Science. She writes in the areas of lawyering theory, race studies, and law and society.

BRADLEY McCALLUM received his BFA from Virginia Commonwealth University in 1989 and his MFA in Sculpture from the Yale School of Art in 1992. During the past decade he has created site-specific community-based artworks built from a collaborative process of gathering oral histories and testimonies that are then utilized as the primary material for his sculptural installations. His past works include an installation at the Wadsworth Atheneum in Hartford, Connecticut, entitled *The Manhole Cover Project: A Gun Legacy*.

ANDREW ROSS is a Professor and Director of the American Studies Program at New York University. His books include *No Respect: Intellectuals and Popular Culture* (Routledge, 1989), *Strange Weather* (Verso, 1992), *The Chicago Gangster Theory of Life* (Verso, 1994), *Real Love: In Pursuit of Cultural Justice* (New York University Press, 1998), and *The Celebration Chronicles: Life, Liberty, and the Pursuit of Property Value in Disney's New Town* (Ballantine Books, 1999). He has also edited many anthologies, most recently *No Sweat: Fashion, Free Trade, and the Rights of Garment Workers* (Verso, 1997).

JACQUELINE TARRY brings to the visual arts a background in both philosophy and logic, two influences that imbue her conceptual art practice with methodical precision and a yearning for truth. She received a Bachelor of Arts degree from State University College in her native Buffalo, New York. Raised in the heart of the city, Tarry approaches artistic production with an acute awareness of urban dynamics and the role of violence and conflict within the inner city. She also forged a professional partnership with artist Bradley MacCallum, with whom she shared a vision of public artwork that addresses sociopolitical issues by infusing art with civic dialogue.

SASHA TORRES is the Second Decade Society Faculty Development Chair and Director of the Program in Film and Media Studies at Johns Hopkins University. She is the editor of *Living Color: Race and Television in the United States* (Duke University Press, 1998) and author of *Black, White and In Color: Television, African Americans and the Production of Natural History* (forthcoming from Princeton University Press.) She is a co-editor of *Camera Obscura*, serves on the editorial boards of *Meridians*, *Aztlan*, and *Gay and Lesbian Quarterly*, and has commented on media matters for Fox News, National Public Radio, and numerous newspapers and magazines.

JENNIFER R. WYNN is the Director of the Prison Visiting Project for the Correctional Association of New York and author of a forthcoming book about her work with prisoners at Rikers Island, New York City's principal detention facility.

Index